D0055577

My Utmost

My Utmost

୶

A DEVOTIONAL MEMOIR

Macy Halford

Alfred A. Knopf

NEW YORK   2017

THIS IS A BORZOI BOOK
PUBLISHED BY ALFRED A. KNOPF

Copyright © 2017 by Macy Halford

Library of Congress Cataloging-in-Publication Data
Names: Halford, Macy, author.
Title: My utmost : a devotional memoir / by Macy Halford.
Description: First Edition. | New York, NY : Alfred A. Knopf, 2017.
Identifiers: LCCN 2016029736 (print) | LCCN 2016042547 (ebook) |
ISBN 9780307957986 (hardcover) | ISBN 9780307957993 (ebook)
Subjects: LCSH: Halford, Macy. | Christian biography. |
Chambers, Oswald, 1874–1917. My utmost for His Highest. | Evangelicalism.
Classification: LCC BR1725.H1835 A3 2017 (print) | LCC BR1725.H1835 (ebook) |
DDC 270.092—dc23
LC record available at https://lccn.loc.gov/2016029736

Jacket photograph by George Baier IV
Jacket design by Peter Mendelsund

Manufactured in the United States of America
First Edition

For my mother and my grandmother

My Utmost

I

ॐ

A river touches places of which its source knows nothing.

—SEPTEMBER 6

Dallas, 2011. The slender blue book had been lying on my bedside table for years before I started reading it, ever since the night of my baptism, when my grandmother had presented it to me as a gift, a sort of token of my entry into religious maturity. I'd tried to read it then but hadn't gotten very far. At thirteen, I was a keen enough reader, and *My Utmost for His Highest* was an inviting book— a daily devotional, with a brief reading for each day of the year— but at the start it suffered unfairly from its association with a senior citizen. After one sentence, I'd decided it was old-fashioned, as fusty and tedious as everything else my grandmother liked— the book equivalent of boiled vegetables, potted pansies, needle-point, PBS, Chanel No. 5, and the taupe-colored Chevy she'd been driving for twenty years. All of these things bored me—I think they even bored my grandmother. If she liked them, it was because they were set to her frequency. Once, when I asked her why she never talked about her life, or anything, really, beyond the weather, she offered this as an explanation: "The Macys are a very boring people," Macy being her maiden name and the source of my own. I replied that I hoped she wasn't including me in her assessment, and she smiled and said, "Oh, no, Macy dear, you are always fascinating." It is tempting to read into this comment a slyness or even a bite, but my grandmother's was not a mind given to doubleness. On the rare occasions when she spoke of her own parents and grandparents, who had all lived out their lives "back on the farm," she used the expression "salt of the earth" without irony.

But I shouldn't employ the past tense when I talk about my grandmother. She is still alive. It is merely her mind—or much of it, anyway—that belongs to the past, having begun its final flight several years ago, around her eighty-sixth birthday. Otherwise, she is well and still going about her daily rounds as she always has, in the little red-brick house on Wabash Avenue, in Dallas, Texas, where in the 1980s and '90s she helped my mother to raise me and my brother and my sister, and which I left—to go north, to New York—just after my eighteenth birthday.

It was a recent visit to this house and my grandmother that prompted me to begin thinking about *Utmost*, or rather to begin thinking about it in a different way than I usually did. At that point, I'd been reading the book more or less every day for fifteen years, and so I thought about it often. Or maybe it makes more sense to say that I thought with it, since its presence in my life had become so fixed that I hardly noticed it was there anymore. It wasn't until this visit, when I happened to spot my grandmother's own ancient copy on the kitchen countertop, where we were sitting drinking coffee, that I began to wonder about the fact that we'd both been reading it so long, she even longer than I, and even after losing her mind.

"Do you still read this book, Nana?" I asked, and, after I'd repeated the question, she confirmed that she did. "Every morning when I wake up, bright and early," she said. "Six a.m. That's when I'm up. 'Early to bed, early to rise, makes a man healthy, wealthy, and wise.'" It was my grandmother's short-term memory that had disappeared, not her long, or (alas) the bit where her vast collection of moralizing aphorisms was stored. "Also a woman," I replied. "Just look at you! Ninety years old and still going strong," to which she shook her head in confusion, having apparently forgotten her previous statement. How, I wondered, could a person who couldn't recall what she'd just said still enjoy reading? Wouldn't she have forgotten one sentence by the time she reached the next?

My grandmother took a sip of her coffee, then abruptly turned and left the kitchen. She'd gotten into the habit of disappearing like this, as if she'd been called away by a voice only she could hear. I let her go, the way people are instructed to let sleepwalkers go, and while I waited for her to return I flipped *Utmost* open to the entry for the day: September 6. It was the entry about rivers, the one that contained the line "A river touches places of which its source knows nothing." I smiled, both because the line was apt to the day and because I'd been waiting for it to come around again, ever since the first hint of autumn had swept across New York. It was still high summertime in Texas, and it seemed strange to me to be reading the page on such a hot day, even though it must have been in the summer heat that I first encountered it. I read the words over again, trying to raise the temperature in my mind, but they refused to conjure anything but the crispness of impending fall in Manhattan, the coolness of the rivers that embraced the island. I seldom read the book out of order. Every evening, I opened it to the day's reading, read through to the end, and wondered whether I'd remember it 365 days later. Some entries, like the one for September 6, I always recalled very clearly, as if I'd just read them; others were perpetually new, though I'd read them eleven, twelve, thirteen times. I was never sure whether this was because they hadn't struck me as being memorable, or because I'd changed so drastically in certain particulars over the course of the year that I was really reading them with "new" eyes. This possibility had been planted in my mind long ago, when I was a teenager. One Sunday, as I was sitting in a pew at church, reading my copy of *Utmost* and waiting for the service to start, a man had approached me and had begun to tell me why he found Oswald's book to be so compelling (*Utmost* readers tended to refer to its author by his first name only). "It's a book that reads you," the man had said, "rather than the other way around." I'd regarded him coolly, noting the snakeskin sheen of his cowboy boots, the black twine of his bolo tie, the gel-slicked flop of gray atop his head. His comment struck me as a silly, unmanly thing to say, particularly for a man dressed as he was dressed, but over the years, as various of my Texas-born prejudices had fallen away, I'd come to see the truth in it. It helped to explain why certain passages seemed to morph over time, and why people tended to read *Utmost* for decades on end. It was certainly a large part of the book's appeal, this strange mutability. How many books had the power to evolve with a reader over the course of a lifetime, never growing tiresome? The Bible, perhaps, along with certain others—the works of Dante, Milton, or Shakespeare, Whitman, Melville, Joyce, or Woolf. But *Utmost* was in a special class. It was holy, and when I was a kid I'd often heard it mentioned in the same breath as the Bible. There had even been a disclaimer printed in a version that came out in the 1990s—nearly seventy years after *Utmost* had first been published, in 1927. The disclaimer read:

This book is not the Bible—it is intended to point you to
the Bible.

But my own edition, from the eighties, contained no such
warning, and I'd quickly succumbed. *Utmost* sat on my bedside
table right on top of my Bible, the minute grooves in their soft
leather jackets locked together. Actually, the leather *Utmost* was
bound in was faux—midnight-blue "leatherette"—and the gilded
lettering of the title was fake as fool's gold. But to me, it was the
real thing, fine and fancy and all mine. It was The Book, the one I
reached for first, always. I used it in the way I knew many people at
my church used it (for it was from them that I'd first learned how
to read *Utmost*, in a manner that was close to praying), turning to
it each day for a concentrated dose of spirituality, meditating on
its insights, committing them to memory. Now, I can admit that I
was probably guilty of using it as a placeholder when there wasn't
time to get right to the source. But back then I was convinced that
it was just as good. After all, each entry opened with a Bible verse,
so it wasn't exactly true that in reading the book one *wasn't* reading the Bible.

I hadn't been much bothered by this issue until I got to New
York and encountered a different breed of Evangelical from the
one I was used to. This breed, which might be called "Evangelical
intellectual," appeared during my senior year of college, in the form
of a young man from Kentucky. He was a student at Union Theological Seminary, which was located a few blocks from Columbia
University and my own school, Barnard. I met him one Sunday at
church—I was going to Riverside Church, which was a politically
liberal, quasi-interdenominational congregation with ties to the
Baptists (the Northern ones), the Church of Christ, and the Civil
Rights movement, such strange mixtures being commonly occur-

ring phenomena in Evangelical Christianity, which has never yet brought forth a "pure" example of its type—and struck up a brief friendship with him. He was, I soon discovered, extremely serious about his religion, by which I mean extremely snobby, and when I told him about my *Utmost* habit, he lashed out. Devotionals like *Utmost* were disgusting, he said. They pretended to do the work of interpretation for the reader, excusing Christians from what he considered their most pressing task: to grapple with Scripture in all its mystical, rhetorical, contradictory glory. If he could have his way, every Christian on the planet would be reading the Bible in the ancient Hebrew and the ancient Greek, followed by the *Summa Theologica* and then Luther and finally Calvin (there wasn't really a need for anything else in the way of Christian literature, he thought, and besides, those four could fill more than one lifetime). He hadn't read *Utmost* himself, but it was his understanding that it was a book full of dubious theological equations, fitting into no particular tradition, something he regarded as evidence of a lack of intellectual rigor on the part of its author. (Here, I'd interrupted to offer the boy the author's name: it was Oswald Chambers, and he was a Scot who'd been born in the late nineteenth century and died in the early twentieth.) It was beyond him why so many American Evangelicals—tens of millions of them—had embraced the book, except he knew that most American Evangelicals were uneducated and hopelessly lowbrow. "These are people who send all their money to swindling television preachers and use what's left over to go to the water park," he said.

His words hit home. Wally Amos Criswell, the preacher of my own childhood church, a massive congregation known as the "jewel in the crown of the Southern Baptists" (the denomination to which it belonged), had been both a fixture on television and a very successful fund-raiser, and I'd always had summer passes to the Wet 'n' Wild. But I resented my friend's accusations, particularly the accusation of anti-intellectualism. I thought *Utmost* was a smart book for smart people. It was certainly better than many of the Evangelical offerings on the shelves when I was growing up, books like *Dare to Discipline, Love Must Be Tough,* and *The Satan Seller.*

From my current vantage point in the kitchen, I could see that the books I remembered from my childhood were still on display in my grandmother's tiny library, in the same order they'd always been in. Perhaps they hadn't been touched in two decades. The Bible and *Utmost*—those were my grandmother's lodestars. She still read them regularly, and she still professed to love the activity of reading. I'd never understood why she limited her range so drastically, though it might have had to do with how she viewed her own capacities. She'd told me frequently when I was growing up that she wasn't smart—despite the bachelor's degree (in home economics) she'd earned in the 1930s, and the master's degree (in nutrition) she'd earned in the 1970s, after her husband died. She'd earned those, she thought, merely by working hard. "I'm not clever like you, Macy dear," she'd say, though I thought that she was very clever. True, she lacked a sharp tongue and a high humor, preferring instead the even keel; and, yes, she'd turned away from much of the cultural product of the twentieth century, maybe out of fear, perhaps out of discernment. But I'd observed her for more than thirty years, and I knew that she knew very well how to exist in the world, helping others, doing no harm, peaceful in mind and body.

Now it occurred to me that there was only one intellectual "product" that appealed to each of us in equal measure. The thought came to me as I sat in the kitchen waiting for my grandmother to return, staring at the shelves of books I remembered from my youth, and thumbing through her old copy of *Utmost.*

I called out, thinking I would discuss it with her, but she didn't answer—perhaps she'd forgotten to put her hearing aids in. I jumped off the stool to go look for her.

It was always a shock, coming back to this house. As I walked through the rooms, it unfolded as it had throughout my childhood, in a familiar succession of doorways opening into low-ceilinged, dim spaces. But in the past, they'd been alive, filled with people. They were empty now. There was the den, with wood paneling, dark gray carpeting, and the television—this was the room that held the library, the one that was visible from the kitchen—followed by the bedroom where I'd slept with my little sister and which always made me shudder. The precise color of paint on the walls of this room, a sort of purplish rose, still seemed to me the color of captivity, and it didn't help that as I walked through it now I could see the red, white, and gray of my high school cheerleading uniform peeking from the open closet door. I shut the door as I passed by and hurried on to the middle bathroom, tiled in beige and orange and avoided during my childhood by everyone except my grandmother, who didn't mind the roaches that crawled frequently out of the drain in the shower. These were enormous roaches, a local species known as Texas ride 'ems, immune to the efforts of the exterminator who came several times a year. They'd always paralyzed me, but Nana would crush them with a bare foot and toss them into the toilet. She knew no fear of such things, having performed infinitely more noxious tasks in her childhood—decapitating chickens, drowning mice, neutering cats (using nothing but a rubber band)—all the bloody, necessary acts that went along with farm work. This bathroom gave way to the front bedroom, where my brother had slept, then to the hallway with the piano, and, then, finally, to my mother's old bedroom.

Suddenly, I was in a different house. The bedroom marked the beginning of my mother's domain. She was an interior designer by profession, and she'd never been able to stay long in a space without refashioning it to her liking. In her old bedroom, a queen-size canopy bed held court, flanked by oil paintings and a heavy walnut desk with lion's paws at the ends of its legs. On the opposite wall, a massive armoire, carved from only a few pieces of golden oak, gave off a sharp, wooden scent, so that when you entered the room, you felt as if you were somewhere else, somewhere ancient and forested—if you were to enter that armoire, it was easy to wind up far away, in Narnia, perhaps, which is where I'd inevitably gone when I played in it as a child. Leaving my mother's bedroom, you entered the white-tiled, brightly lit bathroom she'd installed in the nineties. This led into the living room, which was exqui-sitely appointed with cream-colored sofas and Persian rugs, and then into the dining room, where there was a table made of one vast slab of porous white marble, a Russian samovar, an antique Chinese tapestry, and a hollowed-out ostrich egg, perched atop an ornament—a small ring set over four more lion's paws, this time in brass. A small oil portrait of Christ at Calvary hung above it.

Was it odd, I wondered, that my grandmother had made no alterations to my mother's décor after my mother moved out? She seldom used these rooms. They were too fancy for her, not func-tional enough. In the past, she'd entertained in them, but since her dementia and hearing loss had set in, she'd had few visitors, which isn't to say that she'd ever had many. She'd always been a solitary person, self-contained and self-sufficient. "I never get bored, and I never get lonely," she liked to say—enviable qualities, to be sure, but I'd always sensed that there was a vehemence to her self-control, a defiance. It had always been impossible to think of drawing my grandmother out of her little world, and even now, when she needed help badly, it was difficult to know how to help her. All of my family's attempts at installing home health aides had ended in failure. My grandmother would order them out of the house, scream at them, even throw things. Or so I'd heard. I'd always been far away when these dramatic scenes were unfolding. I had a hard time picturing my grandmother in such an extreme emotional state. Extremes were not her style.

But where had she gotten to? For a moment, I lingered in my mother's lovely living room, remembering one Christmas when I'd hidden behind a sofa in the hopes of catching them—my two mothers—playing at Santa Claus. I'd wanted to confirm a certain suspicion, which was that the real Santa Claus would never have stuffed our stockings with toothbrushes, oranges, and underwear that came in a tube—not least because Santa didn't shop in bulk at the local Sam's Club. I'd waited a long time, fighting off sleep, and was rewarded when my mother and my grandmother emerged, as expected, with presents in their arms. I began to nod off as they went about their business, but right before I lost consciousness, I heard my mother say, "Oh, Mom, not underwear *again.*" They had such different styles.

◈

I shook myself out of the memory. If my grandmother was not in the house, she must be outside in the garden. And indeed, I found her there a few minutes later, kneeling in a large flower bed, a blanket of purple pansies spread out before her, a spade in her hand. She looked up, confused, as I approached.

"Macy dear!" she said. "When did you get here?"

"A while ago," I told her. "Don't get up."

She stood anyway, brushing the mud from her khaki shorts. I recognized them as the same shorts she'd gardened in in the eighties. There were mud stains in virtually every fiber, but otherwise they were in remarkably good shape.

"Don't be silly. We'll have a cup of coffee. You've come all the way from New York City!"

I followed her inside for another cup, thinking that it was a good thing she brewed her coffee so weak.

After we were resettled at the kitchen countertop, two watery cups of Maxwell House steaming before us, I once again held the copy of *Utmost* out to her.

"Nana," I said. "Why do you like this book so much?"

She took the book from my hands and turned it over, studying it. Her blue eyes widened, as if in comprehension, then narrowed again—cornflowers unfurling and folding, sun to shade.

"Nana," I repeated. "Why do you like this book?"

"Oh, it's very good," she said. "Very, very, very good. I read it every morning, bright and early. 'Early to bed, early to rise—'"

"But what about it makes it good?" I said.

"Well, it's very real."

"Real?"

"Yes. You know what I mean. It's all about Jesus."

"Is it?" I said. This was curious to me. "Isn't it about a lot of things?"

"No. It's about Jesus," my grandmother said. "That's why I like it."

She flipped the book open to July 5, then asked me what the date was.

"September sixth," I told her.

She found it and began to read aloud, her voice fragile and sweet.

"'September sixth. Diffusiveness of Life. "Rivers of living water." John 7:38. A river touches places of which its source knows nothing, and Jesus says if we have received of His fullness, however small the visible measure of our lives, out of us will flow the rivers that will bless to the uttermost parts of the earth. We have nothing to do with the outflow—"This is the work of God, that ye *believe*. . . ." God rarely allows a soul to see how great a blessing he is.'

"Isn't that nice?" my grandmother said, and I agreed that it was. The entry was one of my favorites. I felt peaceful, confident, whenever I heard it, and any anxiety instantly vanished. That was one thing that *Utmost* did better than any other book I'd read: it threw you back into the river.

"Do you want me to finish it?" I asked her, but her mind seemed to have gone again.

"Did you know," she said at last, "that your great-great-grandmother memorized a different Bible verse every single day of her life, and every day she'd come over to our house—this was my father's mother, mind you—she didn't live with us, their farm was down the road—she'd come over every day and recite it to us children. And that's how she learned the entire Bible. She was a very Godly woman. Salt of the earth."

"Why did she come over?" I said.

"Who?"

"Your grandmother, why did she come over to your farm every day?"

"There wasn't anywhere else to go."

"But why did the people from the other farm come to your farm to eat? They didn't want to eat on their own farm?"

"It would be doubling the work. It wasn't easy cooking every day for so many people. Biscuits and gravy, eggs, waffles, potatoes, coffee. That was breakfast. Four a.m. That's when she came over."

I stayed quiet, hoping she'd continue. It was as much as she'd ever told me about her life, and I could sense the delicacy of the thread floating in the space between us. She went on, her eyes steady and fixed on mine.

"During the Depression, we hunted for pennies in the floorboards. But we were lucky, always had plenty of food on the farm, never lost the farm. You know I still have the farm, don't you? And I had my pony, Moxie, that I rode to school every day. Have you seen pictures of Moxie?"

I nodded. Moxie was immortalized in a photograph that hung on a wall of family photos.

"She was a sweet pony, and so trustworthy. She'd take me through the highest snowfall, without so much as a whinny. And she'd stand outside the schoolhouse, waiting patiently until two o'clock, when the bell rang. Patience is a virtue, you know. I don't know if an animal can be virtuous or not, but Moxie was a virtuous pony."

She went on like this for a while, painting pictures of a stark early-twentieth-century midwestern childhood (she'd grown up in Missouri). A little white schoolhouse in the middle of a blank, snowy expanse, and radiating out from it, like spokes on a wheel, eight deep black lines, the pathways trod by the eight students and their ponies, each issuing from the direction of some faraway farm. Astonishing, really, that that schoolhouse had been my grandmother's portal to higher education, and in a sense to mine as well. I studied her as she spoke. Her face was remarkably unchanged from what it had been when I was young—a testament, I supposed, to the efficacy of the regime of Ivory soap and Pond's cold cream she'd followed for at least fifty years. There were few lines, and her features, all dainty, all pretty, hadn't been lost to gravity. She'd been considered a great beauty when she was younger and had even been named Barnwarming Queen during her junior year of college. Her eyes were light and small, and they spoke to the sweetness which nearly everyone noticed in her. Everyone (with the exception, perhaps, of the home health aides of late) had always loved my grandmother. She was an utterly innocuous being. Sweet, simple, pretty, pleasant.

"And that's why we all had *M* names," I heard her say. "My mother was Matilda Macy, but she went by Matie; I was Marjorie Macy; my sister was Mary Macy; and my pony was Moxie Macy. She was Mary Elizabeth, and that's why you are Macy Elizabeth, but you know my brother's son named his daughter Mary Elizabeth Macy, so you've got some competition."

The bit about the names prompted a recollection, about all the car trips we used to take to the farm to see this brother and his family when I was a girl. I'd hated nothing so much as going to the farm, where there was nothing to do and the water wasn't safe to drink. I'd especially hated my cousins' friends, big farm boys on roaring four-by-fours who taunted me about my name. "What's your name?" they'd say. "Macy Macy?" And then they'd laugh as I angrily denied it. I'd hated boys with all my heart back then. "Born cruel," my grandmother would say when I'd cry about them, and my mother would always shrug and say, "Boys tease, girls whine."

I tuned back in to what my grandmother was saying.

"Yes, what my mother gave us was good habits. You're no better than your habits, you know."

"I know," I said.

"That's why I always eat so healthy. Plain, simple food. Meat, potatoes, and vegetables."

She fell silent, then sighed.

"Are you okay?" I asked her, but she didn't answer. She stood up and, once again, walked out of the kitchen without a word. This time I followed her, out to her flower beds, where her spade still lay in the dirt, waiting. She picked it up, resuming the work she'd probably been trying to finish all day, and I looked down the street, into the canopy. Evening was coming.

"Okay, Nana," I said, touching her on the shoulder. "I'm going. I'll see you tomorrow."

She turned around, confused again.

"Oh, Macy dear," she said. "Do you want to come inside?"

There was pain in her face, a kind of pleading I'd noticed during every visit I'd made since I'd first gone away to college. She wasn't asking me not to go, she was telling me not to: *don't* leave. But it was always necessary to leave. That decision—the decision not to spend my life in Texas, not to spend my life with her—had been made long ago.

"No, no," I told her. "You finish your gardening. I'll see you tomorrow."

I took my hand off her shoulder, and she turned back to her work. She'd stay there a long time, I knew, digging and redigging holes, moving earth from one flower bed to the next, as she had when I was a child, though then she'd done it only when it was necessary for the upkeep of the garden. She still had all her old habits, though now they were merely that—habitual, devoid of any grand purpose. They were like the scaffolding surrounding a half-dismantled house. How strange that they'd endured, I thought. Why had they endured, when she hardly seemed to understand what she was doing? What part of her did these habits belong to?

I said goodbye again and walked up the hill toward my mother's new house, another red-brick ranchburger on Wabash Avenue, just a block up from the one I'd grown up in, the one where my grandmother still lived. It was small, but my mother knew how to expand spaces beyond themselves. Even from this distance, I could sense the full light from her kitchen drifting down the street, brightening the path. Could my grandmother feel it, too? I turned to look back at my grandmother, but dusk had settled and all I could see were the leafy black branches of the pecan trees, dropping like a curtain over the scene—house, garden, grandmother, and all.

II

❦

Think of the healing and far-flung rivers
nursing themselves in our souls!

—SEPTEMBER 6

Dallas, 2011. Later that evening, as I lay drowsing, *Utmost* open on my belly, the curtain rose again on the little red house on the corner. This was an earlier edition: the trim on the windows was still beige, rather than white, and the old tire swing still hung from the branches of the pecan tree outside the kitchen, as it had until the late nineties, when the rope my uncle had secured it with a decade before snapped, sending me tumbling to the ground. The memory of falling jarred me awake, and I climbed out of bed and walked— softly, so as not to be detected—to the western wall of the room, the small room I always slept in at my mother and stepfather's house. It was 9:00 p.m. I pressed my ear against the wall, waiting. From across the divide, I could hear my mother and my stepfather talking in the animated voices they always used when they talked politics and, amplified behind them, the sound of Bill O'Reilly waxing, as ever, indignant. For the past thirteen years, every time I was home for a visit, I'd been sent to bed early by Bill O'Reilly, who had become a closely observed evening ritual in the house. Sometimes, if dinner ran late, I felt an obsolescent hope raise its tattered feathers: the hope that we'd simply missed the program. But there was no such thing as a discrete event anymore, not in the land of television. The cable was set to record *The Factor* automatically. No matter what the hour, Bill was in the box.

Fortunately, the walls in the house were thick, and if the volume got too loud, I could always put on headphones and watch the antidote—Jon Stewart—on my laptop. This evening, though, I found I hadn't mustered sufficient outrage at the day's news to require catharsis, and I went back to my book. It was still the entry for September 6. I was running a line through my mind—the line about the far-flung rivers that nursed themselves in our souls. I thought the line must have been important to me in my teenage years, because a feeling came over me when I read it, a very old sensation, of suddenly comprehending my soul as a *part* of myself, separate in some way but still inside of me, and of being startled by the discovery. I recalled suddenly having the sense that grand, incomprehensible forces were marshaling themselves someplace deep in my body—whole rivers, like the mighty Mississipp', which I'd drifted down one summer in an old-timey steamboat during a family vacation—and that these forces would eventually fling themselves out, fling *me* out. They'd carry me, I was sure, all the way to the horizon of my world, then tip me over, like a raft over rapids, into the black, glassy waters of the future. My idea of this future, back then, had not been specific. It consisted mostly of intense longing and vague images: of romance, of the streets of Manhattan (I'd never been to New York, but I imagined it constantly, always glittering, always under the cover of night), and of some kind of artistic expression—acting, singing, reading, writing. The sense that I must go to New York and pursue a higher life than the one I led in Texas was so strong that I was certain it came from God. Yet it also seemed impossible (it was the sense of impossibility which made the desire so intense), and I wondered, as perhaps every teenager wonders, how such a future would be accomplished. Oswald's words contained an answer: through the soul where rivers which mysteriously fed themselves were already bearing me along to my destination.

I switched off the lamp and lay back on my pillow, appreciating it. It was a cotton-stuffed pillow of just the right size—not too big and not too small—purchased ahead of my visit by my mother, who'd recalled me saying something over the telephone about liking medium-size cotton-stuffed pillows. That was how my mother was: infinitely generous and thoughtful. Even the television watching in the evenings was an act of generosity, because she knew that my stepfather loved to discuss the news with her, in a kind of two-way, three-way conversation with Bill. It wouldn't have been much fun for my stepfather to sit alone with the set, sipping his scotch. In fact, I was happy for them to watch it together—or, more precisely, I was happy for them to be happy together. It was strange for me, though, since I'd hardly ever seen my mother watching TV when I was growing up (she'd remarried only after I left for college). But then, everyone in the family took in more screen matter than we used to, I more than anyone. I was, by profession, a blogger, and I lived in front of the screen. This was true even though I blogged about books, a subject which one might reasonably suppose immune to the twenty-four-hour news cycle. But anything which wished to live on the Internet was obliged to play by its rules. I wondered whether, when I had children (*if* I had children), I'd be able to adequately describe the total, life-altering effect of its advent, or if I'd be as poor a storyteller as my grandmother, who couldn't muster more than a few sentences about the coming of electricity and automobiles to her family's farm. But these things are difficult to measure when one is living through them.

I switched the light back on—it was too early to fall asleep—opened my computer, and pulled up the Bible passage that began the day's entry in *Utmost.* John 7:37–38:

> In the last day, that great day of the feast, Jesus stood and cried, saying, If any man thirst, let him come unto me, and drink.
>
> He that believeth on me, as the scripture hath said, out of his belly shall flow rivers of living water.

I rested my hands on my belly, scooting the computer down my legs. It was curious to think of the belly being the place, but thanks to my upbringing the first reading I gave a text was always the literal one. Nothing mattered to Southern Baptists like the proper interpretation of Scripture, which began for them in the literal one and moved grudgingly (inevitably) on from there. I'd stopped being able to keep myself from discerning shades in Scripture some time ago, but there was fun in literal readings, particularly of verses like this one. I read it again, imagining the Spirit churning alongside dinner, a Holy Ghost in the machine.

The sound of laughter came from the next room—Bill's outrage must have reached comical heights, as it was bound to do at least once an episode—and I picked up *Utmost,* flipping through the pages. They were folded and scarred with red pencil, fifteen years' worth of notes. Underlined bits flashed before me, reminding me. It was a luxury to lie around reading like this, thinking like this—to have time to think like this. Lately, my moments with Oswald had been rushed, the day's entry squeezed between blog posts and social engagements and subway rides. Usually, my visits home were working visits. But my conversation with my grandmother earlier in the day had put me in a reflective mood, and I'd decided not to work this evening. I wanted to try to recapture some of the earlier life, the life my grandmother still seemed to be leading: measured, repetitive, still. The evenings I'd spent in her house had seldom featured television, and most political discussions had taken place over breakfast, which was when the newspaper arrived, bearing the full twenty-four-hour news cycle inside its finite yet entirely adequate pages. The hours after dinner had been filled with the kind of ritual I'd just been engaged in—reading and thinking and praying, the three activities hardly distinguishable from one another. No television, no Internet—no such thing as Internet. Sometimes, the telephone would ring, and sometimes there would be a friend on the other end of the line, but this always stopped by nine. Afterward, it was quiet time.

Or rather, as I'd recently learned, it was *the* Quiet Time. The Quiet Time was perhaps the sweetest and most endearing of all Evangelical rituals, a moment in every day set apart for private praying, reading, thinking, dreaming. It was also, like all Evangelical rituals, unofficial and entirely voluntary, Evangelicals wishing at all costs to avoid legalism and anything else which might throw them into the company of the papists, for whom many retained a sincere loathing. Such dread did members of my own childhood congregation have of "empty" ritual and regulation that they avoided using the term *religious* to describe themselves, and even eschewed *Evangelical* and *Baptist,* preferring instead *believing, Bible-believing, Bible Christian,* or, simply and best, *Christian.* A set of actions like those constituting the Quiet Time, performed daily for the purpose of honoring and communing with the divine, veered dangerously close to ritual, so people took pains to explain how it was supposed to differ. Even Oswald, who'd believed that time alone with God was necessary to the Christian life ("It is impossible to conduct your life as a disciple without definite times of secret prayer," he wrote), had advised Christians to "make a habit of having no habits." "Your god may be your little Christian habit, the habit of prayer at stated times, or the habit of Bible reading," he wrote. This was a sign that one was performing them too consciously. The ideal was to turn the entire life into a spiritual life, to carry the lessons and visions from times of worship and prayer out into the world, and to do so naturally, automatically. People who insisted on worshipping God *only* during set times became "spiritual prigs," and people who refused to participate in real life because of their devotional time were even worse. "'I can't do that just now, I am praying; it is my hour with God.' No, it is your hour with your habit." Ultimately, Christianity was about a personal relationship—between Christ and the individual—and it was meant to be a fantastic relationship, filled with uncertainty and excitement and desire, with trust and love. The private devotional times were where that relationship developed, and what went on there was nobody's business but one's own: what happened in the Quiet Time stayed in the Quiet Time.

That, at least, was the ideal. In reality, I remembered, I'd frequently been asked by Sunday School teachers and other concerned adults if I was keeping up with my prayer and Bible reading, and admonishment had followed if I didn't reply in the affirmative, leading to the onset of what has aptly been diagnosed as "Quiet Time guilt." At the time, though, I thought it very natural that such a question would be put to me, because reading and praying in private seemed natural remedies for a variety of emotional and spiritual ills, the way chicken soup was a natural remedy for the common cold, and church was a place which—again, *naturally*—concerned itself with emotional and spiritual ills. It was the responsibility of the adults there to ask if something was wrong and to propose a solution, and the solution they proposed was, very often, the Quiet Time. I remember always being grateful for the advice, if only after the fact, since it always worked.

And yet (it seemed amazing, thinking of it now), this all-important devotional time had never been named when I was a child. I'd learned the title one day not long before I'd left for this trip to Texas, from a book I was mindlessly thumbing through at the library while avoiding the work I was supposed to be doing.

From the 2010 edition of *The Oxford Handbook of Evangelical Theology:*

> Most Evangelicals would agree that certain spiritual disciplines are necessary for the formation of the godly life. A text frequently cited in support is 1 Tim 4:7: "Train yourself in godliness." If asked to list what they regard as the most important spiritual practices, they are not likely to differ very widely in their answers. Topping the list would be the daily personal devotion or the Quiet Time consisting of about twenty to thirty minutes (it used to be longer!) of spiritual exercises of Bible reading, study of and meditation on a passage, and prayers of praise and intercession. . . .
>
> The Quiet Time grows out of the deep conviction that the Bible is God's word. As one Evangelical puts it, "No Spiritual Discipline is more important than the intake of God's Word." Reading the Bible followed by prayer is the way one "hears" from God even in matters of personal guidance. In their practice of prayer, Evangelicals have generally preferred extemporaneous or free prayer to set

or liturgical prayers. This is because personal relationship is thought to be best expressed in personal conversation rather than using a prepared speech.

Having grown up in an Evangelical house, I can vouch for the general correctness of this definition, though I would add that reaching a *perfect* definition of any Evangelical practice is difficult precisely because the foundation of the Evangelical religion is personal relationship: in a sense, there are as many Evangelical Christianities as there are Evangelical Christians. But it was true that, in our community, the Bible was the centerpiece, and prayer and reading were free (or personal) conversations. When it came to prayer, the passage we took as our guide was Matthew 6:5–8:

> And when thou prayest, thou shalt not be as the hypocrites are: for they love to pray standing in the synagogues and in the corners of the streets, that they may be seen of men. Verily I say unto you, They have their reward.
>
> But thou, when thou prayest, enter into thy closet, and when thou hast shut thy door, pray to thy Father which is in secret; and thy Father which seeth in secret shall reward thee openly.
> But when ye pray, use not vain repetitions, as the heathen do: for they think that they shall be heard for their much speaking.
> Be not ye therefore like unto them: for your Father knoweth what things ye have need of, before ye ask him.

This was how my mother and my grandmother and I had prayed in the red house on the corner: Often in the evenings, after my mother had tucked me in, I would slip out of bed and tiptoe to the kitchen for a glass of milk. On the way, I would pass by the door to my grandmother's bedroom, which was always open a crack for the cat, sending a tight block of light across the floor in the hallway. I would see her sitting stick-straight in the hard little bed that was just big enough for one, turning the pages of *Utmost* or the Bible or shutting her eyes momentarily to let a prayer issue from her lips. Then she would switch off the light to sleep. My grandmother always slept flat on her back, without a pillow, and would not move till morning, not even when the cat curled itself up on top of her face, something we knew had happened by the sudden muffling of her snores, which were deep, resounding, and rhythmic, like waves breaking on a shore.

Then I would go to my mother's bedroom. Her door was often closed, but at the bottom was a vent with slats wide enough to see through. I would lie on my belly in the darkness and watch her for a moment while I drank my milk. She was always the same: afloat on her queen-size canopy bed, enthroned by a dozen fantastical pillows—pillows with green silk ruffles and paintings of nude women in the bath, pillows in the shape of a ball or a cylinder, pillows with white feathery strands, like eyelashes. Propped up on these pillows, a single pink Velcro curler atop her bright blond head, she would read, cracking sunflower seeds between her teeth. The Bible sat on her knees, just above the big plastic cup she used as a spittoon. When she was done, she would floss, drop the strand into the cup, switch off the light, and begin to intone her prayers, whispering into the darkness. My mother and her ways had always made me laugh, and it would not be long after I'd arrived at the base of her door that I would see her smile, turn her head, and say, "Come on in." I'd slept in the bed with my mother, taking turns with my brother and my sister, until I was already in high school.

It was around the time I started to sleep alone that I'd begun to read *Utmost*, which was a book given to me specifically for my bedtime devotional. Again, from the *Oxford Handbook:*

> The Quiet Time may be supported by a wide range of devotional aids in the forms of books, tracts, and magazines, but increasingly by using the latest in electronic storage and delivery systems and the internet.

Reading this, I couldn't help but be glad that I'd come of age in the time before "electronic storage and delivery systems and the internet" and was able to become completely absorbed in my book. The fact that *Utmost* was its own physical object was important, I think, since it was not simply a book like any other but a ritual, a measure of time and activity intended to lift the mind and body into a higher, more sublime realm—the realm of the divine—and this was a realm which, for me at least, had always been easier to access in a space set apart from the common round: in a house of worship, in a natural setting, in a ritual, in a book. I recalled the feeling, when I would spy on my mother and my grandmother during their devotions, that the atmosphere in their bedrooms was much altered from what it was at other times, and all because of the fact that they had a certain book open on their knees and were locked into it. Time slowed around them, grew palpable. They grew powerful. One could almost see the words lift themselves off the page and work themselves into their memories. This was another reason *Utmost*'s objectness was important: it was a very memorizable book, a book with strong aphoristic qualities. Its individual words, sentences, and paragraphs seemed to have been strung together almost haphazardly. There were spaces all around them, spaces into which one could slip oneself, one's own ideas. But in the electronic edition, I'd noticed, it hardly ever happened that one bit presented itself more forcefully than another. The words blended into a single dimension, and I found myself clicking away just moments after I'd read them.

When I'd first started reading *Utmost*, at the tail ends of days filled with the activities that are the unique domain of the American high school student—with cheerleading and show choir and math team and cross-country, with Young Life meetings and watching the boys in their bands, with late-night drives to the lake, lying wide to the clouds out on the pier, smoking cigarettes, and later-night study sessions at the IHOP—I would read to tie it all together. I would relate (to use Oswald's word) everything I'd experienced over the course of twenty-four hours to the vision. The vision was a work in progress, a bit of it completed every day, and *Utmost* was the frame.

Those had been good days. Full days, cozy days.

I let the memories go with difficulty. Now I lived alone, in Queens, and in general life had gone on strangely. The visions I'd had of the river carrying me north into a dazzling artistic life had materialized. But the reality was of course different in many respects from the visions. There were city streets, romance, and writing—but each of those things was more complex than I could have imagined. What I'd imagined, as it turned out, were the pretty façades of half-built buildings, buildings I hadn't understood would be mine to complete, buildings for which there were no blueprints.

And as reality had advanced on vision, I'd changed as well. Had I believed, back then, that the girl with rivers running through her, the rivers she believed to be the same as God, would enjoy the approval—perhaps even the admiration—of the Christians who had raised her, since she had so boldly thrown her raft into the river, taking the much advertised leap of faith? Had it seemed that peace and certainty would certainly be hers? I couldn't quite remember, because I couldn't quite remember that girl. I hardly ever had visions anymore, and when I did they were shallow things. Now, when I thought of God, the noise came flooding immediately in, the voices of a thousand pundits and politicians and preachers, the flickering images of a dozen holy wars, all lit by the eternal light of the screen. But this was the calamity that had befallen us all—all spiritually minded citizens of the twenty-first century.

I slipped once more from bed to press my ear against the wall. O'Reilly was still talking, on and on, as if on an endless loop. Where was the river, I asked, the river that could carry me across this divide? I sent the question up in a silent prayer. Then I poked some earplugs into my ears and went to sleep.

III

❧

Simplicity is the secret of seeing things clearly.

—SEPTEMBER 14

New York, 2011. Sometimes in the city, the divide narrowed of its own accord. *Utmost* was often present during these moments, generally because I would bring it up. I'd raise it, as a bridge or maybe as a defense. This was what happened one night shortly after I'd returned from my trip to Texas.

It was not often that my childhood religion made an appearance in my New York life, though the possibility was not as unlikely as it might seem. Despite having been born, in 1845, out of schism with the Triennial Baptist Convention, largely over the question of slavery and whether or not the Bible endorsed it (the Southern leadership was insistent that it did), the contemporary incarnation of the Southern Baptists did enjoy a presence north of the Mason-Dixon. There were in fact several Southern Baptist churches in the city, as well as a large and diffuse Evangelical Christian community to which many Southern Baptists, current and former, in some sense or another belonged, together with members of untold thousands of other denominations and non-denominational gatherings, Evangelical Christianity being a hydra with too many heads to count. Still, I would not have expected to see Southern Baptists in the place I did that night in September, because it was one of my usual haunts, and I did not make a habit of haunting places popular among Southern Baptists. When I'd first moved to the city, this had been a matter of choice: I'd wanted a new life. But now it was simply how things were. I no longer would have minded running into people from my old world—for years, I'd been developing a complicated nostalgia for it—but one didn't simply run into Southern Baptists in New York the way one did in Dallas.

It wasn't a run-in but an invitation which brought me into their company that evening, an invitation I wouldn't have accepted were it not for the venue: Keens Steakhouse, on West Thirty-sixth Street. Keens was a favorite watering hole of certain members of the copyediting department of *The New Yorker* magazine, where I'd worked since 2004, until 2009 as a copy editor, after which I'd moved to the Web department, where I wrote and edited a blog about books. Keens was particularly popular after late closings, when nothing but a glass of Macallan would serve to wipe away the commas and broken lines of text squiggling mercilessly across our fields of vision. Keens had started its life in the nineteenth century as a private pipe club for men and had retained much of its original character. Inside, its famous scotch bar and three dining rooms were appointed with brass railing, dark wood, and taxidermied busts of animals. Meat, mostly red, was what was on the menu, and it was still possible to order the namesake dish, a large mutton chop. But the real draw was the ceiling, decorated with fifty thousand clay churchwarden pipes, many of which had belonged to illustrious former members. Here, Teddy Roosevelt's exhalations browned the walls; here Albert Einstein, Babe Ruth, and General MacArthur swilled their scotch before the fire. I was never certain if I was imagining it, but every time I went to Keens, I thought I saw men, their cheeks rounded with scotch, gazing at the ceiling as if wistful for a simpler time: in 1905, the club had been compelled by judge's decree to admit women, though in my experience of the place, it seemed a largely pointless ruling. Men always outnumbered women by the dozen.

If Keens was an odd choice of watering hole for my copyediting department (which, like copyediting departments the world over, was almost entirely female), it was a much stranger venue by far for the women who gathered there this evening. These were members of an upstart networking and support group devoted to women who worked in Christian publishing. There was already a branch of the group in Dallas, which counted among its members a church friend of my mother's, and now they were expanding northward. A few days after I returned from my trip, my mother had phoned to ask if I'd mind attending the inaugural meeting, as a favor to her friend, and to her.

I told my mother that I did not work in Christian publishing and hoped to leave it at that. But the next day, she called again. The group, she'd learned, had decided to redefine its mission ahead of its first meeting. Instead of an association for women who worked in Christian publishing, it would be an association for Christian women who worked in any kind of publishing at all. They were changing their mission precisely to attract people like me, holy souls heaven-sent to labor among the heathen. I was an Esther, my mother reminded me, able to please the kings and queens of the mainstream media, while secretly remaining loyal to my people. "This group needs women like you," she said, ending her speech as she did every speech in which she mentioned Esther: "Who knows but you have been sent to the kingdom for such a time as this?"

Knowing I wouldn't appease my mother without an argument, I laid one out. This group, I told her, might be changing to include people like me, but I was absolutely certain there would be no one else at this dinner who worked outside of Christian media. Not because there weren't Christians in the mainstream media (in America, there were Christians everywhere), but because each wing of the industry had its own groups and associations, none of which overlapped with the others. New York was a big city made up of tiny, introverted villages—social and economic and cultural enclaves whose walls made them as impenetrable as medieval fortresses—as I'd had ample occasion to learn in my current job. If this organization was a networking organization, then only people who could benefit from contacts in the Christian-media world would join. It also suggested that they would be suspicious of anyone from the "lamestream" media, which was, after all, their avowed enemy (Sarah Palin was now deep into her career as a reality-TV star, but my recent visit to Texas had confirmed that the unfortunate term she'd coined was still in vogue). Not, I added (climbing, against my better judgment, onto my soapbox), that *The New Yorker* was mainstream. As one of the last bastions of long-form literary journalism, it was undeniably niche, even if its impact was often outsize, and even if it had a big corporate owner. If the right-wing media detested it for its political leanings, as I knew it did, then it seemed to me I was better off steering clear of any situation in which I would be forced to defend it or, worse, to defend myself. I'd had to account for my cultural choices to hostile listeners often enough back home to know how uncomfortable it could be, and how fruitless.

"I am not Queen Esther," I concluded, with a dramatic flourish, wanting to add "nor was meant to be," but I held my tongue. I knew I was coming off as a snob, something I'd been warned about repeatedly during visits back home.

"Well, of course it's up to you," my mother replied. "But you'll be blessed if you go."

I sighed.

"Where is it?"

"A place called Keens."

"Why didn't you say so?" I pictured a toasty glass of Macallan: amber courage. "I'll go."

A few days later, I found myself climbing the plush carpeted stairs that led to the second-story dining room. I was quite literally vibrating with anxiety, unable to silence the questions running through my mind, particularly the question of what on earth I'd find to talk to the other women about. Ostensibly, we were coming together because we shared three very important things: a religion, a gender, and a profession. But I knew that these were the very topics I needed to avoid. Each of those designations contained within it many variations, some of which diverged so wildly from the others as to render the overarching categories meaningless. It was almost impossible to know exactly what someone meant when she said, "I am a Christian" or "I believe in God" or "I want to empower women." What kind of Christianity did she practice? Who or what did she think God was? What did she think a woman was *for*? These were pertinent questions, but they were dangerous questions to raise if one wanted to keep the peace. As John Locke put it, "Every man is orthodox to himself," and he meant that every man, when forced to defend his particular brand of orthodoxy, is like a wild animal backed into a cage.

I didn't want to find myself backed into a cage that evening, but I feared it was inevitable, given my dilemma. This dilemma had many aspects, but at its heart was the fact that, although I'd made it into mid-adulthood with my Christianity intact, I was not the *kind* of Christian I was supposed to be, by which I mean the kind my childhood community had raised me to be. That I wasn't quite right had been communicated to me over the years in many subtle and not so subtle ways—even by my grandmother, who during my twenties had always asked if my current romantic interest went to church—and it was something I could see plainly for myself. I didn't dress or speak like the Christians who'd raised me. I didn't read what they read or watch what they watched. I didn't vote as they voted, and, apart from an hour each Sunday, I didn't surround myself only with other Christians; despite my best efforts (among them joining singles' Sunday School groups and eHarmony), my romantic interests *never* attended church. The difference went all the way down. I didn't seem to think as these Christians thought. Yet the difference wasn't total, and therein lay the dilemma. I still recognized myself in my Southern Baptists— the earliest, closest version of myself, the girl whose visions had fueled the adventure—and when they prayed aloud, in a church service or a Bible study, I heard in their prayers echoes of my own. Surely, we were speaking to the same God.

But it was a curious fact of contemporary life that God seemed less sticky than culture when it came to binding people together. My mother had compared me to Esther, a girl of divided affinities. But Esther had lived in a time (or at least in a Book) when one's God was synonymous with one's culture and one's people, and her dilemma—whether or not to risk her life in order to save her people and her culture, and to honor her God—was too clear-cut to map onto my own. Certain groups, I knew, still thought this way, but I didn't. My education (liberal) and experience (plural-istic, globalized, democratic, commercial) had taught me to value the spaces of exchange, the spaces where variety jostled with similarity, where multiplicity met unity. I'd learned to question any group claiming to have a monopoly on God and on the correct interpretation of Scripture. Yet I'd been raised in such a group (nothing, as I've already said, was more important to Southern Baptists than the correct interpretation of Scripture), and I still felt its pull. I still heard the voice of Wally Amos Criswell, my childhood preacher, railing against rationalists, atheists, Northern intellectuals, and strains of Christianity that engaged in the dreaded "higher criticism of Scripture" (i.e., literary or historical readings). And when I say railed, I do mean railed. In 1987, the year I turned eight, Criswell preached a sermon that contained these lines: "You know, that's an unusual thing: the difference between academia and good common sense. You can be a learned, graduated idiot and absolutely know nothing in the earth. I've gone to school with them by the uncounted numbers, graduated in the same class with them: idiots, stupid idiots."

In our church, the ideal was to "preach the Word and nothing but the Word." I'd been taught early to turn to Scripture in moments of difficulty and had often found sustenance there. But when I went looking through the Bible for examples of people trying to perform the kind of cultural tightrope walk that defined my adult life, no single hero or heroine emerged. Rather, it was the story of Naomi and her two daughters-in-law, Ruth and Orpah, that caught my attention. Ruth, the good daughter, who, following the death of her husband, decides to remain with Naomi, declaring,

Whither thou goest, I will go; and where thou lodgest, I
    will lodge:
thy people shall be my people, and thy God my God.

Where thou diest, will I die, and there will I be buried:
the Lord do so to me, and more also, if ought but death
part thee and me.

While Orpah, turning prodigal, kisses Naomi goodbye and van-
ishes from the story.

Stay or go—the story dealt in decisiveness, in finality—Ruth
or Orpah. But I could not choose. To me, it was Ruth *and* Orpah,
two faces on a two-faced coin. That coin was inside me, turning and turning, and had been for a long time. Perhaps the issue
would have resolved itself had it ever been forced by external pressures, but although I lived (as all Americans did) in the midst of a
very old and ongoing culture war, it was generally easy for me to
avoid confrontation. This was the benefit, and perhaps the curse,
of living in a secular society in which freedom of religious expression was both paramount and tricky to exercise—or rather to
enjoy—in the common, secular sphere. It was like a currency one
could not spend. Of my many friends in New York who had grown
up religious, there were only two who practiced now, the rest having accepted the obvious: that it was extremely difficult to bridge
two warring worlds.

But I (apparently) was a glutton for difficulty. That night at
Keens, as I arrived at the top of the steps, I found my anxiety quieted somewhat by an old hopefulness: that I would find among
the women that evening a kindred spirit. I spotted the group right
away. They were, predictably, the only women in the room, and
they were seated at a large round table beneath an oil painting
of a tiger in repose. They were perhaps nine or ten altogether,
and every one of them was blessed with good posture and shiny
straight hair. Their clothes were uniformly corporate Christian:
red blazers, gold-cross necklaces, and tiny flag pins abounded.

Briefly, I regretted my own attire, which was what one might call global-culture-worker chic: black from neck to boot, enormous horn-rimmed glasses, plum lipstick, and a frizzy bun plopped in the French style (carefully careless) on top of my head. I hurried over—I was the last to arrive—and, as I sat, one of the women suggested we hold hands and bless the meal, since the salad course had already been served. There was no Macallan in sight, and I suddenly realized that of course there wouldn't be. It was a meal planned by a Baptist—sure to be full of sound and fury, but dry, so dry. How had I forgotten?

"Heads bowed, eyes closed," the woman, whose name tag identified her as Rhonda, said, and, joining hands, we obliged.

I'd always been amused at the sight of the masculine evening crowd at Keens quaking at the females in their midst, but now I realized that until that very moment I'd seen nothing. Already, several of the men seated around the dining room had been eyeing our table, but, as the sound of the prayer caught their ears, every head in the room turned in amazement in our direction. Forks heavy with dripping chunks of sirloin hovered on their way to open mouths; scotch glasses clinked and remained suspended. Even the waiters stopped what they were doing. Out of respect? Curiosity? Horror? I wondered when last the august walls of Keens had been shaken by the sound of prayer. Never, was my guess, not even in the good old days when the rulers of the nation were sincere Christians. Surely even a devout believer like Teddy Roosevelt had left religion out of the clubhouse.

"Heavenly Father," Rhonda prayed, her voice ringing out, so loud I was sure they could hear her in the kitchen. She had a deep, pleasing, muscular Southern accent. "We gather before you today with joy in our hearts. Thank you, Father, for bringing this amazing group of ladies together to honor and serve you. We pray, Lord, that you will touch our minds and our hearts tonight as we discuss the work we do, that you might teach us how best to honor and glorify you in that work. We know, Father, that we are but small voices crying out in a world deafened by the noise of the Deceiver, and we know that you have given each and every one of us a unique opportunity to spread your Word. Bless this meal, Lord, bless these fine women, and"—here her voice grew even louder—"bless everyone in this restaurant and lead them to the light. In Jesus' name, we pray, Amen."

"Amen," we all said.

I raised my head in time to catch the other diners hastily averting their eyes, and I smiled with satisfaction. I truly admired people like Rhonda, people who were unembarrassed and easy with themselves. I'd always been such the opposite.

At the table, there was a general clattering of utensils and water glasses, and the eating commenced. I introduced myself to the woman who was seated next to me. Her name, she said, was Jenny. She was perhaps a decade younger than I—in her early twenties, I guessed—and she was formidably pretty, with glossy black hair, green eyes heavily circled with black eyeliner, and soft white freckled skin. Her blazer was not red but green, just a shade deeper than her eyes, and the gold cross around her neck was large and heavy and suspended on a long chain. It dropped precipitously into the V of a white T-shirt.

"Where do you go to church?" Jenny asked.

"Trinity Episcopal," I told her. "Down by Ground Zero."

"Oh," she said, wrinkling her nose. "Well, I guess we're all in this together. That's the important thing to remember."

"Do you work in publishing?" I said, hoping to change the subject before things got out of hand.

"Sort of. I'm an ambassador for a group called Models for Christ. Sometimes I do print ads."

"Models for Christ?" I asked. "What's that?"

"Oh, you know." She moved some lettuce around with her fork. "We get together to talk and pray. It's a support group."

I asked if there were many Christian models in New York, and Jenny raised one perfectly sculpted eyebrow, a gesture which conveyed a large amount of irony and a clear denial: *No.* While I was thinking that she must be a very good model, since she was able to create such communicative facial expressions, it occurred to me that her plight must be quite difficult.

"What do you model?" I asked.

"Intimates," she said. "Bras, panties, stuff like that."

"Corsets? Garters? Teddies?"

"What?"

"Never mind."

We finished our salads in silence. Or rather, I finished mine while Jenny continued to push hers around. Eventually, the waiters came to clear the table, and Rhonda tapped on her water glass with a fork. She gave a brief speech about the mission of the group (to support women who worked in Christian media in all their professional endeavors—apparently she hadn't got the memo about the change in focus), and then she suggested that we go around the table and introduce ourselves. She asked us to state where we worked and what we did to get the Lord's message out.

"Also," she added, "I'd love it if you'd give one example of how the Lord has blessed you at work this year, and one way He's challenged you."

One by one, the women shared their stories. Most of them worked at small Christian newspapers, magazines, and radio stations in the tristate area, and they all reported challenges of a similar vein. These mostly concerned the difficulty of finding advertisers for religious content and the nightmare of dealing with hate mail, which seemed to arrive at their various publications as often as tidy handwritten notes containing gleeful grammar "gotchas" arrived in the mailbox of *The New Yorker*'s copyediting department. I tried to listen attentively, but my pity for the women—it really was absurd for an advertiser to ask a Christian paper if they wouldn't mind printing the word "Jesus" a bit less frequently— was swallowed up in my own anxiety. My heart was pounding by the time it was my turn to speak, but somehow I managed to convey that I worked at a magazine in midtown, where I wrote a blog about books. As my challenge, I named coping with the negative comments that often appeared on my blog posts, and, as my blessing, I named a supportive working environment. I was lucky, I said, to work among friends.

"Do you blog about Christian books?" one of the women asked.

"No," I said. "But I usually don't blog about *anti*-Christian books, either." I paused. That had sounded suspicious, and was it even true? Had I really never written about Richard Dawkins? Christopher Hitchens? I couldn't remember. I knew I'd met both men, out at the readings, out at the parties, and I certainly knew the contents of their books, but it was possible that I hadn't read them—at least, not cover to cover. Part of being in the literary world was knowing things like that without really knowing them. There was a cultural shorthand one acquired, perhaps by osmosis, and there was a cultural guilt, too, at not having read *everything*. It was important to be able to pretend that one had. Just a few weeks before, someone had left a copy of a book called *How to Talk About Books You Haven't Read* lying on my desk. As a joke, I supposed.

Of course, I didn't plan on reading it, and anyway I didn't need to. But surely, I hoped, I'd remember if I'd *written* about books I hadn't read. With the Internet, the women would be able to check my facts in a second. Was that my blogger's paranoia kicking in, or my Baptist paranoia?

Blinking these questions away, I continued: "I do literary stuff, history, fiction, mostly fiction," I said. Was fiction offensive? Of course it was. I'd recently reviewed a book about a man who falls in love with an ape. Thank heavens, I thought, that it was a female ape. But what about those gay penguins at the Central Park Zoo? Surely I'd written about them at some point: year after year, they were the subjects of the most banned book in America, even though it wasn't *precisely* fiction and even though (as the tabloids had reported) the gay penguin couple in question had split up.

"But which magazine do you work at?" someone said.

With great difficulty, I forced myself to answer. The women all began speaking at once.

"How impressive!"

"You must be the only Christian!"

"Why were they so mean about W.?"

"You're such an Esther!"

"They were mean, weren't they?"

"How lucky we are to have you there!"

"That's a Jewish magazine, isn't it?"

I threw a dazed smile across the table, hoping it would hit all of the women at once, and, in an effort to avoid answering their questions, I nodded and shook my head, first this way and then that, until I was dizzy. To my relief, the main course arrived, and the focus shifted to the food.

As I cut into my steak, I relaxed a bit. The introduction hadn't been so bad, though I was always surprised by how intransigent our partisanship had become in our reading material. I wondered if it had really gotten worse, or if I'd just become more aware of it as I'd gotten older. I was by no means immune to its effects. I subscribed to the liberal periodical canon—*The New York Times,* the *LRB, The NYRB, Harper's, The New Republic, The Atlantic, n+1, The Believer,* et al. I also from time to time read more thoughtful Christian journals like *Christianity Today* and *Relevant.* My family, in contrast, were devoted consumers of a genre that included print publications like *The Weekly Standard* and *The Wall Street Journal,* and my mother sometimes read niche fare like *Acts & Facts,* a creationist monthly (sample article title: "New Chromosome Research Undermines Human-Chimp Similarity Claims"). We could seldom stand to read each other's publications, though my mother was more open-minded than I. The year I'd sent her a gift subscription to *The New Yorker,* she'd read it, becoming in the end a big fan of Malcolm Gladwell's. I'd thrown *Acts & Facts* across the room after two paragraphs—prompting my mother to chastise me (perhaps justifiably) for jumping to conclusions before I'd considered all the arguments.

The waiters arrived to clear the table for dessert, and Rhonda once again tapped her glass, this time instructing us to change seats. I took my napkin off my lap slowly, wondering whom to approach. Perhaps the woman from Jersey who worked at a free Christian daily called the *Love Express.* How unwelcoming could someone from a paper with a name like that be?

Before I could rouse myself to action, Rhonda had swooped into the chair next to mine—I got the impression that she always swooped like that, always moved without hesitation. Extending a hand in greeting, she told me how happy she was that I'd come, and that she hoped I'd come again. I took the hand, studying her. She was a youthful woman in her mid-forties, with red lipstick that matched her blazer. She had a broad, lively face, the kind which suggested she was ready to be everyone's friend.

"Blogging about books must be so much fun," she said, leaning in, her voice soft.

I nodded, apprehensive.

"Do you keep up with Christian publishing at all?" she asked. "I'd love to have some of your recommendations."

"No, I don't," I told her. "Unfortunately, keeping up with regular books takes up every bit of time I have."

Regular books? Had I just said that? What was a regular book? Seeing Rhonda's frown, I added hastily, "But you know what? I still make time to read *My Utmost for His Highest* every day."

This had the desired effect.

"Get out of here!" Rhonda said, pushing on my shoulder with her fingertips. "That is my favorite book of all time."

"Mine, too," I said. It genuinely pleased me to encounter other *Utmost* aficionados, and I was satisfied, also, that my assumption— that Rhonda would be one of them—had proved correct. The book had often saved me in situations like this.

"How about that," she said, still smiling. "Oswald Chambers. You know that his wife wrote it, don't you? Biddy Chambers. Some people don't know that."

"I don't think she actually wrote it," I said. This was an old claim about *Utmost* that popped up from time to time. I didn't know the answer, but I'd heard convincing arguments to the contrary. Also, it seemed unlikely to me that in the era of transparency the secret wouldn't have come out.

"Oh, I think she did." There was slyness in Rhonda's voice. Turning her face to the side in a dramatic gesture, she slowly lowered one heavily shadowed eyelid, then raised it again. A wink. I couldn't imagine what it meant—maybe something along the lines of "Behind every great man there's a great woman"—so I said nothing.

"Well," she said, after a moment. "That is fabulous, just fabulous. Praise God. And you've given me an idea. I'm going to pull it up on my phone and read from it. I always like to read from *Utmost* at things like this. Isn't it always perfect for every occasion?"

"It is," I agreed. Being mysteriously applicable to everything was one of *Utmost*'s chief qualities.

"It's like the little black dress of books!"

I laughed; I hadn't heard that one before. Rhonda took an iPhone out of her pocket and tapped an icon. To my surprise, it opened onto the original, or "classic," edition (the same one I'd always read) rather than the updated version. Ever since it had first appeared, in 1992, the updated edition had been more popular than the original. I despised it, though not because it was a bad book. On the contrary, I thought that the "translator" had made a very nice-sounding product. But I'd never understood why a translation had been necessary, except from a marketing point of view. True, Oswald hadn't always expressed himself in perfect English, and certainly not in clean, contemporary, American English. But he had expressed himself in *his* English. He'd had that most elusive of writerly qualities: an original voice. I imagined that the updated version sold so well to Americans because it was marketed to them, not because they actually found it superior to the original. In fact, I'd met several readers of the updated edition who'd had no idea that they were reading a translation, perhaps because the original was barely stocked anymore. Often, when I visited a bookstore, I would ask for the original at the desk and would inevitably be told that they didn't carry it. What they did carry were assorted *Utmost* tie-ins: *Utmost* in pink (presumably targeted at women), *Utmost* for kids. *Utmost* journals, calendars,

Bibles. There was even an abbreviated version. Had people's attention spans disintegrated so far that 250 words a day were 200 too
many? It all upset me terribly.

Rhonda once again called for attention, and I shook myself
out of my grumblings. I was, I felt, the most ridiculous of contemporary beings, a blogger who was also a Luddite. Plus, there
was no point in being grumpy around somebody like Rhonda: her
enthusiasm was intoxicating. Now, she held her phone in the air
and asked the women if they'd heard of *Utmost*. They all nodded
that they had, and she began to read aloud. September 14: "'Imagination versus Inspiration.'" I'd read the entry that morning, but it
was nice to hear the words spoken in Rhonda's Southern accent.
"'*Sim*plicity,'" she said, "'is the secret of seeing things clearly. . . .
You cannot think a spiritual muddle clear, you have to obey it
clear. In intellectual matters you can think things out, but in spiritual matters you will think yourself into a cotton wool.'"

She went on for a while, and when she came to the end, she
gave her interpretation. It was, she said, a powerful reminder for
people like us, people who spent so much of our time thinking
about what to say and how to say it, wondering whether it made
us sound smart or dumb.

"I know none of us wants to sound dumb, ladies!" she said,
and we all nodded in agreement. I myself spent most of my waking
hours trying not to sound dumb—one of the hazards of having a
job as a critic. In the back of my mind, I heard my grandmother's
voice, telling me how she'd never been very smart. "Not clever like
you, Macy dear."

Rhonda continued.

"What I want to communicate to you is that we don't need
to overthink things when it comes to getting God's message out.
I know that, as women, we like to beat ourselves up, and maybe

we work with guys who aren't so supportive. Maybe we work in a boys' club, and we don't feel smart enough to challenge it. But what does the Bible say? 'Lean not on your own understanding.' Listen to Oswald here. He says we have *spiritual* messages to impart, not intellectual ones. God's mind, not ours. Male, female—it doesn't matter. And even though our intellects are important, it is very easy—much easier than we know—to overcomplicate things by worrying about them too much. At some point, it stops being God's message and it starts being ours. We get in the way of ourselves, we get in the way of God. We lose objectivity, we lose truth, we allow fear to win. Like Oswald says, we get into a cotton wool, and you all know what happens when that happens: you can't see, you can't move! I want to urge all of you to throw the heavy weight you carry in your jobs onto God. A big theme of this book is that if we want to be of use to God, we have to be real. *Spiritually real.* Let's be real, ladies. Let's tell it like it is. He alone is strong. He alone is sufficient to *all* our needs. He has put us just where He wants us, and He *will* accomplish His goals. Amen?"

"Amen," I said, impressed that Rhonda had been able to put together a sermon like that off the cuff.

One of the women asked Rhonda if she could take a look at the copy of *Utmost* on her phone, and Rhonda passed it to her. I sat back in my chair, gazing up at the tiger and listening to the chatter. It was pleasant, sitting and listening. There was a time, I remembered, when I'd expected to grow up and belong to a group just like this one, to be a woman just like these women. It was strange that I hadn't. Turning into one of them—into a woman like my mother or my grandmother—would have been the obvious thing.

The waiter arrived, carrying a silver coffeepot. A chorus of spoons clinking against china rose above the steady murmur of conversation, and as I stirred some milk into my coffee, I looked up and saw that the woman seated directly across from me was reading *Utmost* aloud to the woman next to her. I couldn't make out which entry she was reading; she was reading softly, as if to a child at bedtime.

Suddenly, I felt perfectly at home, among people who were, once again, *mine.*

A memory came to mind, of a summer afternoon at my grandmother's house decades before, and of several women sitting around a glass coffee table, fanning themselves with the front covers of a book. They all had the same book, a small book covered in midnight-blue leatherette. Sweat showed in the armpits of their silk blouses, which were all in pastel colors, soft blue and light pink and chickadee yellow, but the room smelled only of perfume. Anyone would love to linger in that room with those women, at least at that moment. But there was a box of Kleenex on the table, which would undoubtedly come in handy as their session continued.

Then I heard the voice of one of the women, speaking to the others: "The first thing you have to know about Oswald is that you can trust him," it said. And a small girl—me—who had been hovering in the doorway came running into the room to sit at the woman's feet.

IV

༄

"And the parched ground shall become a pool."

ISAIAH 35:7, JULY 6

Dallas, 1986. The lump in the ground where they'd buried Spoofer, our mother's Old English sheepdog, was still visible, though now it was covered over with dry brown grass. My brother, Preston, and I stood on top of it in our bare feet, picking burrs out of the hard grass and arguing about whether or not the lump was smaller than it had been. Our uncle had told us that down in the earth Spoofer was disintegrating, that every bit of him was going back to ashes and dust: his long white hair, his bright blue eyes, his wet pink tongue, his glassy yellow teeth. Even the worms that were eating him would eventually turn to dust, along with the parts they'd ingested. Our mother said that her brother hadn't dug the grave deep enough, and that if she'd been here to supervise, she would've made sure he did a better job of it. But we'd gone to California, where Spoofer couldn't come because of the hills and the stairs. He was old and sick and had bad hips, and so he'd stayed here, on flat land with Nana. Preston and I had said a prayer for his soul beneath the lemon trees. Our mother had had Spoofer for a long time, since before we were born. She liked to tell us how he'd ridden shotgun in her red Mustang convertible, and how she'd taken him everywhere with her.

It was a hot, dry July afternoon. Preston and I had nothing to do—not for the rest of the summer, now that the Fourth had come and gone. We'd been outside all day. Already, we'd taken our bicycles down to the creek, where the bamboo grew into a forest, and had eaten a picnic with turkey sandwiches and oranges and honeysuckle. Then we'd hidden in the alley to spy on the neighbor's new wife. She was his third, Nana had told us, and the second who'd come out of a mail-order catalogue from China. She never set foot outdoors. The neighbor kept the skulls of enormous animals on a post of wood mounted by his back door. His entire house was painted the color of split-pea soup, and he'd planted so many tall bushes around it that you couldn't see a single window. Instead of grass, he'd covered the yard in thick black-green ivy that grew in tangled stretches between beds of small white rocks, and in one corner he'd placed a statue of a little man who was bald just like he was. The Buddha, our mother said, an idol. Preston and I had crouched in the alley by his back fence for an hour, until finally a woman's face appeared, half hidden by a screen door. We'd screamed when we saw her, and she'd vanished.

Now we were home and bored and beginning to fight. Preston stood next to the mound where Spoofer was buried, scraping it with his foot.

"It isn't smaller," I said. "He's still under there."

"No he's not," Preston said. "The worms ate him."

He picked up a stick and stabbed it into the ground, right into the middle of the lump.

"Stop it!" I screamed.

The door on the back porch opened, and Preston was gone in a flash, around the house and down the alley, leaving the stick behind him.

"What's going on?" my grandmother said. She was wearing her green apron, and her hands were coated in flour. "Your mother's group is meeting now. We're not going to have a ruckus."

I tossed the stick into the bushes.

"Nana," I said. "I want to come in. I'm hungry. It isn't fair."

"Well, you are red," my grandmother said. "Come on in and I'll give you a snack. But you've got to be quiet."

Inside, the house was warm and still. I lay down on the gray carpet in front of the television. It wasn't on, and anyway it didn't get any channels, but it was my favorite object in the house. I stretched out on my back and lifted my legs, pressing my toes against the VCR. From the living room, the sound of a woman's voice drifted, so soft and low that it almost seemed a whisper, and then another woman's voice, almost identical to the first. They were far away, down a hallway and behind a door, but I could tell from the quality of their voices and the stillness of the house that they were praying. I knew what about: men and children, children and men. I'd met these women before. They came over sometimes to talk and pray. Sometimes, they came with their children, and then I had someone to play with; sometimes they came alone, and then I hid in the hallway to listen. They were all nice women from church, and they all belonged to the single parents' Sunday School group.

My grandmother came into the den to tell me that my snack was ready. I jumped up and followed her to the kitchen, groaning when I saw what she'd prepared: apple slices with unsweetened peanut butter and a glass of milk. Since we'd moved into her house, four months earlier, we'd been eating cheap and healthy. Our mother had said that it was because Nana was a dietitian, and also because she'd lived out the Great Depression. She understood how to monitor pocketbooks and stomachs. Every day at dinnertime, Preston and I dutifully reported what we'd eaten for lunch at school, and if it was determined that we hadn't had sufficient units of milk and roughage that day (three glasses, three servings), Nana would watch us while we made up the difference.

After I'd finished my milk, I slid off the high stool and went to stand near the doorway that led to the living room, taking care to stay out of sight. The women were laughing now—about what, I couldn't tell—and there was a crinkling sound, as if something was being taken out of a paper shopping bag. The conversation grew louder and louder—everyone was speaking at the same time—and then all of a sudden the chatter stopped and a single voice took over. I knew the voice. It belonged to my mother's friend Sherri, whom I adored, because she was beautiful and sweet. Sherri had white-blond hair that reached halfway down her back, and her makeup was always perfectly matched to her attire. She sold Mary Kay, and whenever she came over she'd help me choose a lipstick—I was a spring, she said—painting it carefully onto my mouth. She was so good at her job that she'd been given a pink Cadillac, but my mother had told me that she wasn't rich at all, that the car didn't really belong to her.

"Let's all read along with the day's entry," Sherri said, and she began to read. I stood very still behind the door, listening to the words without understanding them. It seemed to go on for a very long time. When she was finished, she said, "Okay, ladies, the thing y'all gotta know about Oswald is that you can trust him. He is *real.* He's tough, but in a good way. Some people find him a bit too smart, but I think y'all are gonna like him. You are *very smart ladies!"*

I poked my head around the doorway to see if they were finished. Sherri was seated in the middle of the long white sofa, in between my mother and another woman. She sat right on the edge, with her spine stick-straight, so that the back of her pink silk blouse floated free—she'd often told me that a lady's back should never touch the back of her chair. Her legs were crossed, and I could see the toe of her pink suede pump peeking over the edge of the coffee table. Her hands were in her lap, and in them she held a small blue book. She was talking with my mother now, just the two of them, and I wanted very much to hear what they were saying. I stepped out into the doorway, to catch her attention. Sherri smiled and waved, and I ran over.

"Here comes my pretty girl," Sherri said. "With hair like a princess. All the boys are gonna be falling all over themselves when you grow up." She pulled me down to the floor at her feet, gathered my hair up into her hands, and began to braid it. She did the most perfect French braids. I felt sorry for her that she only had a son.

"Sherri," my mother said.

"Oh, come on now, Debbie," Sherri replied, and I looked nervously at my mother. She didn't like it when people called her Debbie. Her name, as she always tried to tell them, was Deborah. The Judge. But nobody in Dallas could ever seem to remember it. They always said to her, "Debbie Does Dallas!" And they always said to me, "Macy, like the store." But it wasn't. It was Macy, like my grandmother, Marjorie Macy, and like her mother, Matilda Macy. But mostly, it was Macy, like the first Macy, Thomas, who came to America in 1639 so he could be a Baptist, free from persecution. He was famous for letting Quakers into his house one night when the Puritans wanted to cut their ears and noses off and hang them and burn them, and for buying the island of Nantucket afterward with a bunch of other people who wanted to live in peace. Preston and I had memorized part of a poem, by John Greenleaf Whittier, about it:

> And yet that isle remaineth
> A refuge of the free,
> As when true-hearted Macy
> Beheld it from the sea.

Sherri pulled my hair straight, to smooth the braids.

"Are you excited that you're going to be a big sister again?" she asked.

I nodded shyly. Sherri placed a hand on my mother's belly.

"Gonna be here before you know it!"

On the coffee table in front of me sat a copy of the book they were all reading. I reached for it.

"Here, darlin'," Sherri said. "Let me show you how to use it."

She took the book and flipped it open.

"You see? Here's the page for the day: July sixth. Can you read the words at the top?"

"Of course I can," I told her. "I can read anything."

Sherri laughed loudly, and I hid my face. Had I said something funny? Then she pointed at the part I was to read.

"'Vision and Reality,'" I read.

"Very good!" Sherri exclaimed. "And here's the Bible verse, Isaiah 35:7: 'And the parched ground shall become a pool.' *Parched* means dry, like when the ground here gets really hot and all the grass turns brown and all you wanna do is jump in the swimming pool. I bet you go swimming a lot."

I nodded, even though I didn't. We didn't belong to the country club, and we didn't know anyone with a pool.

"And this is talking about how the things we want, God will help us to make them real, like water coming up from nothin', just from the dirt."

"Oh, Sherri," my mother said. I turned around.

"There, there, sweetheart," Sherri said. She placed her hands over my mother's. "It's gonna be all right. God is faithful."

"God is faithful," my mother said.

"Let's pray again," said Sherri.

They closed their eyes. I looked away from them to the book, at the words printed there. They rose off the page, hovered for a moment, and disappeared:

Let Him put you on His wheel and whirl you as He likes, and as sure as God is God and you are you, you will turn out exactly in accordance with the vision. Don't lose heart in the process.

V

〜

We see like children; when we try to be wise we see nothing.

—SEPTEMBER 14

New York, 2011. "Excuse me."

I turned. Jenny, the lingerie model for Christ, had placed a hand on my shoulder.

"It's just my bag," she said. "It's caught under your chair."

I looked around. The women were gathering their belongings: evidently, the meeting had come to a close. The tables surrounding us had reached varying states of depletion. White-wine glasses had given way to red, now drained to silt; mutton bones recently bereaved of meat decorated otherwise empty plates. But the candles were only half gone, and the easy flow of conversation rising above them meant that the night—for some, at least—was just beginning.

"Are you headed home?" Rhonda asked, pulling on her coat.

"I'm off to a book launch," I told her. A thought occurred to me.

"Rhonda," I said, as we made our way toward the staircase. "Earlier, when you said that we needed to be real—spiritually real—what did you mean?"

"Oh, well, you know: *real.* It means that you've accepted Jesus as Lord of all. That you trust Him totally, instead of trusting the wisdom of the world. Also that you've been tried and tested—that's very important."

"And how do you know if you're real?"

"Oh, Macy," she said sadly. She shook her head. "If you're real, you just know."

We stood for a moment at the top of the stairs.

"You should read Oswald," she went on. "He's very good on this question."

"I've been reading him for fifteen years," I told her.

"Then I guess you better keep reading him."

We reached the street, and I shook Rhonda's hand, thanking her for the evening. But when she asked whether I'd be back for the next meeting, I told her I couldn't make any promises.

"I'm so busy," I explained. "You know how it is."

"I think I do," Rhonda said. "God bless you, Macy. I'll be praying for you."

After we'd parted ways, I turned for a moment to admire the Keens house. New York was full of pretty nineteenth-century buildings, but this one was one of my favorites. Maybe it was the proximity of Madison Square Garden and the abomination that was Penn Station, but Keens seemed to have a rebellious air about it, as if it had survived merely as a rebuke to its surroundings. I felt a twinge of envy for the men who had been its members in the olden days: how nice it must have been for them. Of course, there were some men in the city who still belonged to clubs like this one, clubs where women weren't allowed past the foyer. The father of one of my boyfriends, a kindly man who toiled long hours at an investment bank and kept his family in a penthouse on Fifth Avenue, had belonged to one. And his wife had belonged to an all-female club, though naturally he had paid her dues. This had been a source of worry to her and, obliquely, to me, since it was hinted that such luxuries (responsibilities?) might one day also be mine if things stayed on track. It was all a matter of keeping the family name in the Social Register.

I, alas, was fated to remain unregistered.

As I began to walk in the direction of my next destination, an apartment in the East Sixties, I reached instinctively for my phone. I liked to call my mother whenever I was walking in the city, and I generally spoke to her once or twice a day.

"How was it?" she asked.

"Fine," I told her. "They were very nice. But I want to ask you something."

"Of course."

"Do you remember telling me that you didn't know how I could have understood *Utmost* when I first started reading it?"

"You mean when you were a teenager? Yes, that is not a book for beginners. No way. It just makes beginners feel bad, like they could never be holy enough. I mean, *My* Utmost *for His* Highest? Also, it's too intellectual. I've recommended it to so many friends over the years who are, like, 'I do *not* get this.' And for a girl of fifteen . . . Although, you were very bright."

"Thanks, Mama. But do you remember the word you used to describe people who could understand it?"

"No."

"Sure you do," I said. "You said that only people who were"— I paused, to indicate the blank she was to fill in—"could understand it."

"I'm not sure," my mother said. "Let me think."

I walked on in silence, while she mumbled quietly to herself.

"Well," she said at last, "I suppose I might have said that only people who were real could understand it."

"That's it!" I said. "That's it! But what did you mean by it?"

"By *real*? I guess what I meant is: you got the good, you got the bad. You got both sides, you've seen them, you know they're in you, you know that the only thing in existence that can save you from the bad is Christ. You know what it's like? It's like that movie *Black Swan*. Did you see it? It was gross—your brother walked right out of the theater. But I have to say, I kind of got it. I mean, yes, they played up the sexual stuff, but I understood what they were trying to say. She's got the bad in her and the good, and she doesn't know what to do about it. Of course, the ending was ridiculous. She's like, 'Perfection is possible.' Please! Not this side of heaven, honey. And then she dies!"

We both laughed.

"Okay, I gotta go," I said.

"Off to another party?"

"Yep."

"Oh, the life you lead. Have a wonderful time."

I walked on, remembering. When I was younger, I'd known exactly what was meant by the idea of a "real Christian." People at church had used the phrase often, and often in describing my mother. "Oh, you're Debbie's daughter," they would say. "I love her; she's so real." They'd meant, first, that they saw Christ in her, and also that she'd been tried and confirmed—born once and born again (the latter event had taken place in the mid-1980s, just after she'd gotten pregnant with my sister, and just after my father had left). They'd meant that she was outspoken about her beliefs and about how she'd come to them, that she "witnessed" freely about her journey and about the saving effects of Christ on her life. They'd heard how she'd been in California at the time of her crisis, about how my father had moved the family there for a job, then left, and about how she'd felt so hopeless that she'd decided to go to church one Sunday, though she was long out of the habit. The church she chose was the First Presbyterian Church of Hollywood, or Hollywood Pres, as it was known. It was a famous church, a powerful Evangelical church, and it was alive with a kind of spirituality that had been entirely missing in the dry genteel little parish she'd belonged to as a child in Illinois. She hadn't known before that this kind of Christianity existed. Hollywood Pres was a church of rousing song and charismatic preaching, of vibrant community and toothy morality. She heard the preacher—Lloyd Ogilvie, who in the future would serve as the chaplain of the United States Senate (following his predecessor at Hollywood Pres, Richard Halverson, into the position)—and she was filled with conviction. All of a sudden, as she'd put it to me many times over the years, "I knew that I knew that I knew."

I smiled, thinking how that phrase had also been clear to me in younger days. Now, I had little idea what it meant, just as I had little idea what "real Christian" meant. There were layers of meaning in those phrases, though the words they contained were simple. It was strange, I thought, that even though I couldn't define *real*, I felt certain that I *wasn't*—not in the way my mother or her church friends were. But why? Why should I feel that way, when I knew myself to be a Christian? It was true that, having been born into the faith, I'd never had a single, stunning moment of rebirth. If being born again meant being *converted* to a personal faith in Christ, I saw clearly that I'd never achieve it: How could a person convert from same to same? But I'd asked Christ into my heart as a very young child and had enjoyed a relationship with Him ever since. Surely, this counted for something.

I arrived at the building where my party was being held and was directed by the doorman to take the elevator to the penthouse. As the box rose noiselessly into the sky, I tried to shake thoughts of religion from my mind. It would be necessary now to shift gears.

The moment the elevator doors opened, I knew I'd worried for nothing: there was plenty here to lull me into forgetting. As I stepped into the apartment, a tuxedoed servant offered to take my coat, while another handed me a champagne flute. The liquid inside was both golden and pink, and at the bottom sat a cluster of small red berries, trembling slightly in the bubbles.

"An autumn cocktail," the servant said. "Organic cranberry, rum, and champagne, with a touch of simple syrup, made from organic cane sugar."

"Thank you," I said. I lifted the glass into the light. Then I lowered it slowly, my eye drawn to what lay beyond.

Beyond the mannequin guests, artfully grouped in threes and fours, two walls of windows converged at a ninety-degree angle. I made my way past a table that held free copies of the book whose release we were celebrating—a book written by the apartment owner's wife—and went to stand in front of the windows, marveling at the construction. The panes of glass had been joined almost seamlessly, so that if you stood directly between them, in the corner, you felt as if you were being thrust out over the city, in a strange, angular spaceship. Here, we were higher up than anything nearby, and below, as far as the eye could see, were dense constellations of light, the park breaking in the west like a gasp. Who needed stars above, I thought, when one lived like this?

"There you are."

I turned to find Tom, a freelance reporter, book reviewer, and sometimes friend. We often showed up at the same parties.

We kissed hello and clinked our glasses.

"This place," I whispered. "It's nuts."

"I know, right?" Tom said. "The guy's a hedgehog. But kind of a sweet one. He actually embraced his wife after her speech. Nice move missing it, by the way."

"Is the book any good?"

Tom snickered. His eyebrows, fine and black and twitchy, rose and fell, and his small black eyes darted over the crowd until they found the author. Twin bats, seizing on a prey.

"I'd say we'll never know."

I shrugged, uncomfortable. We were invited to these things only so that we'd publish reviews. But this book wasn't suitable for the blog I ran, and I felt as though I were there under false pretenses—even if it was ethically questionable for the author to have invited reviewers in the first place. But Tom reassured me, as he had many times before. It was the way things were done, he said. I should view it simply as a joining together of forces: we were all book people, after all, and we were a dying breed.

"Also," he went on, "they don't really expect you to review it. They just want to be able to point around the room at all the publications they've managed to entice, so that their friends will think they're culturally legitimate. Tonight, you're not you, you're Miss *New Yorker*. You certainly look the part."

"Gross, Tom," I said.

"Oh, come on. Tighten that bun and follow me to the bar. Or, if you insist on seeing corruption everywhere, go home and read a Victorian novel."

I followed him to the bar: I was long out of Victorian novels. As we waited for the bartender to assemble our next round, I found my previous thoughts returning to me. "Do you ever have the feeling we're not living in the real world?" I said to Tom.

It was a rhetorical question, and a facile one, but I was in the mood to ask it. Tom glanced around, his eyes alighting on the servants, in their tuxedos; on the guests, in their Brooks Brothers and tweed and black; on the stacks of books glistening seductively on the table.

"Two things. One: this isn't our world. And two"—he raised the flute to his lips—"there's no such thing as the real world."

"I'll drink to that," I said. "But maybe there's such a thing as reality."

Tom gulped back his champagne and shook his head violently, as if the bubbles had shocked him.

"You speak in riddles, and I cannot stand riddles."

So I began to tell him about the dinner at Keens, and about my grandmother and *Utmost* and all of my current worries. Tom listened, his head cocked in sympathy. He understood, he said. He'd been born in Iowa, into a Church of Christ family.

"I was baptized in the river by the preacher man. And when I came up, I felt different. I really believed it had done something to me. I thought I'd believe forever."

"Then what happened?"

"Then I grew a brain."

"Come on," I said.

Tom smiled and gazed dreamily out the window, dropping his head onto my arm. We'd moved to a long leather sectional that faced toward the west, and by now we'd had sufficient amounts of champagne, enough to make all troubles dwindle to their proper proportions.

"I was baptized in a swimming pool," I said.

"Poor baby."

"Do you think I'll ever grow a brain? Or is it too late?"

"Oh, too late! Much, much too late. There's no hope for you."

We were quiet for a long time, looking out over the city. Then we heard a voice.

"May I get you anything else? The bar is closing."

I looked up to see one of the servants standing over us, as calm as when I'd first stepped out of the elevator. If he was tired, or annoyed by our continuing presence (now Tom and I were among the last remaining guests), he gave no sign.

"Another round of those intoxicating autumnal concoctions," Tom said. "We are in the *rum*-inative mood."

The servant turned without a word.

"Listen," Tom said. "If you're so worried about all this stuff, about that woman telling you you don't understand your favorite book and you're not a real Christian and whatever, then you've got to get to the bottom of it. I'll tell you what my favorite editor always tells me when I'm confused. Don't whine. Don't wonder. Just do the work. Replace hypotheticals with facts. What's the deal with this book? What do you know about the guy who wrote it, about his context? Maybe you're not the one who's reading him wrong."

"I doubt it," I said. "He was a preacher, an evangelist, one of these people who's on fire for Jesus. I'm sure he has much more in common with the fundamentalists than he does with someone like me. I mean, there's a reason *Utmost* is W.'s favorite book and Jerry Falwell's favorite book and the guy who ran the National Prayer Breakfast. Clearly, I'm the one who's misreading."

"Wait, wait, wait," Tom said. He set his glass, empty once more, on the table. "You're telling me you have the same favorite book as George W. Bush and Jerry Falwell?"

"Yes," I said. "But it's not only—"

"Egads." Tom placed his hands over his eyes. "I think you'd better keep that one to yourself."

"I usually do."

We walked toward the elevator, where the servant stood holding our coats and bags. After I'd organized myself, I glanced one last time at the wall of glass, at the lights on the ground and the hazy expanse stretched over Jersey. God's gray earth. I felt suddenly sick from the champagne.

"This building is too tall," I told Tom.

"Nowhere to go but down," he said, and he pressed the button for the lobby.

∾

Out on the street, I kissed Tom goodbye—he was headed to Brooklyn—and I started for the subway. But when I arrived at the station, I found I wasn't ready to stop walking, and I hooked my way around Bloomingdale's toward the east. It had been true, what I'd said to Tom about keeping *Utmost* to myself. I'd been keeping it to myself around people like him—which is to say, my friends and colleagues—for seven years. In that time, I'd only ever brought it up among family or to significant others, though as of yet I'd never dated anyone who had the least bit of interest in it.

But it wasn't their fault, I realized now—my shyness about *Utmost*. There were reasons why my reticence had begun when it did, and none of them had to do with friends or colleagues, or not directly. They had to do, rather, with the year I'd started my job—2004—a strange year for me and an even stranger one for *Utmost*. That year, we'd traveled to Scotland, Oswald's homeland, together. That year, we'd lost a love and an election, but we'd gained a career. That year, we'd committed ourselves to a certain mode of existence, a highly secretive, highly protective mode. I'd never in my life lied about my beliefs, but I'd certainly learned how to skirt the issue.

Now I found myself wondering if it had been the right choice: Were secrecy and omission ever the right choice? The East River came into view, and I made my way to the bench that looked out at the bridge. I sat, facing Queens, and thought back to Scotland, as it had been when I'd visited, seven years before.

VI

ᕁ

Most of us live on the borders of consciousness—
consciously serving, consciously devoted to God. All
this is immature, it is not the real life yet. The mature
stage is the life of a child which is never conscious.

—NOVEMBER 15

Glencoe, Scotland, 2004. "Put that away, please, I beg you."
I shut my computer and looked out the car window. On the side of the road stood a sign in the shape of a large triangle, rimmed in red and bearing the silhouettes of two hunched figures, a man and a woman, the man holding a cane, the woman with a hand placed gingerly on the man's back, as if, in stouter days, they'd had a different kind of relationship. And beneath, another sign: ELDERLY CROSSING. The signs were hilarious, and necessary. All week long, Munro and I had been dodging Madge, a ninety-year-old hellion who lived across the loch from his parents' farm, and who liked to go to town in her motorized wheelchair, traveling slowly and with magnificent imprecision down the single lane, so that it was impossible to pass her. Each time her electric buzz came within earshot of the house, we could hear Farmer Willie, the crofter whose family had held the tenancy on the land for

centuries, cursing, though neither Munro nor I could understand what he was saying. We'd had a brief conversation with him when we arrived, Willie speaking his Gaelic, Munro speaking the posh English he'd learned as a schoolboy and never been able to shake, and I stammering in a twenty-first-century American which suddenly seemed egregiously anachronistic. I'd never been anywhere in the Old World that hadn't been retrofitted for tourists, but Willie, hands red and swollen, boots caked with dung, face rippling out from the central features in radial bands, belonged to a different age. Willie smelled of salt and dung and a mineral that didn't exist anymore where I was from, if it ever had—something dark and medieval. That we'd somehow arrived here from our different points on the continuum, to stand face to rugged face, seemed impossible. And indeed, Willie, when I'd met him, had looked right through me to his flock, waving, in a gesture I'd taken to mean "Keep away"—though who should keep away from whom was unclear. The flock, yellow-gray puffs thirty strong, had started when he'd waved, moving as one to the top of a hill, then dropping noiselessly down the other side. This was a key feature of this part of Scotland: there were few hiding places in the landscape, yet things vanished and appeared with ease.

"Can you see them?" Munro asked, leaning across the passenger's seat. "There, in that crevice. Two brontosauruses, sauntering toward the horizon."

"Sauntering?"

"Oh, yes. Brontosauruses always saunter, especially when they're with their sweethearts, especially in this part of the world. The brontosaurus is the most romantic of all dinosaurs."

I caught my breath as the glen came fully into view, and took his hand.

"I've never seen anything so . . ." I said. "Not in my entire life."

Then I was quiet, because it would have been embarrassing to say what I was thinking, and perhaps intrusive to Munro's own thoughts. Deep, deep ran the valley to the horizon, and high, high rose the hills. Distance was difficult to measure. Length seemed to dominate height, though height was also very present. The earth was folded and tented in strange ways, and the sky overhead was heavy and wet but also wide. It was a wet green world, swollen and quivering and silent. If the color green had form, I thought. The summits were powerful but also gentle. How were they so gentle?

"Let's go," Munro said, pulling the car into a small lot. "We'll walk down through the valley, then up there—the Aonach Eagach."

He climbed out and went around to open my door.

"How are those feet?" he asked. Kneeling, he took my legs in his hands, guiding them to the ground. Then he took the top of a boot and tugged.

"You're too kind," I said. They were his mother's boots. I locked a finger in a curl of his hair. It was so much redder against the green. In London, it was yellow as ginger.

"That's all right," Munro replied. "You've got to have dry feet, haven't you?"

We walked from the car down into the valley, Munro snapping photographs as he went. Everywhere he went, the big black Nikon went first. I outpaced him after a few moments, pushing toward the summit.

"I'm sorry," I called, as the ground began to slope upward. "Munro, I'm sorry!"

"What for?" he called back.

"For everything!" I shouted.

He shook his head, about to speak, but said nothing. Instead, he raised the camera, and when he was done he ran to catch me.

"You look happy here," he said. "Like you belong here. Look."

He held out the camera, and in its tiny window I saw a figure in tweed and bright blue boots, high in the green, smiling, pale, hair wild as the grass underfoot. It did look as if it belonged. Briefly, I imagined what my childhood would have been like had it been spent in argyle and Fair Isle, hiding from the rain, rather than dodging the sun in neon plastic shorts and a Rebels cheerleading uniform, trying with great futility not to burn. If I'd been raised away from Neiman's and highlights and Get in Shape Girl in the starkness of the loch; away from the Red White and Blue in the green and gray. Was there Scots in my blood? My paternal grandmother's maiden name was Burns. Perhaps I was one whole quarter Scots, and perhaps even Highland Scots. Perhaps my ancestors had been forced out in the Clearances in the Age of Mass Migrations, the long nineteenth century; or indentured into servitude in the colonies a century before. Or maybe they'd been from the Lowlands and had left of their own accord. I knew nothing of that side of the family, except the rumor that my great-grandmother Lola had run a back-alley abortion clinic in Oklahoma in the fifties, and that she'd taught the boys in the family to swim by tossing them into the lake. Well, the Scots were known for being tough and pragmatic, weren't they? But almost no one lived here anymore. The Highlands covered more than half the landmass of Scotland, but there were only 230,000 people, just 9 per square kilometer. You could walk for days in the Highlands and see nothing but green and sheep.

But it hadn't always been this way. They said that if you paid close attention, you could sense the vanished settlement lines— the patterns etched out over the course of a millennium by the clans and the crofters, before the houses and the farms had been abandoned, razed, forgotten, so that what one saw, when one looked out over certain stretches of the Highlands, was not empty space but emptied space. Violently emptied. And if you watched very closely, for a very long time, they said, you might almost see it fill up again.

"Borderlands," I said. "Now I think I know where his obsession started."

"Who's that, then?" Munro asked.

"No, nothing."

It had been an awkward period for me with *Utmost*, and for the moment I wasn't speaking of it to anyone. Not even Munro. Especially Munro.

"You'll tell me about it later," he said. He turned, letting the shutter close on the valley at his feet, and I started again up the path, keeping the summit of the Aonach Eagach in view.

∾

Later that night, I sat cross-legged on the bed under a woolen blanket fragrant with age, a glass of Oban on my knee. I was alone in the room. In the kitchen, I could hear Munro going about the business of making lamb stew, and, since this seemed to be a rather involved undertaking, I'd decided it was safe to proceed. As quietly as I could, I leaned to fetch *Utmost* from my bag, then pulled the blanket up over my head so that I was completely hidden.

I'd been reading the book for nine years. That evening, I'd decided to give myself permission to read it out of order in pursuit of a theme, since it was the only book by a Scot I'd ever read, apart from *Treasure Island* and *Peter Pan*. The morning's entry had touched on the theme I was interested in: consciousness and childhood. Oswald wrote often of Jesus' warning, in Matthew, that only those who became as little children would enter the kingdom of heaven, and he always cast childhood as a state of semiunconsciousness. A child didn't worry about how well he was obeying God's will, a child *was* God's will. In a similar way, a child was a prayer, able, through his unconscious faith, to follow Paul's command to "Pray without ceasing." A child didn't worry about the future: though uncertain "of what God is going to do," he was nevertheless "certain of God." To His grown children, God was mother: "A child's consciousness is so mother-haunted that although the child is not consciously thinking of its mother, yet when calamity arises, the relationship that abides is that of the mother. So we are to live and move and have our being in God." Childhood was a dependent state, but also a free state, a joyful state. Most of all, it was a *natural* state. The child behaved naturally and was also (this had been in my mind earlier in the day) in tune with nature. "If we are children of God, we have a tremendous treasure in Nature. In every wind that blows, in every night and day of the year, in every sign of the sky, in every blossoming and in every withering of the earth, there is a real coming of God."

Yet becoming as a child, though it was in some sense the easiest thing to do, was also difficult. It represented the mature stage of the Christian life. Before this stage, there was necessarily a struggle of will. Habits had to be developed and doggedly maintained before they became natural; focus had to be won, imagination trained. The treasure that lived in nature was hidden from those who cast their eyes upon idols: "Is the idol yourself? Your work? Your conception of what a worker should be? Your experience of salvation?" Oswald asked. The "greatest gift God has given us" was imagination: it was the condition of attaining the perfect peace of Isaiah 26:3 (in Oswald's own translation of the verse, "Thou wilt keep him in perfect peace whose imagination is stayed on Thee"). But imagination was often "at the mercy" of impulse, and the childlike wonder at nature was forgotten. Most of us, Oswald wrote, our imaginations sullied, only ever reached the borders of mature childhood, came only to the cusp of losing consciousness. We were not afloat, as we should be, on the great swelling tide of God's purpose, but tethered and troubled by purposes of our own.

When I was finished reading, I poked my head out from beneath the blanket and dropped the book gently into my bag. The scotch, like the blanket, was fragrant and warm, and I felt a prayer go up, carrying itself to the tops of the hills. But it was of little effect. Hardly ever in my life had I been so troubled, and on so many fronts at once. And it was foolish! So foolish, I chided myself. Because what it came down to was that, after three and a half years of searching, I'd finally found a good job. The path had been halting, disconcerting. I'd lived at home for a year, temped for a year, nannied for a year, despaired. Over and over again, I'd asked God if He had different plans for me from the ones I'd always imagined. Darker plans. A darkness had hung over each of those years, and a darkness had ushered them in. They'd begun, properly, on September 10, 2001, three months after my college graduation. On that day, I'd arrived at Heathrow Airport, in London, on a flight from JFK, to begin a master's program in medieval history at Cambridge University—this was where I'd met Munro, on the eleventh, in a Latin class cut short by news of the attacks. I'd been so hopeful about the course, but in fact I would never finish it. I would abandon it before the year was up, as well as the plans I'd made to continue on for a Ph.D. This had seemed the right decision at the time (I was not cut out for academia, I'd decided), but soon I'd begun to fear that I'd thrown myself off the path, the only path which might have allowed me to become a writer, because I loved writing history and had thought it was my calling. But all through the year in Cambridge, I'd been unable to write a word, a new, terrifying experience. Ideas had crowded in too quickly, refusing to resolve; my old faith that order would naturally and eventually triumph over the chaos in my mind was shaken. That was the darkness—the blinding darkness of the blank page, the "darkness which comes from excess of light," as Oswald put it— that had stayed with me ever since. Ever since Cambridge, I hadn't been able to put pen to paper, though getting back to writing was all I ever thought about.

And then, just over a month before I'd left for my trip with Munro (a trip long in the planning), morning had broken. A friend from college had called to say that she was leaving her free-lance gig as a nighttime proofreader at *The New Yorker*, and she wondered if I might be able to fit it into my nannying schedule. It was twice a week, Tuesdays and Thursdays, beginning at 5:00 p.m. I'd gone for the interview, taken the proofreading test, and gotten hired. Two weeks later, I'd been offered a full-time position in the copyediting group. This was what even my skeptical friends had called a miracle. My mother and I had cried for days over the telephone and plotted out a professional wardrobe. It was nearly four years since I'd graduated college, and it was high time (I felt) that I found a job which might justify the funds she'd borrowed to put me through Barnard. I got the job at the beginning of October. By the fifteenth, my nannying days were behind me, and I belonged, suddenly, to a different world.

This was what I was having such a hard time explaining to Munro. In fact, I hadn't even tried to explain it, since I feared it made little sense, and Munro was an eminently rational person. This new world I'd been pulled into—a dream world, or rather a dream-job world—had disoriented me to such an extent that every idea of the future I'd had before, every promise I'd made, now demanded revision. In this new world, edges were sharp, opinions paramount, and stakes very, very high. The fate of the world seemed to hang on the strength of the arguments presented in the magazine's pages. I'd read *The New Yorker* before, but finding myself inside it was something else—not least because I'd been under the illusion that my new office would feel something like the world of a Woody Allen movie: twee, literary, comical, anxious in a comical way. In fact, it sometimes did feel like this (particularly on Tuesday mornings, when the cartoonists came to sell their wares), but not always, and not at first.

It so happened that I'd joined the staff at a strange moment: the tail end of a presidential campaign season which had been, as an editorial in the magazine put it, "as ugly and as bitter as any in American memory." This editorial, which was one of the first pieces I ever proofread, represented a major break with *New Yorker* tradition. It was the first time in its seventy-nine-year history that the magazine had endorsed a political candidate, a change motivated by all the reasons detailed in the endorsement, the tone of which was outraged, worried, nearly mournful. It was a wartime election and the first presidential election since 9/11. It was an election in which the incumbent was a Republican, a representative of a style of government much despised by all liberals and most New Yorkers, and, in the opinion of the editorial, a quasi-legal holder of the office, having stolen by Supreme Court fiat the election of four years prior. And it was an election in which faith had played a significant role (or an even more significant role than it usually did):

As a variety of memoirs and journalistic accounts have made plain, Bush seldom entertains contrary opinion. He boasts that he listens to no outside advisers, and inside advisers who dare to express unwelcome views are met with anger or disdain. He lives and works within a self-created bubble of faith-based affirmation.

I'd sent an email to Munro the day I read the editorial. We'd developed an epistolary romance—indeed, this was our only romance, since he lived in London and since, during the year we'd both been in Cambridge, we'd been just friends—which had been like a lifeline to me over the past year, my one outlet for writing, my one connection to what I'd left behind. I'd written to him that I was looking forward to our trip, and I'd joked about the piece I was reading, that my new colleagues would somehow guess that faith-based affirmation was a fuel I ran on. I'd joked that it was lucky no one could see the image which kept flashing through my mind: an image of a framed and autographed photo of George and Laura hanging above a toilet (my *parents'* toilet). I joked (with Munro it was necessary to joke about these things, since he was a devout atheist), but in truth the possibility of being discovered frightened me. I was not a supporter of Bush's, but I wasn't sure this was enough to distance me from what people at my new place of employment hated about him, and I could not allow myself to be hated. If the stakes were high in the land of political journalism, they seemed impossibly high for me. Failure would mean a return to nannying, to not knowing, to darkness. This wasn't school; it was real life. It was my *only shot* at real life.

Munro had soothed me with the calm indifference of a seasoned and jaded consumer of media. I was taking it all too seriously, he assured me, and much too personally. The press would argue as it would argue, but I wasn't required to agree with everything it said, not even if I worked for it; indeed, he was certain that a place like *The New Yorker* wasn't interested in hiring people without minds of their own. The piece, he said, had nothing to do with me. Bush had nothing to do with me. His religion had nothing to do with mine. I'd thanked him and conceded that the last point, at least, was almost certainly true. My religion was *Utmost*-based, and Bush's, it seemed, was self-created. I'd relaxed, picturing *Utmost* resting on my bedside table. However roughly faith was to be handled by the media in this election, my own, personal faith was safe.

Maybe it's rare in life that we are provided the opportunity of correcting a pleasant but mistaken belief nearly the moment it takes hold, and in that sense I suppose I ought to have been thankful for what appeared later that week in *The New York Times:* an op-ed detailing Bush's habit of reading a devotional called *My Utmost for His Highest.* The instant the familiar contours of the phrase had caught my eye, I'd known I was in trouble. What good, I'd thought miserably, could possibly come of *The New York Times* mentioning Oswald's book, probably for the first time in its history, perhaps for the last, at the end of one of the "bitterest and ugliest Presidential campaign seasons in American memory," particularly one in which faith had played such a divisive role? None, was the answer I'd soon arrived at. The purpose of the op-ed, written by Robert Wright, was threefold: to inform the readers of the *Times* that the president read a daily devotional (a book which they'd apparently never heard of, though it was one of the best-selling books of all time); to give an overview of its contents; and to connect some of the president's recent mystifyingly horrible decisions to certain passages. I was short of breath as I read it. It was well written (indeed, I would come to love Wright's books in the future), and the bits of Oswald it quoted did sound, in that context, completely insane. A passage in which Oswald talked about how setbacks in our lives were often part of a grand purpose was interpreted like this:

Some have marveled at Mr. Bush's refusal to admit any mistakes in Iraq other than "catastrophic success." But what looks like negative feedback to some of us—more than 1,100 dead Americans, more than 10,000 dead Iraqi civilians and the biggest incubator of anti-American terrorists in history—is, through Chambers's eyes, not cause for doubt. Indeed, seemingly negative feedback may be positive feedback, proof that God is there, testing your faith, strengthening your resolve.

My palms were soon black with print. Oswald interpret ten thousand dead civilians as *positive* feedback? As *proof* that God was there? Oswald had abhorred it when people explained away tragedy as God's will (this was like issuing a "rebuke" to suffering, he said), and he rarely spoke of "proof" when it came to God. He believed in God; he did not try to prove Him. True, he'd thought that God was present in darkness as in light, and, yes, he'd believed that difficulty, in addition to being an inevitable part of life, could have a strengthening effect, and that this in some sense revealed the hand of God. But this was hardly an uncommon idea, nor did it seem a sufficient explanation of the president's military strategy.

As soon as I'd finished with the op-ed, I'd begun Googling Bush and *Utmost.* Within moments, I'd found an interview the president had given *The Washington Post* from the campaign trail, in which he said that his goal was never to push religion on the people, but that he himself was a believer, and that he read *Utmost.* "If you've read Oswald Chambers," he explained, "you'll understand that Oswald Chambers is a pretty good gauge to test your walk." Then I'd found another opinion piece on the subject, this time in *The New Republic,* dated the previous year (Bush had apparently been talking about *Utmost* to the press for quite some time, per-

haps because it was bound to resonate with so much of his constit-
uency: "religious coding," this political tactic is called). This piece,
written by the venerable literary critic Leon Wieseltier, was more
poetic than the piece in the *Times,* but the message was much the
same. Chambers, the author wrote, was "infatuated with crisis"
and his book was "an extended assault on the legitimacy of doubt."
For the latter observation, Wieseltier provided numerous smoking
guns—even I'd had to admit that, sitting on the screen of *The New
Republic*'s website, they appeared damning. In particular: "Never
ask the advice of another about anything God makes you decide
before Him. If you ask advice, you will nearly always side with
Satan"; and "If there is the slightest doubt, then He is not guiding."
For Wieseltier, "Bush's most embarrassing quality is his derision of
doubt. . . . A contempt for doubt is a contempt for thought, and a
strange humility." This might have been true of Bush, but *Utmost,*
it had always seemed to me, was very pro-thought. Its warnings
against doubt made sense within the book's larger context of faith,
where the two ideas were necessary corollaries of one another, for
how could one speak of faith without also speaking of doubt? And
how could someone write of Oswald's thoughts on the subject
without noting the clear distinction he made between doubt in
intellectual endeavors, which he advocated, and doubting *God*?
He'd cautioned strongly against, as he put it, "believing one's own
beliefs." When he said that God was not guiding where there was
doubt, he meant to caution, to encourage reflection before acting.
Or so it seemed to me. I'd always found Oswald to be a model of
humility, and not a strange one, either. But Wieseltier and Wright
had not seen it, and they had the final word—perhaps the only
word about *Utmost* that would ever reach non-Evangelical eyes.

Certainly, I'd decided, closing the browser, the word wouldn't

come from me. As unpleasant as it was to encounter these critiques of *Utmost* (had I believed, all this time, that it was a book
my intellectual friends and colleagues would appreciate, if they
were only made aware of it? That it might make Evangelicals a bit
more respectable in their eyes?), it would be more unpleasant by
far if my own attachment to it were known. And what, after all,
could I say to two big names like Wieseltier and Wright? I suspected that I knew the book better than they did. They'd probably
read it through quickly once, for the express purpose of attacking
a political enemy, an odd way of approaching a book meant to
be experienced ritually, over time, by members of a specific community. But I also knew that we were all outside readers from time
to time—or at least that we ought to be—and anyway, who was I?
I'd never written anything but school essays, and I was only two
weeks liberated from nannying—a noble profession but one which
schooled its practitioners in the wisdom of concealing their true
opinions. Wieseltier and Wright, in contrast, were intelligent, seasoned critics, paid to opine, paid to convince. For a brief moment,
they'd even convinced me. I'd felt myself grow fearful that they
were right about the book, and then I'd been ashamed. And then,
since shame was not an emotion I could allow myself to feel in
relation to *Utmost,* I'd taken the book from my bedside table and
removed it to a drawer. This, I'd decided, was where it would live
from now on, in a place more secluded, more secret, than it had
been previously. Tomorrow, the newspaper would be recycled.
Next week, the election would be won and lost, and soon everyone
would forget the weapons that had been deployed during its awful
opening act, *Utmost* included. Until then, and long after, I'd keep
my head down and devote myself to my new job.

And this was what I'd been doing for the past month, even

here with Munro—in Britain, where I'd been thinking about moving, before.

I'd brought with me on this vacation my new laptop, along with a book I was supposed to review: my first review ever, my big return to writing. It was a minor affair, just 160 words, unsigned, but I was driving myself crazy with it anyway. I'd read the book three times and underlined nearly every sentence. I'd refused to leave the computer behind even during our drive to the glen. Was it monstrous, the way I was behaving? Perhaps, but certain things had come into focus for me over the past few weeks. One was that I wanted to stay in New York—to *make it* in New York, a goal which had suddenly become attainable again—and another was that, for the time being, my secrets were safe with one person, and one person only. "Never show the deeps to anyone but God," Oswald had advised. I was beginning to understand what he'd meant.

"Stew!" Munro called at last, his voice advancing. "All hail the chief of the mighty clan *uan*."

He appeared in the doorway in a pungent cloud of steam, hair wild, torn blue shirt sauce-stained. I saw him there, and also in the pub on that first day in Cambridge, the grim little pub where our Latin class had gone after it had broken up early after news had come of the attacks in New York, to drink bitter brew and stare at televisions that usually displayed cricket matches. I remembered how kind he'd been when another student, Saul, had begun to speak, leaning into me, of how it was America's turn, how we deserved it, how we never understood, how *I* didn't understand. I'd removed myself for the tenth time to the public telephones, where I'd painstakingly typed in the numbers on an international calling card, followed by the number of my boyfriend in New York, repeating it again and again when it didn't work, then trying friends. Boyfriend, friend, friend, boyfriend. And when I'd finally given up again and returned to the table, I'd heard Munro, huddled with Saul, calming, reprimanding, shielding. I'd been grateful— some men could hear only the voices of other men—and in that moment the loyalty and affection which now ran deep had taken root. It had always been the law in my church and my house that Christians should love only other Christians, since God would bless only relations between Christians and since in the war which was ongoing it was necessary to bond together: Paul had stated it clearly, and those who had ears to hear had heard. In friendship, in politics, in romance, even, if possible, in business, this was the law. I knew well the price of breaking it, since my father wasn't a Christian, and this was why (the story went) he'd left, and why my mother had been punished, for yoking herself unequally, why we'd all been punished. But in that moment, I'd started to love Munro without wanting to, though not not wanting to, either. The year that followed had been a long year of not not wanting, for I was from that first day in a constant state of anxiety, and wherever he went, peace attended.

As I rose from the bed, letting the blanket drop, I found I could imagine it easily, our life together. I gathered my scotch glass and followed him into the dining room, where two bowls of stew sat steaming pleasantly, side by side. I could imagine rising and fol- lowing him like this day after day, the bowls emptying and filling and emptying. I could imagine walking to the village each Satur- day for market, our pace slackening over the years, until, finally, we walked hunched over, cane in hand, hand on back, a hazard to oncoming traffic. I could imagine the years passing imperceptibly amid the hills, outside of time and our awareness of it. I could see the green faces of the dinosaurs at the horizon, the yellow flocks rising and falling, Willie on his thousandth birthday, Nessie in the loch, babies in the heather, the Spirit moving on the face of the waters. It was all quite easy to imagine here, on the far side of reality, in this land where no one lived.

No, I thought, raising a spoonful of lamb and carrot as Munro bent his head to his bowl, no one lived here.

Not yet.

VII

∽

You cannot think a spiritual muddle clear,
you have to obey it clear.

—SEPTEMBER 14

New York, 2011. By the time I rose from the bench, it was well after midnight. I started for the subway, thinking back over the evening. I was thinking, particularly, about Tom's comment about my brain—that it was too late for me to grow a new one. It was an intriguing idea. Recently, I'd read a book by an anthropologist from Stanford who'd gone to live among the Evangelicals like Jane Goodall among the chimps, and who'd come to the conclusion that Evangelicals "train the mind in such a way that they experience part of their mind as the presence of God." It was a similar conclusion to the one Charles Darwin had reached over a century before, though he had written of the mind *being* trained:

> Nor must we overlook the probability of the constant inculcation in a belief in God on the minds of children producing so strong and perhaps an inherited effect on

their brains not yet fully developed, that it would be as difficult for them to throw off their belief in God, as for a monkey to throw off its instinctive fear and hatred of a snake.

Of course, Darwin (like Tom, like millions) had been able to throw off his belief, and who knew but there had been dozens of snake-loving monkeys through the ages: there were, after all, many possible variations. But me? Perhaps long ago, I'd trained my mind or had my mind trained for me. Or maybe this was how God operated, descending into the gray matter, etching out new wrinkles, setting up camp in the nooks and crannies. Either way, it was clear to me that the part of me which believed was deeply ingrained. Even in my most doubtful moments (and I did doubt), when tragedy or mystery began to overwhelm me, I found myself, reflexively, praying. The prayer seemed to come of its own accord, as if it were praying itself. It prayed that I might learn to live, as Oswald might put it, in acceptance of the mystery. Like Darwin, I could not "pretend to throw the least light on such abstruse problems," since "the mystery of the beginning of all things is insoluble to us." But where Darwin was "content to remain an Agnostic," I was content to remain, on all abstruse subjects, a believer.

This did not mean, however, that I was not also a seeker, or that I wished to leave my spiritual beliefs unexamined. All believing people, if they do not turn back in fear, are bound, at one point or at many, to cross a line: the line between living their faith and considering it. I had long fancied myself a bold transgressor of this particular boundary—bold because I had always wanted to turn back when I came to it. To cross over was to risk destroying something fundamental to self, and therefore to survival. Not a fear of destroying God or a belief; a fear of destroying *self*. So often in the modern discourse about religion, the focus was on intellectual acquiescence and rationalism, on how people could accept certain scientifically unsupportable premises: for instance, that the world had been created in just six days. But this did not strike at the heart of why, even in an age when science provided so many answers about what we were and how we'd become what we were (though not *why* we were), people continued to identify themselves as religious. Religion, and the kernel of faith it ideally enclosed, was many things at once: a set of beliefs and principles, and also of rituals; a cultural identity; a personal identity; a historical framework; an inheritance (sometimes the only inheritance); a responsibility; a map; home. Most of all, it was a style of being, by which I mean a style of confronting an aspect of the human predicament which was common to all, religious and not: the fact that there are limits on what we know and what we can know; the fact that we all must learn to live with mystery, however clever we are, however much of it we dispel. Faith was most often spoken of as an object, as something one "had," but it was more properly a verb: "to faith." It described a method of confronting the unknown which was uniquely flexible and universally applicable. It precluded nothing in particular, admitted nothing in particular, but absorbed, cast off, evolved with a person over the course of a lifetime, becoming, in many cases, inseparable from that person. Or perhaps it was a language, as close as that to a person's mind, a thing she could not think without. Either way, to the person of faith, faith was substance, not accident.

Yet as inextricable and hardy as faith could seem to the faithful, it also carried stipulations. If it was an action or manner of going through life, it was one which required exercise, upkeep: one got better at faith the more one practiced it, and the opposite was true as well. Faith, like self, could fall apart through neglect, or be torn apart. And in this knowledge lay the fear of examination. One had to have great faith in one's faith (or rather, to note a distinction Oswald always made, in God) to dive into, for instance, the darker chapters in Christian history or geology textbooks or modern philosophies or works of biblical criticism or novels in which the shackles of religion were heroically cast off: part of what it meant to be religious in the twenty-first century was to live in a time when many (though by no means all) possible pathways *away* from faith had been abundantly, courageously, and beautifully documented. There was no shortage of compelling arguments. To examine any one of them without one's own conclusion in mind—not only, that is, for the chance of proving it wrong— was a risk, and it was a risk a great many faithful were not willing to take. If only, Oswald had said, Christians would *think*.

I'd never considered myself among the trepidatious (perhaps I'd even allowed myself to feel superior in my boldness), but tonight, as I'd walked from the party to the subway, my head still light with champagne, I felt forced to admit that, though I'd poked my nose into many dark corners, there was one I'd never dared disturb, not even when the opportunity had presented itself. The opportunity had presented itself many times, and in my stupor I'd realized that it had come around again that evening. It had come in my conversation with Rhonda, in her quip that I didn't really understand *Utmost;* in the little lecture Tom had given me on not knowing much about Oswald or his context; in my mother's suggestion that I hadn't been mature enough to read *Utmost* at fifteen. Suddenly, it had seemed crazy to me that I'd spent so much time learning the history of certain strains of Christianity in college but had never thought to look at my own, specific religious tradition—at *Utmost* and where it fit in, at where I fit in.

In part, I knew, I hadn't wondered about this because my

church had taught that there *was* no tradition worth studying. I'd been raised in the Old Time Religion, a phrase which lent itself to the title of my pastor's most beloved sermon. This sermon, which Criswell delivered many times over the years, had always ended with him singing, a cappella, a rousing rendition of the famous song:

> *Give me that Old Time Religion*
> *Give me that Old Time Religion*
> *Give me that Old Time Religion*
> *It's good enough for me.*

As a child in his sanctuary, gazing up at the white-gold hair glinting in the spotlights, I'd thought that the song meant "old-timey." The sermon began with a reminiscence of Criswell's days preaching in a one-room church house on the Oklahoma plains, a church house heated by a potbellied stove. But as I'd grown older, I'd come to understand that "Old Time Religion" actually meant "All Time Religion." It was a phrase that carried with it a curious idea of history: that all history was Christian history. Bible Christians understood themselves as practicing a first-century, biblical Christianity, not a twenty-first-century Christianity, and this required intense focus on one book, and one book alone. I'd often been asked, by non-Christians, how Evangelicals could possibly look at the world as they did; how their perceptions of reality could be so different from the "mainstream." I'd also been asked by Evangelicals to explain the reasoning of liberals and atheists, which seemed so foreign to them. The answer I'd settled on was that the two groups lived inside two different historical narratives, and that, whether we liked it or not, historical narratives strongly shaped our perceptions: of the past, the present, the future, and of ourselves. Different narratives might overlap in certain places, but it was possible to live one's life in ignorance, that is, without knowing that one's own idea of history was not the *only* idea.

The Evangelicals I'd known had plunged themselves deeply into a single narrative, which is to say into the Bible. A constant effort was needed to bring this book to life in the present day, and I'd witnessed this effort firsthand, in the ultraserious, three-hour-long women's Bible study at my church; in my mother's and my grandmother's nightly reading habits; in the AM/FM kitchen radio that was constantly set to KCBI; in the car radio, always set to the same, always broadcasting a sermon; in the devotional habits I'd been encouraged to keep throughout my childhood. It wasn't that people in the church didn't read beyond the Bible—it was that they didn't read *far* beyond it. In the sermons at First Baptist, when other theologies and philosophies were mentioned, it was generally for the purpose of proving them wrong—or, more accurately, for using them to prove the Bible right. "Biblicism," this "particular regard for the Bible," had been labeled by the Evangelical historian David Bebbington, in a now classic study from 1989. It was one of what he'd termed the "special marks" of the Evangelical Christian religion, those marks which for over three centuries had bound together a theologically diverse, doctrinally motley, racially, economically, and geographically miscellaneous collection of churches and organizations. The other marks in Bebbington's "Evangelical quadrilateral" were

> *conversionism,* the belief that lives need to be changed; *activism,* the expression of the gospel in effort . . . and what may be called *crucicentrism,* a stress on the sacrifice of Christ on the cross.

Over time and in different places, these marks had been expressed in greater or lesser degrees, one presenting itself more forcefully as another retreated, then fading in its turn. At First Baptist in my childhood, conversionism had been important, but Biblicism had been king, and a very specific sort of Biblicism, a late variety or offshoot of the original mark. This was commonly called "factual inerrancy," or "infallibility," and it was held by fundamentalist Evangelicals, those who believed that every word in the Bible, having been breathed into the minds of the writers by God, was certain not only in a literary or spiritual sense but also, even primarily, in a scientific sense and a historical sense. These people studied the Bible in the ancient Hebrew and Greek: they were serious scholars in their own right (Criswell, who had gotten a Ph.D. from Southern Baptist Theological Seminary, was nicknamed the "Prairie Intellectual"). They believed that science and history, if pursued correctly, would correlate with Scripture, and that all discrepancy was a matter of improper pursuit on the part of those who, like most scientists and historians, were thinking with unsubmitted minds—that is, minds which had not been born again into Christianity, and which therefore placed their *own* understanding above God's. Lacking humility and blinding themselves to the truth, they'd eventually been cut off from God, for God, it was thought, did allow His children to give their minds over to Satan and to become handmaidens of Antichrist (these were words used not infrequently at my church). From thence, the thinking went, had flowed all the primary abominations: modern science, history, philosophy, and art, and the liberal, atheist agendas to which they were in thrall.

The particular regard for the Bible that had held sway at my church had extended to other books as well. It was the reason why I'd been given a Bible-centric book like *Utmost,* a book in which every entry opened with Scripture. And it was why I'd never thought of looking at it too closely, the way I wouldn't have tested Scripture too closely. The particular regard I'd had for the Bible had been *Utmost's,* too.

Yet *Utmost* itself never endorsed a devotion to the Bible that demanded a shrinking away from other works of literature. The truth was that, in failing to examine it, I'd given in to fear: to the fear that I'd anger the Evangelicals who'd raised me, and also that I'd distance myself from the intellectuals who'd nourished me and given a much-longed-for space and respect to my ideas. I'd also given in to the superstition that, once *Utmost's* secrets were spilled, whatever magic the book had always held for me would simply dry up, and with it all that I held dear of my childhood religion—for I did still hold it dear.

As I walked, pertinent passages from *Utmost* came to mind: "Always make a practice of provoking your own mind to think out what it accepts easily. Our position is not ours until we make it ours by suffering." "Determine to know more than others." "God is making us spell out our own souls." These were Oswald's call to intellectual arms, and they were of a piece with a major theme of *Utmost:* the importance of action, and of active learning, taken from 2 Peter 1:5: "Giving all diligence, add to your faith virtue; and to virtue knowledge." Oswald, for whatever reason, had been very concerned with Christians' tendency to use God as an excuse not to try, not to think. In *Utmost,* he often sounded downright exasperated: "We are in danger of forgetting that we cannot do what God does, and that God will not do what we can do." "We have to take the first step as though there were no God." "God will not shield us from the requirements. . . . It is always necessary to make an effort to be noble."

These passages arrayed themselves before me as I walked, carrying with them a sense of urgency, and one of them in particular. June 8, one of my longtime favorites: "You are not to spend all your time in the smooth waters just inside the harbour bar, full of delight, but always moored; you have to get out through the harbour bar into the great deeps of God and begin to know for yourself, begin to have spiritual discernment."

How long, I'd asked myself, had I been inside the smooth waters, full of a delight I had not won? What chances had I missed to brave the deeps? By the time I'd reached the subway, I'd made a decision: I'd get out of the harbour and into *Utmost*, as soon as I possibly could.

VIII

⌒

*Expect Him to come, but do not expect Him only in
a certain way. However much we may know God,
the great lesson to learn is that at any minute He
may break in. We are apt to overlook this element of
surprise, yet God never works in any other way.*

—JANUARY 25

Wheaton, Illinois, 2012. The young man in the picture looked sad,
as if his hands, draped one over the other upon an open Bible,
were absorbing all the desolations contained therein. His eyes
were closed, his face downcast. Behind him, a window opened
onto a craggy shore, so high it nearly blocked out the view of the
sea, though in any case the young man was not looking out. The
chair in which he sat held his body at an angle, as if he'd not been
built for sitting, as if he were uncomfortable in the world, or in his
own skin.

I was surprised by this likeness of Oswald, but I'd been surprised by many things since embarking on my journey. I was
surprised, for instance, to find myself in Wheaton rather than in
Scotland, where I'd sincerely hoped to return on my search for
Oswald. It had been nearly eight years since I'd been there. But

Oswald was not in Scotland anymore, not a bit of him. Not his homes or his family, not the Bible college he'd attended in the Western Highlands, not his grave. The grave was in Cairo, in the War Memorial Cemetery where so many British military personnel had been buried during the First World War. His books were in Grand Rapids, Michigan, at Discovery House Publishers, which owned the global distribution rights. And the rest of him was here, in the Billy Graham Center for Evangelism, at Wheaton College, a.k.a. "the Harvard of Christian colleges."

I'd spent the morning in these archives, scanning as many of the hundreds of documents in his boxes as I could tolerate in a single session, and then I'd made my way downstairs, to the Rotunda of Witnesses. It was here that I'd encountered the portrait. In fact, it was a larger-than-life rendering embroidered on a tapestry panel, hung among eight others in a darkened, circular room. Oswald was in excellent company: the Apostle Paul, Justin Martyr, Gregory the Great, Francis of Assisi, John Wycliffe, Martin Luther, Blaise Pascal, and Jonathan Edwards completed the set. I thought it a bizarre grouping, not only for the inclusion of a pope, but perhaps even more for the inclusion of Oswald, who, for all the fame of *Utmost*, had made a much smaller impact on Evangelicalism than, say, John Wesley or George Whitefield (two of the fathers of the movement, mid-eighteenth-century contemporaries of Edwards) or— if a twentieth-century figure was wanted—Dietrich Bonhoeffer, the brilliant German Lutheran who'd resisted the Nazis and died at their hands, and whose ideas (particularly his "religionless Christianity") Evangelicals adored. But the rotunda clearly reflected someone's personal preferences, and this, I thought, was as it should be: it was a true Evangelical creation.

Ahead of my trip, I'd attempted to track down Oswald's path

to Wheaton. How had someone like him—a Brit whose thinking belonged squarely within a late-nineteenth-century tradition— wound up so totally the property of twentieth-century America? It wasn't that he'd had no institutional ties in his own kingdom. For two years in the last decade of the nineteenth century, he'd been a student at the University of Edinburgh. He'd resided, on and off, at a Bible college in the Highlands for nearly a decade after that, before running a college of his own, in London. Finally, he'd served as a chaplain to British troops during the war, under the umbrella of the YMCA. The time he'd spent in America, as a missionary preacher and as a teacher, at God's Bible School, in Cincinnati, Ohio, was relatively paltry, totaling no more than two years, and these had been spread out over several trips. Oswald, it seemed, had posthumously followed the drift of Evangelicalism to America in the years after the First World War, the cataclysm that had accelerated (some might say secured) the decline of Christianity in Britain and in Europe.

There had not been such a marked decline here, and Oswald had benefited from that fact. Somehow, seventeen years after his death, he'd made his way, via *My Utmost for His Highest,* into the cozy, ample bosom of mainstream Evangelical publishing, an industry which had been robust since the very beginning of the movement. In the mid-eighteenth century, John Wesley, the father of Methodism, had been a self-publishing powerhouse, setting the example. His followers had established the first denominational publishing venture in the United States, the Methodist Book Concern, in 1789, putting out a wide variety of sermons, Bibles, Sunday School literature, magazines, newspapers, and spiritual guides. In the years that followed, Evangelical literature had found distribution along the lines of missionary networks, with their nodes of churches, schools, societies, and outdoor "camp" meetings. They

Oswald Chambers in 1906,
about to set off on a mission trip
to America and Japan

were networks that would eventually span the globe, operating on a nonprofit model that was eminently sustainable (the American Bible Society, for instance, which began in 1816 in New York, is still operational, as is the American Tract Society, founded in 1825; *God's Revivalist and Bible Advocate,* the journal of God's Bible School, which contained much of Oswald's first published writing and which began in 1888, is also still in existence). Much of the work was distributed for free or sold in churches, but Evangelicals were also savvy about getting their wares into bookstores, both Evangelical and mainstream, a multipronged approach which they have maintained to the present day.

Utmost had been particularly lucky in its early years. It was by no means the only popular nineteenth-century-style devotional, nor was its author the most famous Evangelical to produce such a book (indeed, Oswald was virtually unknown during his lifetime). There were Charles Haddon Spurgeon's *Morning and Evening* devotions, which Oswald probably read in his teenage years (his father, Clarence Chambers, had been ordained as a minister in the Baptist Church by Spurgeon, and Oswald had been "born again as a lad" after attending a service at Spurgeon's church in London). There was *Our Daily Homily*, by F. B. Meyer, a popular preacher who spoke at Oswald's college in the Highlands, and whom Oswald adored. There was L. B. Cowman's *Streams in the Desert*, a book which Cowman compiled some years after she'd worked with Oswald as a missionary in Japan. And there was *Daily Light on the Daily Path*, a masterpiece of biblical collage, which was fantastically popular throughout the Victorian era, and which, together with Joseph Hutton's 1828 *Daily Devotionals*, served as Oswald's own devotional. Tracking the number of printed copies of these books was difficult, thanks to the unorthodox distribution methods embraced by Evangelical publishers, but *Utmost* was certainly a star. Discovery House, its current distributor, had won the North American distribution rights to the book in 1989, entering into an agreement with the Oswald Chambers Publications Association, a nonprofit, charitable group based in England which had first been incorporated in the 1940s and which still existed (though now primarily in an advisory and grant-making capacity). By 1997, roughly eight years after it had gained the rights, Discovery House was reporting sales of 1.5 million copies of *Utmost* "and associated titles" (all the various tie-ins). And they were simply one distributor. Until very recently, numerous houses had been printing and distributing the English version, thanks to some murkiness about the copyright, and there were over forty foreign translations. Many of these had been published continuously since the 1930s. "Tens of millions" was the guess I'd been given by a member of the Oswald Chambers Publications Association when I'd pressed for the total figure of *Utmosts* printed.

A crucial element in *Utmost*'s success, it seemed, was its early readership. It had fallen into the right hands as soon as it arrived in America, in 1935, seven years after its British publication. The list of names associated with it in its early days in the States reads like a who's who of the conservative Evangelical movement. The top four were Richard C. Halverson, Henrietta Mears, Bill Bright, and, of course, Billy Graham. Halverson's was probably the name most closely associated with *Utmost*, thanks to the introduction he penned for an edition put out in the 1980s. As he related in that introduction, he'd gotten his first copy of the book in 1936, right before he enrolled as a student at Wheaton, and he'd been reading it ever since. Halverson had gone on to serve as a pastor at Hollywood Presbyterian (the church my mother had attended in California, and where she was born again), before moving to the Fourth Presbyterian Church of Bethesda, Maryland, a church that was popular among DC politicians. In 1956, he'd become involved with the National Prayer Breakfast, the annual event at which religious and political leaders, including the president, meet for a morning of communal prayer. In 1969, he became the executive director of the Fellowship Foundation, the semiclandestine asso-ciation which organizes the Prayer Breakfast and which has often been characterized (most notably by the journalist Jeff Sharlet in his book *The Family*) as one of the most powerful, and secretive, groups in Washington, the group that "makes" conservative presidents. Finally, in 1981, Halverson ascended to the chaplaincy of the U.S. Senate, a post he held until 1995, the year of his death.

Halverson had been famous and connected to powerful people, but he was simply part of a larger picture. The Fellowship was founded in 1935 (by the man who also founded Goodwill, Abraham Vereide) as a response to Franklin Roosevelt's New Deal, which conservatives had hated for its socialistic undertones. During the Cold War, with fears of communism widespread, members of the Fellowship had envisioned launching a "worldwide spiritual offensive," a Christian assault that would be carried out across the globe with the help of the political machinery of the United States.

The vision of global evangelism was one shared by the second name on the list, Henrietta Mears, the "Mother of Sunday School," who taught Halverson at her spiritual "retreat," Forest Home, in San Bernardino, California. Mears, who also worked at Hollywood Pres, launched her own publishing venture, Gospel Light Press, which put out Sunday School teaching materials that transformed the institution across the country. In 1937, she founded Forest Home as a place where she might instruct Evangelicals. This mission shifted during the Cold War: from 1947, she wished to *induct* Evangelicals into what she called "the Fellowship of the Burning Heart," a group she envisioned as a worldwide spiritual army. Halverson, together with Bill Bright and the Presbyterian minister Louis H. Evans, Jr., had been present on the night when the Holy Spirit swept down upon Mears, granting her a vision of global revival. "The seeds of destruction," she said in a speech she delivered shortly afterward,

had been long in bringing forth their fruit. Atheism and moral expedience had been at work for centuries before

Hitler's rise to power. There is no mystery as to what has happened to Germany. It can all be traced out step-by-step.

And the same is taking place in America today. There must be a Christian answer to the growing menace of communism. Leaders are predicting that within another generation or sooner we will have entered World War III, which could bring an end to civilization.

God has an answer. Jesus said that we must make disciples of all men. We are to take His gospel to the ends of the earth. . . . God is looking for men and women of total commitment. During the war, men of special courage were called upon for difficult assignments; often these volunteers did not return. They were called "expendables." We must be expendables for Christ.

"The name adopted by those who wish to be expendable in this program of world evangelism," she wrote in a later statement clarifying the group's objectives, "is the Fellowship of the Burning Heart." This Fellowship, unlike the DC Fellowship, was interested in drafting "college-age youths." It was from this commitment that the idea for Bill Bright's organization, Campus Crusade for Christ, arose. Campus Crusade (recently rebaptized as "Cru") would eventually come to include dozens of separate charitable ministries in more than a hundred countries, sweeping millions into its mission. The Fellowship of the Burning Heart also helped to launch Billy Graham's own dizzyingly vast ministry: it was in 1949, during a visit to Forest Home, that Graham experienced his own spiritual rebirth (the one which, among other things, convinced him that the Bible was the infallible word of God).

These were not the only famous names associated with *Utmost* in the 1930s and '40s: it was also a favorite of Bill Wilson and Bob

Smith's, the founders of Alcoholics Anonymous (histories of the group reveal that in the 1930s they read aloud from the day's entry to open meetings). But they were more than sufficient to explain *Utmost*'s immediate and sustained success. Mears, as one of her students recalled in a biography, read it to the teachers she was training, alternating it with Scripture. Bright gave copies of the book as gifts to his early employees, and Graham, in addition to including Chambers in his Rotunda of Witnesses, mentioned *Utmost* on the first page of his own *Utmost*-esque devotional, *Unto the Hills.* Graham's devotion was steady. In the 1960s, Oswald was being quoted in the popular magazines put out by Graham's association. In 1992, the association offered *Utmost* as a "featured premium 'give away'" during a televised broadcast (a freebie for viewers who donated funds): 300,000 copies were sent off.

The reach of these four people—Halverson, Mears, Bright, and Graham—was truly global, encompassing and embracing many languages and media. From the start, they were masters of the modern media universe. Ultimately, one could say that they were the reason why the biggest Evangelical pop stars of the 1990s (including Amy Grant, Sandi Patty, and Michael W. Smith) collaborated on an album called *My Utmost for His Highest;* why George W. Bush name-dropped the book during his campaign for president; and why, in the early 2000s, one could Google "Oswald Chambers" and find references to him on the websites of churches in Africa.

But had *Utmost* really played a part in shaping the global, militarized vision of the interwar years? There was a case to be made. The language for the Fellowship of the Burning Heart had been inspired, first, by Luke 24:32: "And they said one to another, Did not our heart burn within us, while He talked with us by the way, and while He opened to us the Scriptures?" But the link Mears made with militarism could have been taken from *Utmost*, specifically from the March 22 entry, "The Burning Heart." This, in turn, had been taken from one of Chambers's longer books, *So Send I You: The Secret of the Burning Heart*, a book published posthumously, in 1930, with an introduction by S. M. Zwemer, better known as the "Apostle to Islam." Zwemer, a professor at Princeton Theological Seminary, had caught the global bug after the First World War, devoting himself to planning missions to the Middle East, with the goal of converting Muslims to Christianity (American Evangelicals had been undertaking such missions to the Islamic world since the turn of the nineteenth century, without ever achieving their aim).

But Oswald had been long dead by the time the book appeared with Zwemer's introduction. He'd been long dead, I'd discovered, by the time all but three of his books, of which there were nearly fifty, were published—and his message, so very pertinent to Zwemer's agenda, to Mears's, to the DC Fellowship's, was perhaps not so very pertinent now. He'd given the lectures that were to become *So Send I You: The Secret of the Burning Heart* to students at his Bible college in London in 1915, hoping to put into perspective the numerous lives that were being called to the front, both as soldiers and as missionaries (he would offer up his own life later that year). The lectures were full of militaristic language, phrases like "missionary munitions," and they spoke of preparedness—of mental preparedness and spiritual preparedness, of reaching a point where one became willing to sacrifice oneself. I could imagine how rousing they'd been to the young men and women for whom they were intended—young men and women whose friends and loved ones had *already been recruited into service in an actual army during an actual war*, men and women who might be recruited themselves, or even, with the institution of conscription the following year, taken against their will. Oswald, who was eager to go to the front as a chaplain, was perhaps trying to encourage his students to volunteer themselves in some way (in fact, several would follow him to Egypt), so that the soldiers would not be without spiritual and psychological support. For Oswald, in addition to being a preacher, had studied psychology for many years and was ahead of his time in understanding that soldiers needed psychological support, which to him went hand in hand with spiritual guidance (maladies such as post-traumatic stress disorder would not be acknowledged until much later, though the psychological toll taken on soldiers during World War I was both obvious and disturbing). So he spoke, in these lectures, of "healing," and of how ministers might help to heal suffering souls. He spoke, too, of art—of how good artists taught the eye to *see,* and of how ministers might employ their own healing art. It was a strange, complex book, one which made sense only in context.

In the case of the Fellowship of the Burning Heart, context—as always in the history of ideas born in one time and co-opted by another—was not king but rather the first thing to go. Context, as I was discovering in the archives, was missing from so much when it came to Oswald. Indeed, *Utmost* itself seemed to be an exercise in contextlessness. I'd been reading *So Send I You* earlier that day and had been surprised to see that it contained a passage from the day's *Utmost* reading, a passage about God's surprises. But it contained only *bits* of the passage. The other sentences in the entry had been taken from different books, themselves apparently taken from various lectures. There were no wholes here, only collections of bits, rather mysteriously assembled.

On my way out of the Rotunda of Witnesses, I paused once more in front of the tapestry of Oswald Chambers. Perhaps it was appropriate, I thought, that he'd been portrayed as a man of sorrows. There were more surprises on the way, of that I felt certain. I was eager to find out what they were.

∾

One of the more surprising things about Oswald's vaunted position at Wheaton College, which was, and is, a very fine academic institution, full of the kind of intellectual Evangelicals fundamentalists tend to despise, was that no one on the Wheaton staff taught him. Nor, apparently, had anyone *ever* taught him, except in bits and pieces, as part of a larger curriculum. This was in keeping with the fact that there were no published academic studies of Oswald's thought. He had, however, been a favorite of V. Raymond Edman, the president of the college from 1941 to 1965. Edman had included a brief portrait of Oswald in a book about his spiritual heroes, *They Found the Secret,* and had often invited Evangelicals from Oswald's immediate religious tradition (the Keswick Holiness tradition, so named for the town in the English Lake District where its yearly meetings take place) to lecture at the college. Since then, despite Oswald's likeness in the rotunda, and the banner with his photograph that graced the entrance to the archives, Oswald had fallen into academic disfavor at Wheaton.

I'd arranged to meet with Larry Eskridge, a professor of history who specialized in American Evangelicalism and who'd agreed to talk to me about Oswald's weird status. I found him that afternoon, in the campus Starbucks.

"Why on earth do you want to write about Oswald Chambers?" Eskridge asked, right off the bat. He'd read him, he said, but he didn't read him anymore. He'd been under the impression that the "Oz-meister" (as Oswald had apparently been called back in Eskridge's day—he'd graduated college in the early 1980s) was distinctly out of fashion. Although, he hastened to add, he'd just seen a quote of Oz's on Facebook, posted there by the kid of a friend.

I asked him why he thought Oswald was unpopular. I myself saw him everywhere, I said, all over the Internet and in bookstores. Even in bookstores in New York, decked out in his pink faux-leather jackets.

Eskridge laughed. He was a large man with a broad, humorous face, wire glasses, gray hair, and eyebrows that were still dark. When he spoke, he was instantly endearing. There was in his manner something that suggested "former hippie," or at least "former country boy"—a mischievousness, a certain looseness of the arms—and his accent was a unique American blend, a bit of the South mixed with a bit of the Midwest. He was, I imagined, all his students' favorite professor.

I wanted to write about Oswald, I said, because my Southern Baptists had raised me on him and I loved him, but I knew nothing about him.

"Ah," Professor Eskridge said, nodding. "Most younger people of the Evangelical persuasion know nothing of their own background. It puts them in really a bad way sometimes, because they see some of the superficial stuff, the problems, but they don't realize the heritage. With Southern Baptists, particularly, you get the problem. I grew up Southern Baptist, too, up here in Illinois, though I'm from North Carolina originally. We came up as immigrants. Round Lake, Illinois, near the Wisconsin border."

At this midwestern Southern Baptist church, he explained, they hadn't studied theology at all, though they'd been very serious about their Bible. So serious, in fact, that when he went into his first literature course, in college (he'd attended Trinity, a small Evangelical college in Deerfield, Illinois), he'd felt instantly adept, particularly in reading Shakespeare, whose language was so close to that of the King James Version. In this respect, he thought the depth of focus on the Bible was a "Godsend." He recalled a comment made by a former Wheaton professor, Mark Noll (whose name I knew: he was the author of a famous book called *The Scandal of the Evangelical Mind,* the first line of which was "The scandal of the evangelical mind is that there is not much of an evangelical mind"), to the effect that Evangelicals, as much as people flogged them for being anti-intellectual, actually did a lot more serious reading than average people, "because the topics they read about are serious things. Bible study, devotional literature, biographies, stuff that tackles bigger, more ethereal issues, which most folks *ain't doin'.*" But Scripture was essentially the only thing the Southern Baptists who had raised Professor Eskridge had taught him to read (this was part of Noll's "scandal": depth but no breadth). And this, he thought, wasn't a good thing. "There's this idea among a lot of Evangelicals that it's all about the Bible," he said, "to the point where they begin to disparage all the other stuff. I mean, Luther was all about the Bible but he also read a lot of other people. Now Evangelicals think, 'It was Brother Paul, then it was Billy Graham, and then it was *me.*' You know, Pastor Jones, up at the pulpit."

But was it this way at Wheaton? I inquired. Was that why no one taught Oswald Chambers?

Eskridge looked thoughtful for a moment. No, he said, that wasn't the reason. Wheaton was an intellectual place, but the professors tended to focus on "old" Christianity, everything up to the Reformation, after which interest tapered off considerably, with Jonathan Edwards being the major exception. It was, he thought, "a function of theological training." There was a feeling, he said, among historians of Christianity that all the "meaty" theology belonged to a few distinct moments in time: the early church fathers, Aquinas, the Catholic philosophers, and "the big guns of the Reformation," who had set the basic Protestant arguments in place. A result of this focus was what he called "a fleeing of the heritage." Most scholars of Evangelicalism had in fact been raised in Evangelical churches, but, being intellectuals, they wanted to get away from it, away from the "superspiritual stuff," which was intellectually "dodgy." It was also a class issue, he thought, and students weren't immune to it. At the moment, he said, he was teaching a seminar on postwar Evangelicalism, and only five kids had signed up. To them, the more recent thinkers were lowbrow, unimportant.

He went on. "The liberalizing force of education is certainly evident here," he said. Just the other day, he'd seen a funny cartoon in the Wheaton student paper. In the first frame, a kid arrives at Wheaton for freshman orientation. He's wearing a "Bush 2004" T-shirt, and he's saying, "I'm going to go to Bible study and spread the Word." In the next frame, he's a senior. He's got on an "Obama 2008" T-shirt, and he's saying, "I should have converted to Catholicism."

"We call it the Canterbury trail," Professor Eskridge said. "The appeal to the liturgical stuff is very strong among a not insignificant portion of students, Anglicanism in particular. I flirted with it at one point many years ago. You read C. S. Lewis; the 'smells and bells,' as Evangelicals derisively say, is appealing; and orthodoxy is great because it ignites this primitivist passion—I'll get back to the earliest church. And there's Granny sitting in the pew reading Oswald Chambers."

But he also saw another reason why Oswald had been neglected. It belonged, he said, to a specific Evangelical tradition—Holiness—which had more or less faded from the mainstream. Its *influence* was still felt, but it wasn't pursued in the same way anymore—not by mainstream Evangelicals, at any rate.

"It's this Victorian Evangelical stuff that's so hard for people a hundred years later to penetrate," Eskridge said. "It's so serious."

"But what is it, exactly?" I asked.

"Oh," Eskridge said, making it clear I'd asked a difficult question. "Chambers has this big Pentecostal thing about him that's sort of swept under the rug."

"But he wasn't Pentecostalist," I said, bracing myself for another big surprise.

He wasn't, Eskridge said, but the groups to which he'd belonged "were really right on the cusp." It was interesting, he went on, that they "didn't flip that switch, because of the language and this desire to have this constant fullness of the Spirit.

"See," he said, "there's this way in which Evangelical types are able to selectively grab hold of people who, if they actually had them present there in their congregations and had them teaching, they wouldn't be quite as happy or comfortable with them, but because they are frozen in print, and they don't know anything about them . . ." He shrugged. "C. S. Lewis is the perfect example. He's no Evangelical."

"And Oswald Chambers?" I asked.

Professor Eskridge smiled. Oswald Chambers, he replied, was a "bomb."

∽

I had one question on my mind as I left Wheaton: If Oswald Chambers wasn't an Evangelical, and if he wasn't Pentecostalist, what was he? It seemed especially pertinent to the matter of "spiritual reality," the precise definition of which I was determined to find. There was an enormous difference, after all, between a "real Catholic" and a "real Evangelical," between a "real Evangelical" and a "real Pentecostalist." These were traditions that flowed from the same source, but, as Oswald put it, a river touched places of which its source knew absolutely nothing.

To follow his stream, I decided, I'd have to hit the library as soon as I returned to New York. The Columbia library was open twenty-four hours a day, and there was a bus that went directly from Queens to 125th Street. I'd live there, I vowed, like I had when I was a student, rolling out only for meals and classes. Only now, I'd be rolling out for work. I'd handle my "real" work during working hours, not at all times of the day and night, as I'd been used to doing. I'd turn the tables on the Internet and become, once again, the master of my own clock. This Victorian Evangelical stuff, as Eskridge had put it, was so serious, and I would have to be, too.

༄

IX

Tell God you are ready to be offered; then let the consequences be what they may, there is no strand of complaint now, no matter what God chooses. God puts you through the crisis in private, no one person can help another.

—FEBRUARY 6

New York, 2012. "I can't do it anymore. My brain is going to explode."

"Maybe someone can help you," my mother said. "It's just so wonderful that you're getting to write a book on Oswald."

"It is," I agreed. "But no one can ever really help another person with writing. It's forged in the soul, and the soul, as Oswald says, cannot be divided or cut up."

I paused, considering what I'd just said. I amended it. "Blogging, though, is different. I think blogging is probably forged in the intellect, not the soul. What do you think?"

The phone was silent for a moment. Then my mother said, "But if you leave your job, what will you do for money?"

I had a bit from the book deal, I told her, enough to last six months, if I budgeted and if I sublet my apartment. I'd figure it out later, after all the research was done—after I'd been to England, after I'd spent the necessary time in the library, after the Internet was no longer the portal through which I viewed the world. There were people I knew abroad, I said, people in England and in France. For some reason, Paris was much cheaper than New York; I'd already seen a sublet on Facebook that looked suitable.

"I'd really like to go back to Paris," I told my mother.

"Oh, you should," she said. We shared a love of the city—we'd both visited it for the first time when we were fifteen, she with her high school French class and I with mine.

"Actually," I went on, "the library there has a surprising number of works about American Evangelicalism, though I can't imagine who in Paris reads them."

My mother laughed. "Well—you! You'll read them. It sounds wonderful, honey. And if you know that you know that you know . . ."

"No, no. I don't know."

I'd heard every dire warning imaginable, I told her. I'd heard that I'd be losing my salary and my health insurance and my retirement plan, that I'd be losing my public platform. I knew all this to be true, but I couldn't stay anymore. It wasn't just trying to do two things at once that was getting to me. It was the city itself. For so long, it had seemed the only place on earth big enough to hold my vision, but somewhere along the way, it had dwindled to a tiny point. I lived in a small town now, I told her: nearly everyone I knew was a writer or an editor. I loved these people (they were my people, now), and I loved my job. But there was something in the margins, something that had been nagging at me for years. It was true that the city I lived in was famous, and also the magazine I worked for. It was true that I was in some sense a part of these things. But I felt like they'd *earned* their fame, while I'd done very little, either to contribute to it or to merit the benefits it conferred upon me. Perhaps I'd be nothing without them. Perhaps my writing wouldn't gain notice on its own. But in the final reckoning, I didn't care. There were questions I needed to answer, and people I needed to find, and somehow I knew that I wouldn't find them in New York. Would it be a mistake? Possibly.

"Also," I said, "if I go to one more publishing party where the topic of conversation is the latest *Atlantic* cover story on why women in their thirties have no chance of getting married, I'm going to rip my hair out."

"It sounds to me like you do know," my mother said. "And don't touch that pretty hair."

"Thanks, Mama," I said.

"Let's say a little prayer to bless your journey," my mother said, and she whispered a prayer into the phone.

◌∾

X

To "walk and not faint" is the
highest reach possible for strength.

—JULY 20

Paris, 2012. One of the first things that struck me about the life of Oswald Chambers was that he'd spent a great deal of it outside of his homeland, the land he yearned for whenever he was not there. "Scotland," he wrote in his diary in the summer of 1895—he was twenty, and about to leave London to enter art school at the University of Edinburgh—"Scotland, all hail! How my soul beats and strains and yearns for you, Scotland, Bonnie, bonnie Scotland, how I love you! It'll not be long now afore I'll be amang yer hills and braes and woods, Scotland. Ye'll give me the stedfastness of yer everlasting hills, the strength of yer storm-torn firs, the power of yer mountain streams, the tenderness of yer bluebells, and the faithfulness of yer noble pride." It is in one way an uncharacter-istic passage: though often overcome with emotion in his diaries, Oswald was not given to slipping into Scottish affectation. Yet this passage might have been close to how he spoke in real life. According to friends, he spoke deliberately, in a thick Scots accent, presumably with a luxurious trilling *r* that would turn all those *yers* to poetry. Indeed, he wrote poetry and was prone to begin spouting it at random moments, one of his many Romantic tendencies. A picture of him at twenty tells the tale. It shows him whippet-thin and long-faced, with tidy hair that seems to strain against the confines of its style. In later years, when he was out of his parents' house and his hair had become his own business, hair and passion both would upset the delicate sensibilities of his congregations: "Dinna send us yon lang-haired swearin' preacher!" a letter to Oswald's Bible college from a parishioner at a nearby church read. But many more who saw him would love his intensity and irregularity, his peculiar insight. This, too, is evident in the picture, in the gaze that seems to pass through the camera's lens to a world beyond. "He espied angels," a friend recalled, "where I saw only a fence."

When I'd first come across this remembrance, on a cold summer day in Paris, I'd assumed that its author, George Oxer, a friend of Oswald's in their teens and early twenties, was speaking figuratively. From my perch in salle K of the Bibliothèque Nationale de France (a fascinatingly ill-conceived compound along the Seine in which the books had been placed in hothouse glass towers and the reading rooms sunk in catacomb gloom beneath the street), I'd thought back on my trip to Scotland so many years before, trying to imagine the landscape as Oswald had seen it, with angels peeking through the mist. Try as I might, they would never appear for me there. But when I switched the scenery to Texas—Texas where it was presently a very seasonable 105, Texas where the grass, July-browned, smelled sweetly of pine and pecan—I found it was easy. It was a nice activity for days when homesickness set in, and I thought I understood why Oswald, when he was living in the Egyptian desert during the First World War, had daydreamed so fervently about the land which was his past but not, alas, his future. "When are we coming home!" he wrote to one of his brothers in early 1917, a few months before his death. "We are just like an aching child for its mother's lap. Coming Home! what a Day that will be, back to the cool and the cold, back to the mountains and the streams, back to the sea and the wee greatness of Britain. Why my very being is like a fountain of possible tears at the thought of coming back to the Homeland. (Now that is quite an out burst isn't it.)"

This letter, too, was uncharacteristic. Oswald, I was learning, was not at all prone to negative "out bursts" in his private diaries and letters, especially not about the difficulty of his circumstances. This was in keeping with his theology, a cornerstone of which was the idea that, for the Christian, geographic location and personal comfort were irrelevant, or could become so, as faith progressed. The saint, he wrote, dwelled in the shade of God's hand, no matter where he'd been "dumped down" geographically. This shade, though it brought darkness, concealing even the hand which made it, was a space set apart for the refinement of the soul. Here, one learned to "face anything . . . without wavering," even to relish difficulty. It was like the crashing wave which in the ordinary swimmer produced anxiety but in the surf rider brought "the super joy of going clean through it." To such a rider, "life becomes one great romance."

Perhaps it was the frequency with which Oswald changed hometowns and countries—the upheavals coming one upon another, like waves on a tide—that encouraged the development of this philosophy. Born in Aberdeenshire, on July 24, 1874, he moved with his family to England at the age of three, returning to Scotland four years later, to live in Perth. When he was fifteen, they left again, for London, where Oswald remained until his entrance into Edinburgh, at twenty. At twenty-two, he moved to Dunoon, in the Western Highlands, to begin his ministerial training, a process that spanned nine years and encompassed the launch of his missionary activity. When he left Dunoon, in 1906, on a two-year mission to America and Japan, he was leaving for good, though he could not have known it. He was thirty-two, and he would live his remaining eleven years outside of Scotland—in America, Japan, England, and, finally, Egypt. But it was to Scotland he always hearkened in his mind.

The late desert letter to his brother was one of the rare instances in which Oswald broke from the character he presented in his sermons. I found it odd, having so often taken to heart his teachings on circumstance, to learn that he'd suffered from the exile's craving for home, and so intensely that he'd allowed himself to express it in a medium—writing—which he'd long before sanctified to God: writing, like prayer or work, was for him a devotional activity. But it was also reassuring to hear him speak like this. After all, his circumstances in the desert, where he'd been serving as a chaplain to British troops during the First World War, had been very difficult indeed. The craving he'd felt during that time was not simply a craving for home but for health, and ultimately for life. It was a human craving, a relatable craving. I took special note of the themes he raised in describing it. There were childhood, nature, and imagination, three themes he'd so closely linked in his sermons, and which were nearly synonymous with Scotland in his private papers. I also noted the phrase "mother's lap," which called to mind his strange rendering, in *Utmost*, of childhood as a "mother-haunted" state.

It seemed possible that this had been Oswald's own experience of childhood. He was the eighth of nine children born to Hannah Chambers, née Bullock, and Clarence Chambers, and he was, by all accounts, his mother's son, united with Hannah in temperament (they were both passionate, humorous, spiritual, and kind) and happy to pass afternoons with her inside the house while the other children played outside. According to one brother, the young Oswald was unremarkable in all ways but one: the quality of his prayers, which were so beautiful and original that his mother and siblings would crouch on the stairwell outside his door at bedtime, listening. The bond between mother and son was perhaps strengthened by the specter of the father, a stern Baptist minister with whom Oswald, as his daughter, Kathleen, recalled, "disagreed very, very fundamentally and strongly." Though (she was quick to add), they also loved each other very much, and they shared a strong faith, which at times united them. When Oswald was a teenager, Clarence took him to see the great London Baptist minister Charles Haddon Spurgeon, the minister who had ordained Clarence. Oswald had been so moved by the sermon that he'd dropped to his knees outside the church and, with his father as witness, given himself to the Lord. Yet recordings of such intimate moments between father and son are almost nonexistent, a testament to how very different they were in both personality and perception. Oswald, Kathleen remembered, was a clown, often playing, often joking, often in the company of children, and he believed in a God of grace, mercy, and delight, a God who wished to see His children happy. Clarence, in contrast, "had no interest in anything at all except the Bible and hellfire. God to him had no mercy, no gentleness, nothing. You were condemned to hellfire and that was that, if you didn't believe."

Happily for Oswald, he and Hannah generally saw eye to eye, even when it came to their separation. "My dear 'brick' of a mother," he wrote in 1906, from a ship bound for Japan. "I am . . . more than proud of such a mother":

The enervation caused by the fondness and attachment of home folks has so often been terrible in an outgoing missionary's life. If it is possible, I love you more than ever for being so robust and strong in your mind. Thank God for you and upon every remembrance of you.

It was while I was searching for information on Hannah, the figure who had shaped Oswald's earliest persona, that I began to suspect that his angels might not have been imaginary—at least, not in the sense I'd supposed. There was little about Hannah in the Chambers archive, but she did crop up in an interview given by Kathleen, in 1991, to Oswald's biographer David McCasland. "My grandmother," Kathleen told McCasland, "was Highland, you see, and she was really fey, like a lot of Highland people are. She could see into the future." The gift of second sight was one Oswald inherited, sometimes recording in his diary strong feelings or premonitions, which he believed came from God. With Hannah, feyness was part of her national and cultural identity. She "was steeped in Highland imagery and fairies," Kathleen said, and in stories like those of J. M. Barrie, the Scot who wrote *Peter Pan* and numerous other tales in the Highland vein. One of Barrie's stories, about a girl who is kidnapped by "the little people," came to life for Oswald once. "My father met two old farmers up in the hills," Kathleen told McCasland, "and they said their daughter had gone in the same way. My father had a great belief in the old stories and strange things that could happen and did happen."

I'd become obsessed with these interviews with Kathleen, reading them again and again. They were delightfully unhinged, full of bizarre details that had been omitted from inclusion in any of the biographies of Oswald, all of which were of a spiritual or inspirational kind and were primarily concerned with charting his

Christian journey. The most rapt was the 1933 "group" biography, which his wife, Biddy, had compiled from the written remembrances of dozens of friends, students, and family members. This was an invaluable resource, but it often read more like hagiography than biography, not least because, to many who'd known him, Oswald had been *Saint* Oswald. Biddy's book had set the tone for everything that came after, so that in the library of writings on Oswald Chambers, it was almost impossible to find a negative word.

Through this pristine edifice, Kathleen's interviews scurried like a mouse. Their tone, though always loving and respectful toward her parents, was also combative. Kathleen had clearly been skeptical about people wanting to tell her parents' story. She seemed to suspect their intentions, even as she collaborated with them, giving away the family secrets. Did they want to make money? Did they want to turn Oswald into some false, idealized version of himself? To use him to promote their own gospel? She was happy to upend the tidy narrative (by, for instance, heaping scorn on Christian publishing houses, which she declared inferior, from a business-ethics perspective, to secular ones, her father's books having been distributed by both types through the years). She'd sat for the interviews with McCasland when she was seventy-eight, apparently an ideal age for looking back: sharp enough to recall a great deal, but not so sharp that fact overwhelmed fancy in the telling. McCasland had corrected some of her details in the margins, and had told me when I'd met him that her facts couldn't be trusted entirely (Hannah, for instance, had not been born in the Highlands, but rather in the London suburb of Homerton; her Highland spirit had developed at a later, unspecified date). But I couldn't help myself from reading them. Kathleen had died in 1997, and these interviews were her fullest word on the subject of her father. And they were very good. McCasland was an excellent interviewer, asking engaging questions and letting the tape recorder run. There was a visual aid as well, a series of video interviews made around the same time, excerpts from which were available on YouTube. They showed a plump lady, white with age, reclined in posture, and generally unassuming. But when she spoke, in a high-toned English accent, her eyes lit with mischief—you could see the mouse scurrying behind them—and her right arm, draped pleasantly across her lap, sparkled, the effect of the dozen cheap bangle bracelets which were, according to friends, one of her "vices," of which there were only two: the bracelets, and a love of driving very, very fast through the center of London—"the worse the traffic, the better she loved it." Her face was a wrinkled effigy of her father's, and when she described her grandmother Hannah, and Hannah's daughters (Oswald's sisters), one felt she was describing herself. The women on that side of the family, she said, had been blessed with "an incredible sense of humor." As evidence, she offered the fact that all her aunts had declined to marry (as, of course, had she).

Given Kathleen's affection for humor and narrative, it was impossible to know whether what she'd said about Oswald and the "little people" was true. Had he really had "a great belief in the old stories"? Had he believed that his mother could see into the future? That he could as well? The questions weren't ones I'd ever considered in relation to *Utmost,* since nothing touching on these subjects appeared there, but they were of primary importance to my current inquiry—my quest to discover, once and for all, how Oswald had defined "reality." I'd begun to see that his ideas on the subject, a subject which cropped up hundreds of times across his oeuvre, were many and multifaceted—a collection of prisms, hardened over the course of a lifetime. They'd been shaped by university philosophy and psychology courses; by Bible-college theology courses; by literature and art; by Evangelical revivalist meetings and travels in foreign lands; by war. But they were all rooted in Scotland, in what was possible in the hills, in what he'd learned at his mother's hip.

And what was possible in the Scottish hillside in the last half of the nineteenth century? Perhaps unwittingly, Kathleen had struck close to the truth in her characterization of it. In the old days, she'd said, strange things *could* happen and *did* happen. Speaking from a later time—our time—she'd made a distinction, between possibility and actuality, which was, for most of us, permanent when it came to our understanding of fairy tales. When we read fairy stories (or vampire stories or werewolf stories), we understood that what could happen—inside the space of the story, that is—did not happen in reality. The divide was, perhaps, essential to our enjoyment of these tales. However extensively reality was warped in the telling, we knew it would always spring back into its proper shape when the story was done.

But this was not how fantasy operated in the Highlands in the mid-nineteenth century. In that time and place—which was a modernizing place but not yet a fully modern one—strange things *did* happen. In *Folklore: or, Superstitious Beliefs in the West of Scotland Within This Century*, a helpful compendium first published in 1879 (five years after Oswald's birth), the author, one "James Napier, F.R.S.E., F.C.S., &c.," notes that belief in the tales presented in his volume, tales he'd collected from his fellow countrymen over the course of sixty years, was still enjoying "a vigorous existence, at least in the West of Scotland," though the tales were beginning to die out. The stories Napier presents are curious blends of paganism, Christianity, and mundanities. The one about the child-snatching "little people" told to Oswald by the farmers is a good example. In Napier's version, unbaptized children are stolen from their beds by the fairy queen, who, having pledged her allegiance to Satan, is now obliged to pay him a tithe or tax. But because she can't manage to collect this tax from her own fairies (over whom she rules, in Elfland, like a feudal landlord), she pays it out in babies. The didactic messages of the story are many—baptize your babies and pay your taxes in timely fashion, don't make deals with the devil, don't trust your landlord—but did people really believe it to be true?

Yes, said Napier, his answer providing a nice illustration of mid-nineteenth-century thinking on the nature of truth and reality. While "modernization," "enlightenment," "science," and "education" had released some people from their superstitious beliefs, he wrote, a great many others, trapped in darkness, clung to them still. Such people, he thought, had a very good reason for doing so—instinct:

Our minds instinctively seek an explanation of the cause or causes of the different phenomena constantly occurring around us, but instinct does not supply the solution. Only by patient watching and consideration can this be arrived at; but in former ages scientific methods of investigation were either not known, or not cared for, and so men were satisfied with merely guessing at the causes of natural phenomena, and these guesses were made from the standpoint of their own human passionate intelligence. Alongside the intelligence everywhere observable in the operations of nature they placed their own passionate humanity, they projected themselves into the universe and anthropomorphised nature. Thus came men to regard natural phenomena as manifestations of supernatural agency; as expressions of the wrath or pleasure of good or evil genii.

Even the introduction of Christianity into the pagan world could not release people from their superstitions, Napier thought, because "neither heathens nor Christians had for a long time any clear idea that the overruling of God in Providence was according to fixed laws." Yet Napier's subjects, ignorant though they may have been of God's geophysical language, the clockwork nature of His universe, did believe in other fixed laws—for instance, that carrying a raw potato in the pocket of one's trousers protected against rheumatism, or that placing a cold iron in the bed of a pregnant woman scared off fairies. Christian ideas entered into this superstitious world, but did not overturn it, and from this commingling arose the belief system still in evidence in the Scottish Highlands in Napier's day. The sense in which folklore was "true" for Highlanders was effectively the sense in which Christianity was true, and fairies existed in much the same way as Satan or the Holy Ghost existed: they were all supernatural beings. The spiritual realm to which they belonged, though hidden in some sense, was observable in another. As Napier put it, supernatural agency was *manifest* in nature; nature *expressed* supernatural emotions. The physical universe was like a permeable veil dropped over the spirit world, a veil which both concealed spiritual forces and revealed them (in much the same way that the human body could both conceal and reveal hidden emotions). Humans could not cross over into the spiritual world during their lifetime, but they could influence it: a cold piece of iron placed in a bed had as genuine an effect there as a baptism did, and it mattered not that one ritual was "pagan" and the other "Christian." Napier's Scots would not have made the distinction, nor would they have thought it possible to rid themselves of one set of beliefs without imperiling the other, so entwined had the two become over the ages. In Hannah's time and place, in other words, a good pagan was not a good pagan but rather a good Christian. And a good Scot (as Kathleen suggested) was someone who hadn't entirely abandoned this distinctively Scottish way of believing.

Oswald, in addition to being a good Christian from his earliest years, was also intimately tied to the hills, to the old Scots who lived there, to Scots who had died there. In the 1933 biography, numerous friends noted his fondness for taking long walks in the hillside. All night, they recalled, he'd walk Ben Nevis, so that he could see two sunrises in a single morning: one from the summit, one from the valley. Often, he walked with his dog, Tweed, and often with friends. With George Oxer, the friend of his teenage years, he recited Robert Browning and struggled with the great questions of life. As a Bible-college student, he formed a close friendship with John Cameron, a sheep farmer. When they walked, they hunted rabbits, stopping to pray when the Spirit moved them. Cameron was special to Oswald because he was of a certain type: "the Scottish Covenanters, whose blood dyed our heather red." The Covenanters were Scottish nationalists who, beginning in the early seventeenth century, objected to (English) royal meddling in the Presbyterian Church. Their refusal to accept the king as the head of the Kirk—only Christ could fulfill that role, they said—led to a protracted struggle, and many paid with their lives. Their sacrifice had not been forgotten a century and a half later: indeed, it had become emblematic of a larger Scottish desire to assert their cultural distinctiveness from their English overlords. On the first page of his Bible, Oswald wrote: "For Christ's Crown and Covenant: motto of the Blue Banner of the Scottish Covenanters." The descendants of the Covenanters were independent thinkers, independent Christians. They were people of the hills, men like John Cameron and the farmers whose daughter had been snatched, men who still believed in fairies, men who still believed in Scotland.

As I'd read about Oswald's life in Scotland, a strong sense of recognition had come over me. Imagining him walking in the hills, footsteps trailing the blood of martyrs, attended by friends and angels, reciting poetry, dog at heel, gun at shoulder, I realized how close it was to the image I'd always had of him. I'd always seen him walking, and always in the hills. In *Utmost*, walking was a metaphor for the spiritual life. "The life of faith is not a life of mounting up with wings, but a life of walking and not fainting," he wrote. In life, there was sometimes difficulty and sometimes excitement, but there was almost always monotony (even in the midst of war this was so): "The height of the mountain top is measured by the drab drudgery of the valley." The valley, which for Oswald was the same as the shade of God's hand, was our natural place: "We are not built for the mountains and the dawns and aesthetic affinities, those are for moments of inspiration, that is all. We are built for the valley, for the ordinary stuff we are in, and that is where we have to prove our mettle."

Perhaps the passage had stuck with me over the years because I'd been born in the flatlands, where there was neither mounting up nor descending. Or else it was because I'd been born in late-twentieth-century American city-sprawl, where any amount of walking was a chore, because it was not driving. Drudgery was something I'd thought I understood very well, and Oswald's metaphor had resonated, even while the kind of walking he described, full of the drama of peaks and valleys, of dawns and "aesthetic affinities," of the trials of darkness, spoke to a much more romantic sort of drudgery than I'd ever experienced. It was not surprising to me to discover, all these years later, that he'd spent a good portion of his lifetime mastering hills that were alive with history, with nature, with sprites, with God. God who appeared "in every wind that blows, in every night and day of the year, in every sign of the sky, in every blossoming and in every withering of the earth," effortlessly piercing the veil. In fact, this romantic vision of drudgery had made me look at my own in a different light, to appreciate it and not to fear it. In the valley where I lived, though it seemed that nothing of any importance was being accomplished, that my entire life might spool out in absurdities—in school bells, church bells, football games, household chores, household fights, competitions won or lost (all these seemed like absurdities to me then)—in fact, Oswald said, everything was happening.

Yes, real things were happening in the valley, things we could not see. Or perhaps, from time to time, we could see, as Oswald saw angels and Hannah saw the future, as thousands of Scots had seen fairies in the heather, as they still saw monsters in the lochs. At times, the veil tore, and we saw. These were the moments we remembered best, and the places in which they occurred were the ones to which we wished to return.

It was not until relatively late in my research that I came across a precise definition of *reality* in Oswald's work. His oeuvre was massive, spanning thousands of pages and nearly fifty books, and it was filled with dense, often mysterious theology. It was also, for better or for worse, portable. Each day upon arriving at the library, I pulled up a digital version of his collected works, an object which in real life was hefty as a dictionary, vowing to read ten screens' worth before going for my second coffee. I'd usually start to lose focus after only twenty minutes but would awaken whenever my eye drifted over the word *real* or *reality*, which was surprisingly often. Indeed, the concept seemed to form a backbone of Oswald's thought, though for a long time I could not tell exactly how he was using it. In *Utmost*, it had always seemed to indicate "authenticity" or "truth" or "Christian."

Then one morning, during my reading, I'd seen it. Making a distinction between "Actual" and "Real," he wrote, "By Actual is meant the things we come in contact with by our senses, and by Real that which lies behind, that which we cannot get at by our senses."

In other words, Oswald's "actual" was synonymous with what most of us today would call "real," while his "real" was what most of us would call "spiritual" or "supernatural" or even "not real." It was curious to see him put it this way, because the terminology he used—*real* and *actual*—tended to come up only in philosophical discourse, not in works of popular Evangelicalism. Oswald hadn't bothered to explain the background for his statement: if he'd taken the terminology from Aristotle (and he might have, since he'd been both a student and a teacher of philosophy), he'd redefined it for his own purposes. In describing the nature of reality, Aristotle had made a distinction between actuality and potentiality. A butterfly resting on a leaf, for instance, had the potential to fly; a butterfly on the wing was a butterfly actualizing its potential to fly: the two states together described the shifting, nonstatic nature of reality. Oswald sometimes used the verb *to actualize* in his writing, to present the idea of a fully actualized Christian, one who not only believed but who acted out his beliefs, in just the way Aristotle might have used it. But he also sometimes used the terms simply to separate the material from the immaterial, what we sense from what we cannot sense.

At first, I'd thought that he'd wanted to make this distinction, between the spiritual "real" and the material "actual," because he'd mistrusted the material world. But this wasn't it—not precisely. His goal was to learn to see and appreciate both realms. Focusing on the real while denying the actual was "fanaticism"; focusing on the actual to the exclusion of the real was "materialism." The two realms were separate, but they could be brought together, and this was the life's work of the saint, who had special access to both. The saint was tasked with joining reality to actuality, thereby transforming the actual into the real, for anything touched by reality was made real. God, the ultimate Reality, had broken into this world from the spiritual world on numerous occasions, most notably when He sent His son, and often during the age of miracles (which Oswald considered past), transforming what He touched into something spiritual. Now, God relied on His saints to realize or actualize His presence on earth. The process was not effortless. The two worlds had to be forcefully, physically, brought together. As Christ had entered the world through a fleshly womb, as He had opened the gateway to heaven through human blood spilled on a wooden cross, so God would come now only through the efforts of His (human) children. Often, this implied suffering, and suffering, more than any other activity, was the way the saint actualized his potential. Oswald loved a particular passage of Tennyson's and used it frequently in his discussions of reality:

> *Life is not as idle ore,*
>
> *But iron dug from central gloom,*
> *And heated hot with burning fears,*
> *And dipt in baths of hissing tears,*
> *And batter'd with the shocks of doom*
>
> *To shape and use.*

In this life, Oswald wrote, the saint did not sit idly by. He climbed the mountain and took what he saw there down into the valley, hammering out the heavenly vision with his footsteps. The saint smashed beneath the waves, plunging again and again, until he learned to ride the surf. He opened his lips and forced air through his vocal cords, transforming dead sounds into song or prayer or prophecy. Raising his paintbrush, he transformed meaningless paint and canvas into art. Gripping his pen, he spelled out his soul. Keeping Godly habits, he carved spiritual "grooves" into the "material of the brain." The saint lived by Shakespeare's dictum "Thoughts are but dreams till their effects be tried," and he never failed to try the effects. He pursued God to the ends of the earth, following the vision wherever it led. Again, Oswald thought it was Tennyson—Tennyson who'd labored to make real and perfect every poetic vision he'd been given—who had it best:

> *Not of the sunlight,*
> *Not of the moonlight,*
> *Not of the starlight!*
> *O young Mariner,*
> *Down to the haven,*
> *Call your companions,*
> *Launch your vessel,*
> *And crowd your canvas,*
> *And, ere it vanishes*
> *Over the margin,*
> *After it, follow it,*
> *Follow the Gleam.*

XI

∾

"Behold, He cometh with clouds."

—*Revelation 1:7,* JULY 29

Paris, 2012. One morning in Paris, not long after I'd come across the mention of Oswald's angels, I awoke to a sunny sky and an *Utmost* filled with clouds. Oswald was talking about how God seldom revealed Himself in "clear shining" but rather in mystery, and I was thinking about how mysterious Oswald himself was, and how the process of finding him—the *real* him—had been so odd. It had led me here, to the strange little room in Paris I now called home. It was a quiet room, long and narrow and high-ceilinged, with a twin mattress and a large window; a shower, an armoire, and a desk. It was a room in which everything was of the brightest white, so white that when the sun rose in the morning (the window faced east), everything yellowed slightly—the walls, the floor, the bed, the desk, the glass of the shower door. At dusk, the color changed to pink, quieting to blue at the close of day. There was no kitchen, just a sink and an old microwave oven. The toilet, which I shared with three others, was down the hall and painted battleship gray. A *chambre de bonne*, or maid's room, they called it, or had called it in former days. All the buildings erected under Hauss-mann's scheme, in the latter half of the nineteenth century—Oswald's era—had filled their top floors with them. This lofty position was their saving grace: they afforded magnificent views of the rooftops of Paris.

More than a century after they'd been built, the rooms had for the most part ceased to house maids and had become instead refuges for people like me: artists, writers, immigrants, students—anyone of meager means whose life could play itself out only in a city. Down the corridor from my room, past the second toilet, there lived a handsome young cello player, and next to him a sur-geon from Algeria, a woman in her forties who'd been obliged, by whims of fate and governments, to begin her training again. Around the corner, there was a family from China who had their own toilet, and a madman whose door always opened at the sound of footsteps, revealing walls stained brown from incessant cigarette smoking but never a face. (He was "from an old French family," the concierge had told me, and his landlords felt it would be *pas cor-rect* to evict him.) In the smallest, saddest room, near the service stairwell, there was a Pakistani man who did not work and whose room was so filled with computer parts that the bed was simply a mound of wires and disks and screens, and the walls, hung layers deep in rubbery vines, crawled with tiny winking lights. And there were numerous others I hadn't yet met.

The building was in the Fourth Arrondissement, on the Bou-levard Henri IV, just off the Pont de Sully and the Île Saint-Louis, a boulevard so luxurious that among its few shops were an oxy-gen bar and a shop specializing in *amincissement* (thinning—as in, the thinning of women), which faced the equestrian paradise of the Garde Républicaine, the élite mounted police force which still dressed in the tufted silver helmets and gold brocade of the Napoleonic era, and which every Tuesday paraded down the boulevard toward the Place de la Bastille, accompanied by the clanging of its own brass band. I'd rented the room for 350 euros a month, payable in cash, and cash only. Each chambre was tied to one of the grand apartments below, as it had been in the days of maidservants, and, because the owners of these apartments were not allowed to rent the chambres out without declaring the income on their tax forms (which of course they wished to avoid), we all paid cash and lived without rental agreements—*dangerously, unacceptably* on the edge, the hyperprotective French state would have said. But even France had its secret pockets of pragmatism.

And I, having slipped inside such a pocket, felt fortunate. My life in Paris consisted primarily of three things: sitting at sidewalk cafés, sometimes alone, sometimes with new friends (there was a tidy expat community here); reading about Oswald; and trying to remember what *Utmost* had meant to me at the start. This was one of the reasons why I'd been so eager to get back to Paris. I'd begun reading *Utmost* every morning, ritually, during the summer I'd visited France for the first time, when I was fifteen. It had become important for me to try to remember how I'd read it back then, since my research was uncovering so many unexpected things, piling on layers of context and history that threatened to bury the meaning it had originally held for me—the meaning, I imagined, it held for most of its readers.

Take, for instance, Oswald's habit of quoting Tennyson and other mid- to late-nineteenth-century writers in his discussions of reality. His favorites included Tennyson, Robert Browning, Henrik Ibsen, and the Scottish fantasy novelist and essayist George MacDonald. Other notable names from the period—like Charles

Dickens, George Eliot, Charles Darwin, Friedrich Nietzsche, and Oscar Wilde—showed up, too (if not always favorably). The fingerprints of such popular authors were all over *Utmost,* but I hadn't detected them until I'd gone looking. They were seldom credited in that book, and as often as not Oswald had quoted their work without quoting them precisely. So, for instance, Browning's famous rhetorical question

> Ah, but a man's reach should exceed his grasp,
> Or what's a heaven for?

became, in *Utmost,*

> The proof that we have the vision is that we are reaching out for more than we have grasped. . . . Our reach must exceed our grasp.

While MacDonald's

> There is no heaven with a little of hell in it—no plan to retain this or that of the devil in our hearts or our pockets. Out Satan must go, every hair and feather!

became

> There is no heaven with a little corner of hell in it. God is determined to make you pure and holy and right.

Oswald, it seemed, had been operating in a different context than I'd supposed. It hadn't occurred to me, at the start of my project, that his interest in the topic of reality was not a specifically *religious* interest but rather part of a broad cultural fixation—one driving a major artistic and literary movement of his day: Realism. Realism was the genre in which many of his literary sources, Christian and otherwise, had written, and their influence on his work had been enormous, even those who, like Ibsen and Eliot, were avowed atheists.

This week, I was busying myself with chasing down some of these influences. Inspired by the clouds in *Utmost*, I decided to skip the library and go out in search of one in particular—one which was not literary but rather artistic. At nine, after I'd finished eating my second croissant and reading the *Times*, I tidied the chambre and threw my computer into my bag. Then I set out down the boulevard toward the river, determined to reach the Musée d'Orsay before the crowds grew too large.

∾

The Musée d'Orsay, a museum of nineteenth- and early-twentieth-century art housed in a repurposed train station, lay west of my apartment along the Seine, thirty minutes away by foot. I was headed there today because I had a faint recollection of having seen there, seventeen years earlier, a certain painting by Gustave Courbet, the great French Realist. It was, as I remembered it, an oil painting of clouds above a turbulent sea.

I'd been reading up on Courbet ahead of my outing, since what I recalled most about my first encounter with his work was that some of it had been so shocking, even in 1995, that the museum had felt obliged to place it behind bulletproof glass and to post a guard in front of it. I recalled huddling in a queue with my friend Elodie for a chance to view *The Origin of the World*, a realistic rendering of a (naked) woman's middle portion, and glancing about nervously for our teacher. I remembered the shock at the image, and the even greater shock at my own shock. It was an era, after all, when teenage girls were routinely exposed to detailed drawings of female anatomy on tampon boxes and in sex-ed classes and magazines like *YM,* and when we were expected to become intimately acquainted with (the animal version of) it in biology classes: earlier that year, I'd dissected a pregnant pig. Yet I was shocked by *The Origin of the World,* to see a woman thus dissected (her head and arms were off-canvas, and her torso was twisted into an odd shape) and embarrassed to be standing so close to it with Elodie. It was at once too intimate and too public, too lascivious and, in its pretty gilded frame and elegant museum setting, too polite. It was a fine first lesson in the power of context.

That painting had never been on public display during Courbet's lifetime (indeed, it had only just arrived at the Musée d'Orsay that summer, from the estate of the psychoanalyst Jacques Lacan), but Courbet's other paintings had been shocking enough. He'd called himself a *réaliste,* because, he said, he wished to be "sincere to the whole truth," to paint things as they were, not as the artist or anyone else *thought* they should be (he was also, for the same reason, a *socialiste,* an adherent of a new political movement which aimed to erase old divisions, in the hopes of forming a society in which men might be judged according to their merits rather than their class). A Romantic at heart, he'd embraced that movement's opposition to authority, throwing himself into the Bohemian lifestyle that swept Paris in the unsettled decades after the French Revolution. His Realism was an outgrowth of his Romanticism, a way of pushing past the fantasy and idealism of the latter while maintaining its radicalism, its rebellious spirit. At the salon of 1850–51, two paintings in particular had caused an uproar: *A Burial at Ornans* and *The Stone Breakers.* In substance and in style, the paintings—one picturing black-clad figures surrounding a grave, the other showing men at work breaking stones with hammers— were reviled as much for what they did not show as for what they did. The Académie des Beaux-Arts, an official institution tasked with the "safeguarding and development" of French art (and the promotion of its own vision in annual salons), had declared, in the words of the nineteenth-century painter and critic Samuel Isham, that art should be "ennobling, dignified, representing not accidents of the moment but eternal and ideal forms." Courbet's paintings contained no historical or mythical figures. There were none of the stock characters of Romantic painting: no angels or emperors or woodland nymphs, no Shakespearean heroes or ancient philosophers. There was no suggestion of an afterlife, no glorification of the past. Instead, the figures in his burial painting, common folk, were presented on a scale (life-size) and in an arrangement that were generally reserved for paintings of prominent historic events and their very important actors. This was a political statement— a defiant assertion of Republican values. In the grief-stricken faces of the mourners, one could glimpse, too, a religious (or rather an antireligious) statement. As Isham related, *The Burial at Ornans* "came like a shock to the Parisians, accustomed, as they were, to the conventional suggestions of funeral urns, silver tears on black cloth, and weeping angels, to have put before their eyes the actual facts of death and sorrow, neither refined nor degraded, but as they were known and felt by plain, simple people."

Courbet's landscapes were disconcerting, as well. Artists before Courbet had painted landscapes, but these had tended to improve on their material: their colors were deepened and enriched, their lines manipulated to fit beautifully onto the canvas, following conventions dictated by the Académie and taught at the École des Beaux-Arts. In Isham's view, as in many others', Courbet's canvases were *un*artistic, in the sense that he seemed to add nothing to what he saw. The artist was supposed to interpret reality, to glimpse its hidden, emotive properties. Was it really art if the artist could not see them? Isham, thinking not, compared Courbet to "the amateur photographer." Still, he conceded, the effect of Courbet's painting, if unpleasing to the academically trained eye, was undeniably "truthful," particularly when it came to landscapes:

No one else has given so vivid and unsophisticated a reflection of external nature. From his pictures, you can go directly out into the reality of woodland life and feel that the literal truth has been told. No sentiment has been added, no brilliancy lost. The leaves shine and sparkle in their true colors against the gray rocks, the brooks run wet and clear, the grass has the vivid green of moist pastureland, and the sky shines with a luminous brilliant blue, the true blue of the clear summer sky in a mountainous country.

This quality—"veristic," they'd called it in the nineteenth century, coining the word, which meant art or literature that was "extremely or strictly naturalistic"—was the reason, I suspected, the paintings of Courbet's I'd seen at the Musée d'Orsay seventeen years earlier had stuck with me. I could still see the mottled clouds, the motion-filled sea, the soft foam on the waves (and I could certainly still see the origin of the world).

This afternoon, I arrived at the museum to find a large crowd in the central corridor. Happily, my destination—salle 29, the Preimpressionism gallery—was nearly empty (the tourists, it seemed, preferred van Gogh). I spotted the painting right away. It was on a far wall, and I walked toward it slowly, remembering. Then I noticed that another painting on the wall was also a Courbet. This one showed a peaceful scene: sun shining on a pristine beach, a wall of white cliffs beautifully illuminated in one corner. *The Cliff at Étretat After the Storm,* it was called, and it was like the inverse of the one I'd come to see, *The Stormy Sea.* Both were dated 1870.

This second painting was a surprise. I pulled out my phone and opened the photo app, tapping on an image I'd scanned into it several months earlier, while on my visit to Wheaton. The image filled the screen, and I turned the phone sideways, holding it up in front of *The Stormy Sea.* The painting was similar to the image on the phone—both were realistic renderings of storm clouds and water—though the picture on the phone was a charcoal sketch rather than oil on canvas. Then I opened another image and held it up next to *The Cliff at Étretat.* These, too, were similar, showing scenes of peaceful seashores lit by the sun.

The first image on my phone was titled *Seascape, Crashing Waves,* and the second was titled *Harbor,* and they were both the work of the artist Oswald Chambers.

∽

When I thought back on what *Utmost* had meant to me over the years, what sprang to mind first was the clarity and encouragement it had brought to my creative pursuits. There were many themes in *Utmost,* but this was the one I'd cottoned to most. When it came to describing and analyzing the creative life, there was no one like Oswald. He understood that the source of the artist's joy—what he called the "vision"—carried with it a sense of compulsion and that it was a mixed blessing. The person in possession of a creative vision could know ecstasy in working toward realizing it, but this work was often extremely difficult, and not only the work itself, but the external pressures that were likely to attend it. Demands on an artist's time from loved ones; financial hardship; the non-artistic "drudge" work most artists were forced to perform on the side; critics and naysayers, particularly those who raised the banner of "common sense" (the artist was sure, at one time or at many, to be called a fool). Surviving the onslaught so that she might do her work continuously, over a long period of time, even when success seemed unlikely, required a certain kind of faith. The artist needed to have faith that, however difficult the work became, God had not disappeared. Indeed, she needed to grasp that the artistic creation, originating with God's vision, ultimately belonged to Him, too (art, in other words, was not, at its core, a self-serving or selfish pursuit, but rather a gift the artist helped God to give to the world). Since it was God's, the artist had to learn to hand over to Him, with a great effort of will, the circumstances necessary for its realization. She had to trust that God would look after her relationships, her finances, and the public reception of her work. This did not mean that wealth and success were inevitable, nor that they would come within the artist's lifetime. God's time line was long: He had "all of time and eternity" at His disposal. The artist's reward lay simply in pursuing the vision. If she was willing to make herself "broken bread and poured-out wine," God would break her, God would pour her out.

Oswald was specific on the nature of the artistic pursuit. God, he said, was the God of sweeping inspirations and big ideas, but He was also the God of detail, process, habit. The artist could progress only one step, one word, one brushstroke at a time. The vision was the driving force, providing the energy for the journey, but the artist wouldn't get anywhere until she learned to narrow her focus and to act in the moment, each moment. "You have inherited the Divine nature," he wrote. "Now screw your attention down and form habits, give diligence, concentrate." This was the descent from the mountaintop into the valley. A narrow focus kept the artist from becoming overwhelmed—Peter, Oswald reminded his readers, was able to walk on the water until he started worrying about the wind and the unlikeliness of the feat that he was, in fact, already performing—as did habits, which were the artist's "safeguard." This lesson, which might seem obvious to the practically minded, was invaluable to dreamers, those whose faith often led them to hope that God might accomplish in a single leap what usually required ten thousand steps.

Oswald understood something else as well, something it had taken me many years to accept: that if a person received a creative vision and chose not to follow it—whether out of fear or out of laziness—it would eat away at her. The vision was a gift the artist couldn't return or discard. "If you have ever had the vision of God, you may try as you like to be satisfied on a lower level, but God will never let you." The vision compelled to action, immediate and sustained, and if a person did not act upon it, it turned to "dry rot." You had to "continually bring the truth out into actuality; work it out in every domain, or the very light you have will prove a curse." The vision not followed became a burden, a source of regret.

In undertakings big and small, *Utmost*'s message on creativity had sustained me over the years. But there was a flaw in my interpretation. Oswald, in writing about visions, had not, strictly speaking, been writing to only artists. He'd been writing to missionaries and preachers in training—students he'd taught at a small Bible college in London, in the years leading up to World War I. This was one of the more curious things about *Utmost*: although it was a book of mass appeal, numerous of its entries concerned the life of preachers and missionaries, just as if the book had been intended only for them, as a kind of practical guide to the profession. The visions which these Christian workers received, in Oswald's teaching, were visions not of "art" but rather of Christ's sacrifice and what it meant. They compelled missionaries to spread the word about this sacrifice; to labor among the people, serving them; to lead exemplary, holy lives. Often, the visions compelled them to leave behind their belongings and loved ones, and to journey out into the world with no promise of financial remuneration and no long-term destination. It was a life of tremendous uncertainty. The organizations which encouraged and supported it were not always large institutional churches. They were independent, nonprofit, Evangelical "parachurch" leagues and societies, a type of organization which emerged and flourished in the nineteenth century. In an era when a huge percentage of the human race was on the move—it was the age of the Industrial Revolution, the age of mass migrations, of people displaced from home to foreign land, from countryside to city, from family to solitude; it was Britain's "Imperial Century," the century when its colonies spanned half the globe—in this mobile era, these societies deployed a mobile spiritual force. They were often run along what they called "faith lines." This meant that they survived on donations, vowing to keep their doors open only as long as God provided funding. Often, they survived week to week. The missionaries who worked for them pledged to go out "not knowing whither," not knowing how. This was how Oswald had lived, particularly during his time traveling for an organization called the Pentecostal League of Prayer and, later, in his role as army chaplain for the YMCA. He'd lived poor, armed only with faith that help, should it be needed, would appear.

Utmost was undoubtedly a very good book for people following in Oswald's vocational footsteps. But it had been very good for millions over the years, and not all of them had been preachers or missionaries. What they *had* all been, I imagined, were people of dreams and visions, people with strong creative desires, people who believed that these desires came from God and who yearned to serve Him by honoring them. Whether the creative desire was to craft sermons, help the less fortunate, write novels, raise children, or something less concrete—something like leading a life of grace—didn't matter. *Utmost,* as directed as it could be in speaking to missionaries, was often so vague that it seemed to demand personal interpretation.

Still, I'd always been surprised at how well *Utmost* fit on the artistic life. It fit on much better than any other Christian text I'd ever read. It fit on as if the person who'd written it hadn't been a preacher at all, though the biographical note in the preface stated clearly that he was. It was because of this note that I'd assumed Oswald had had more in common with the professional Christians of my own era than he did with me. That Oswald's teaching spoke to me I'd considered a mercy: here, at last, was an understanding of God as a creator of creative beings (this was what was meant by the Bible's assertion that we were made "in His image"). Here was a book which understood the human relationship to God as an active collaboration. There was in my childhood Christianity a retiring streak: two habitually used catchphrases in my church had been "Just come" and "Let go and let God," phrases which placed a strong emphasis on human corruption and weakness, so as to emphasize God's strength and grace. The idea was present in *Utmost,* too, but Oswald advocated relying on God's strength *only* where human strength was inadequate. The shift in emphasis was key. We *could not* do certain Godly things, he wrote—we couldn't forgive ourselves or save ourselves, we couldn't control every circumstance—but God *would not* do what we could. God had given us bodies and minds, and we were to use them. Oswald seemed unafraid of the possibility that our creative and intellectual urges might lead us outside the bounds of institutional ortho-doxy; indeed, he seemed to welcome it.

All this, I'd thought, was nothing more than a happy accident. The Oswald Chambers I knew was a preacher who happened to speak to artists. It would never have occurred to me that he was an artist who happened to speak to preachers.

∾

"From my very childhood," Oswald wrote in his diary in 1896, "the persuasion has been that of a work, strange and great, an experi-ence deep and peculiar, it has haunted me ever and ever." The year 1986 had been a trying one. It was his second year as a student in the fine arts program at Edinburgh, a course in which budding artists received technical training alongside schooling in pertinent history and philosophy. He'd been supporting himself with his paintings and with freelance work, designing advertisements and illustrating books. But this year, the freelance work had dried up, the paintings had stopped selling, and he could feel it approach-ing: the long-feared moment when, facing ruin, he'd have to give up art entirely. He'd told himself in his diary that he could han-dle it, that he could become ordinary. "I'll just be content to earn my living," he resolved. But no, he decided quickly, "no, that can-not be." He'd always known he was meant for something great. The certainty of it haunted him, even while practical concerns stalked him, many of them through the voice of his father. For years, Clarence, the stern Baptist minister, had been urging his son away from art, considering it a "horrifying" profession. It wasn't only the lascivious, unrestrained culture art seemed to give rise to (particularly, as everyone in Britain knew, on the European

Continent, where Oswald had considered studying) but the product itself. Artists painted horrifying things. They painted nudes, and they painted them from live models, something Oswald had been required to do in art school. According to Kathleen, Clarence "could not believe that anybody could allow himself to be in that way familiar with the human body." He advised his son to follow in his own footsteps, to pursue a practical, decent career in ministry. But Oswald would not be swayed—not by his father, at any rate. There was only one voice he would listen to. "I shall never go into the ministry," he declared, "until God takes me by the scruff of the neck and throws me in."

In the last months of 1896, with no end to his financial difficulties in sight, the divine order came, clear and stern, in the form of a pamphlet advertising a small Bible college in the Western Highlands (his father had requested the pamphlet, though Oswald did not know this at first). As he readied himself for his departure, he felt a sense of certainty, a sense of peace. Still, it was the end of a journey which he'd hoped would never end. He'd been drawing since childhood, encouraged in his talent by his mother, the loving, whimsical Hannah. At seven, he'd distinguished himself in an art class in school, where "a large golden eagle drawn in chalks was shown to visitors for many a day." His education had continued throughout his teenage years, in Perth and in London, where he'd attended classes at an art school in Kensington, enjoying, it seems, much success (a teacher told him that if he was willing to be poor and to suffer, he could become one of the top artists of his day). His specialty was portraiture, and apart from this he liked to paint his beloved Scotland. At twenty, he'd gone off to Edinburgh, ready to seize his destiny. But it had been difficult from start to finish. He'd worked hard and lived cheaply, in a boardinghouse. For lack of time and money, he'd made few friends. He'd simply embraced his fate—art, art, and more art, and the only reward the freedom to keep making it.

That this was enough of a reward for Oswald had much to do with his artistic vision, which was to him a divine vision. Though his struggle with Clarence might seem, at first glance, a struggle between an overbearing, overreligious father and an independent-minded son, it was, in fact, a struggle between two sincere Christians who had two very different ideas of God. Oswald captured the dispute in a poem, the title of which—"Insanity"—hints at the intensity of his frustration. He wrote,

> *Music—insanity?*
> *Only if sanity be that hard, dry,*
> *Mechanical monotony of so-called fact.*
> *But if that mechanical monotony of fact*
> *Be but as the organ case, what then?*
> *The appreciation of the music insanity?*
>
> *Man! Who is man? There's One, his creator,*
> *Who gave those divine essences we call*
> *Music, Poetry, Art, through which God breathes*
> *His Spirit of Peace into the soul.*

That some people couldn't understand that God spoke through art (and Oswald knew that God spoke through art, for God had spoken to him through art) seemed evidence of ignorance, or maybe of something worse. Christian ministers, people who might have had a special connection to art (since they professed a special intimacy with God), instead feared and shunned it. Moreover, they passed this fear on to their congregations. Ministers "know not the love of beauty as an artist knows it," Oswald wrote in a letter to a friend, and could not "instruct the people out of the bigoted notions against art." Materialists were just as bad. They tried to reduce truth to a series of material facts, to "atomize" nature, tearing into lifeless bits that which God had so elegantly put together.

Oswald intended to worship God through art. His ambitions, however, were not limited to his own personal spiritual expressions. They were much grander in scope. Indeed, they were radical, revolutionary. In 1895, he wrote in a letter to a friend:

My life work as I see it, my eternal work, is, in the Almighty strength of God, to strike for the redemption of the aesthetic Kingdom of the soul of man—Music and Art and Poetry, or rather, the proving of Christ's redemption of it. There is much that is already bowed to the Kingship of Christ in these realms, but the spirit of Art is to a sad extent the spirit of immorality. Ruskin struck at the sin of it with the sledge hammer of a champion and the Kingdom of Art trembled. That noble champion is growing old and feeble now, and Art seems settling to the sensually reposeful position of previous ages. As far as my limited knowledge goes, our Master and Saviour has no representative to "teach, reprove and exhort," and an ambition, a longing, has seized me and seized me so powerfully that it has convinced me of the need.

For anyone pondering the life of Oswald Chambers, this letter is of the greatest importance. It reveals his precise thoughts

on the nature of art: it was its own kingdom, the "aesthetic Kingdom," and it was a kingdom of the human *soul.* The letter also
provides the key to a seeming contradiction. If Oswald was intent
on reclaiming the aesthetic kingdom for Christ—on filling the
blank space of the canvas with subjects of a specifically Christian
character—why did he not paint Christian subjects? Why did his
work follow in the style pioneered by Courbet, an artist whose
personal motto was "Without ideals and without religion"? The
mention of Ruskin in this letter points to an answer. John Ruskin,
who was seventy-six years old in 1895, had indeed taken a "sledge
hammer" to the art world in several works of criticism which were
hugely influential throughout the Victorian era and up to World
War I.

A fierce detractor of "convention," Ruskin was particularly
critical of landscape artists who drew "what they thought would
make a handsome picture," instead of what they observed: they
copied nature "like children drawing what they knew to be there,
but not what they saw there." In his view, the artifice these painters
brought to their subject bordered on blasphemy. For him, there
was an explicit link between nature, morality, and God. "No doubt
can, I think, be reasonably entertained," Ruskin wrote,

> as to the utter inutility of all that has been hitherto
> accomplished by the painters of landscape. No moral end
> has been answered, no permanent good effected, by any
> of their works. They may have amused the intellect, or
> exercised the ingenuity, but they never have spoken to the
> heart. Landscape art has never taught us one deep or holy
> lesson; it has not recorded that which is fleeting, nor pen-
> etrated that which was hidden, nor interpreted that which
> was obscure; it has never made us feel the wonder, nor the

power, nor the glory, of the universe; it has not prompted to devotion, nor touched with awe; its power to move and exalt the heart has been fatally abused, and perished in the abusing. That which ought to have been a witness to the omnipotence of God, has become an exhibition of the dexterity of man, and that which should have lifted our thoughts to the throne of the Deity, has encumbered them with the inventions of his creatures.

In Ruskin's view, the purpose of art was to capture reality and communicate it clearly: this was how its moral potential was fulfilled. The artist's job was to avoid getting in the way with his own ideas and ideals, to leave his agenda behind. "The greatest thing a human soul ever does in this world," Ruskin wrote, "is to see something, and tell what it saw in a plain way. Hundreds of people can talk for one who can think, but thousands can think for one who can see. To see clearly is poetry, prophecy, and religion,—all in one."

Poetry, prophecy, and religion, communicated on a canvas by one who could truly *see*—this was Oswald's goal. If God willed it, he would be happy to serve as a new champion of art, a new Christian savior of the aesthetic realm. Like Ruskin, he would embrace critical writing—already, he'd won a prize for an essay at university—and he would keep painting. This would be his "life work," his "eternal work."

Oswald had believed in his calling so strongly that even in 1896, when he'd been forced to leave Edinburgh and begin a life in ministry, he'd found a way of clinging to it: the principal of the Bible college in Dunoon had promised to let him teach a course in art. "This may after all be more conducive to gaining the ultimate end of being an ambassador for Christ in the art world," Oswald wrote in his diary. "God moves in a mysterious way." And indeed, during his first years in Dunoon, as a fellow student remembered, "he was regarded primarily as an artist more than a Christian leader." He taught his classes, and he continued to sketch. He went out into nature to draw what he saw: still beaches, white with sun; rough waves, black beneath the clouds; harbors with small boats. He was generous with his art and his learning. He drew the frontispiece for a book written by the principal, and when this same principal decided to run for the school board, he organized the campaign, designing a sandwich board that he himself wore around town. He established a Robert Browning society, which he opened to students and townspeople alike. He became known as a lover of music. "I especially remember one night," a friend wrote, "which for me was epoch-making, when he played to me the Slow Movement of Beethoven's *Moonlight Sonata* and then read Tennyson's *Maud.*" He did a charcoal sketch of Beethoven, stern and wild-eyed, which hints at the depth of his feeling for the composer. He also sketched Wagner (though with a touch less emotion, since, as his daughter later revealed, he did not actually like Wagner's sensibility). He could be a snob about the education he'd received prior to Dunoon—"1 have," he wrote, "a double authority . . . of knowledge and of God," an authority which, he felt, meant that "men *must* listen" to what he had to say. The students in his art classes loved him, though when the time came for him to begin giving sermons, as part of his ministerial training, he frightened the congregation, sounding, despite himself, just like his father: "He seemed to create a fear of God, in the sense of terror, in his hearers rather than of confidence and love."

But what did it matter if he was not a born preacher? He was a born artist. God spoke to him through art, and through his art to other people. This was Oswald's native language, his mother tongue. He would continue speaking it, even when the canvas before him was no longer an expanse of white muslin; even when he'd fully abandoned the kingdom of the aesthetic for a kingdom of a very different sort.

XII

❧

It is not true to say that God wants to teach us something in our trials: through every cloud He brings, He wants us to unlearn something.

—JULY 29

Paris, 2012. Later that evening, I sat in the chambre reading the old biography of Oswald by the light of a eucalyptus candle, a preventive measure against the mosquitoes that swarmed up from the Seine in the sticky summer months. Parisians, I'd discovered, were in denial about their mosquito population and had neither screens on their windows nor air-conditioning units, both of which would have marred the façade. So August was a horror, and everyone fled, leaving the city to the tourists and, of course, to those residents who lacked means or destination or both. Already, the wealthy people on the floors below me had vanished, along with some of the denizens of the sixth floor. Those who remained were doing what I was doing: keeping still and quiet in the dark. In two hours, nothing had stirred in the blackened corridor outside my room, and, since the temperature there was much lower, I'd moved my chair and candle to the open doorway, settling in there to read.

The evening was progressing slowly. The pages of the book were crumbling and yellowed and the ink faded, making it difficult to discern the words in the low light—a problem reflected in the murkiness of the story I was trying to understand. It concerned the moment in Oswald's life when he'd arrived in Dunoon, ready to undergo training for the ministry but unready to give up on his artistic vision, a decision which had apparently been supported by the principal of his college, as well as the other young men he met there.

It had all gone well at first. Oswald had arrived at school with a kind of sheen about him—most men did not come to this obscure Evangelical outpost in the Highlands direct from a world-class university like Edinburgh—and when he began teaching (art at first and later philosophy), he enraptured his students. "Not even the dullest student could have been long under the influence of Mr. Chambers without acquiring a taste for study and a love for the teacher," one recalled. Another said that, in order to impress Oswald, he'd worked harder than he ever had in his life. And another: "His influence was always with you, more so than you were conscious of at the time." His appeal seemed to lie as much in his teaching style, which was impassioned, authoritative, clear, and demanding, as it did in his ability to shift into the role of intimate companion. He befriended his students, meeting with them in private, sharing laughs, listening to their ideas—even leading them on long treks in winter around Loch Eich, on which he delighted everyone by making a fire out of wet sticks. But this was the least of his magic. "He had a deep interest in us all," one student wrote. His greatest joy, another recalled, was seeing them succeed—it spoke to "the rare faculty he had of rejoicing in the happiness of others."

His allure was not limited to his personality. Physically, too, he was intriguing. A friend recalled:

> The features of the face were distinct and of regular forma-tion; the eyes set under a broad cleft of brow, the mouth firm, with lips rather thin. The whole together might have given an impression of austerity; but on the contrary the countenance was unusually pleasing and inviting. This decided cast of features gave him a look older than his years, you could not guess his age, one moment he looked a mere youth and the next a man of maturer years. When he rose to his feet he was surprisingly tall, and I have since thought that his physical aspect had its corresponding features in the structure of his mind.

Everyone remembered this early incarnation of Oswald as joyful and uncomplaining. "How happy he was in all his human associations, never a shadow on his pathway," a student wrote. And it seemed that, for a time, he was truly happy. "Everything goes with me in amazing prosperity," he wrote in his diary, shortly after arriving.

And then, suddenly, the idyll had come to an end. Something had happened to usher in what Oswald called "four years of hell on earth," a time of "darkness and misery." It was this something that I was trying to pinpoint now, since it had occurred dur-ing a time in Oswald's life that was very poorly documented. A friend later described it like this: "Slanders of all kinds assailed him, he was misunderstood, shunned, avoided and evil spoken of." Throughout, it seems, he'd longed for death: "My thoughts for seven years past," he wrote in a letter to his parents after the crisis had passed, "have never pictured me further on than 35 years of age and if you remember I sometimes used to say I should like to go to more commodious premises then." Not only had he quit painting, but he seemed bent on destroying everything from his past. "I remember seeing him spend a whole morning destroying his diaries, short stories and poems," a friend wrote. "I told him I thought it was a pity, but he was whole-hearted in his belief that the time had come to forget all about them and pass on to new things." He even seemed to have lost his religion. "Either Christianity is a downright fraud," he'd announced in a prayer meeting, "or I have not got hold of the right end of the stick."

What had happened? There was one event mentioned in the record that might have played a role: a woman from a nearby village had accused Oswald of improper conduct. The charge was investigated and he was cleared, but, presuming that he was innocent (and there is no reason to suspect that he wasn't), the shock of being so accused must have been great. He would not have been the first charismatic teacher or preacher to awaken a feeling of intimacy in a student or congregant. Indeed, most of his students felt close to him and adored by him, and it is not difficult to imagine that one might have misunderstood him (how many young people throughout history have fallen into raptures over a teacher who stirs them, *sees* them, as no one has before?). It is also possible, of course, that the woman took offense at a genuine advance. For the past several years, Oswald had had a "girlfriend," Chrissie, whom he'd met in London as a teenager and with whom he'd kept up a regular correspondence. But their association had ended shortly before he was accused, meaning that he'd been, in a fashion, back on the market.

Was his heart broken by Chrissie and then again by his accuser?

Was it really woman trouble that had brought on his death wish and buckled his faith? The full story was perhaps lost with the destroyed diaries, but I imagined that it was more complicated than a broken heart; more complicated even than a public accusation, as horrible as that might have been to endure. Oswald had always been a Romantic, but not particularly *romantic*. He was full of passion and transgression, but these had always found their expression in his art, not in relationships with women. "We must ruthlessly smash the thick-plate glass of human tradition and the ignorance that has clustered around it," he wrote in a letter; it described his feelings about conventions governing painting, not those governing courtship.

Perhaps this statement explained it, I thought now. The ignorance he wrote of was the ignorance of "Christian ministers"—ministers like his father. His art had been his means not only of expressing himself but of freeing himself from his father's grip (*ruthlessly smashing* his way to independence). More important, it had been his divine mission. Armed with a paintbrush, he'd seen himself heroically battling against bad art to reclaim the aesthetic kingdom for Christ, revealing in the canvas the God who'd sent Him. To find himself on the path toward becoming a minister, after such a long struggle, enrolled at an institution chosen for him by his father, might have seemed a failure—not on his part, necessarily, but on God's. His conflation of the two things, art and God, would explain why he'd started to doubt his religion at the very moment his artistic dreams had been dashed.

For Oswald, I was realizing, had been an extremely ambitious person. This was not a trait usually associated with poor preachers (he had been relatively poor throughout his life, and sometimes very poor), but it fit Oswald, and it explained some of the discrepancies of his early time at the college. He was, on the one hand, always surrounded by companions—other people being requisite for competition—but he also wished to be left alone. His secret thoughts on his peers would probably have shocked them. In his diary, he wrote,

> Perhaps the consciousness that I am thought of too highly makes me want to get away at times. They all place me so high that I am weary of it. Oh, that I might be away with Nature, and see and not be seen.

Oswald did, of course, love nature—nature was the face or the language of God for him—yet his longing to escape human society was not straightforward. He would be, he wrote, "content to live in a barrel," so long as "I have my soul with mind and imagination to express somewhat of it," but this was disingenuous. Oswald could play the curmudgeon in his diary, but he did not lead an isolated life; his soul ever required an audience to be expressed *to*. In fact, he was an extremely social person, surrounding himself from dawn to dusk, even welcoming company into his time "alone" with God. "Every morning at six o'clock," a student recalled, "I would hear a gentle rap on my door, it was Oswald Chambers. I would rise immediately and dress, and then go to his room where I would find a cup of tea waiting, then we would spend a blessed hour alone with God." He led numerous groups and organizations, in the college and in the town; he attended services at the local Baptist church; and he generally inserted himself into others' lives.

In short, Oswald's trouble in these early days was not that he was a recluse who had been forced to live in society. It was that he was a social striver who'd landed in the wrong kind of society for striving. In Dunoon, he was surrounded by country folk, whom

he liked better than city folk for their simplicity and wholesome-
ness, but whom he also discounted for the same reasons: they were
fruit that had already been plucked. Shortly after his arrival at the
college, he wrote,

> It is surely better for young men to be taught and person-
> ally influenced by godly men long in the work than to be
> crystallized to clear cold cultural concerns in a University
> curriculum. I have thought lately how fine the experience
> of a few years' ministry in a country place among country
> people would be, despite all the disadvantages. To be out
> of the competition, and to have but to think and study
> and preach, and pray and visit, and then come back into
> the swirl and competition of city life amongst the earnest,
> striving worn-out multitudes.

It was the idea of making a comeback to the city that gave his
"disadvantageous" country sojourn meaning, not as a painter now
but as a preacher. The city was for him like the painter's canvas, a
space to be claimed and fashioned. Both were aesthetic kingdoms
whose salvation he wanted to strive for, and to strive for competi-
tively. He could not, he felt, be a real competitor in Dunoon—
winning the affection of country Christians was not the same
thing as winning lost souls. In truth, he was still fixated on what
he called "clear cold cultural concerns," like those addressed in a
university curriculum.

It was perhaps because of this fixation that he launched such
a curriculum at his new college, an arguably inappropriate venue.
He began to teach philosophy, using a popular compendium called
A Handbook of the History of Philosophy, by a German scholar
named Albert Schwegler, first published in 1848, and in its eleventh

English printing in 1900. It considered the primary arguments of all the major philosophers from the pre-Socratics through Hegel, and it was, for those interested in the subject matter, at least, a very digestible introduction. But Oswald's students balked, saying they found it too "abstruse," a gripe which prompted him to rewrite the entire book in simpler language. He was insistent that his students learn philosophy—whether they wanted it or not.

If Oswald's big problem in these years was his inability to deal with his own self, a self with insistent yet contradictory powers and urges, it was a problem exacerbated by his intellectual pursuits. Much of the philosophy he was teaching concerned the idea of the self, and much of the literature he was reading did, too. One of the most influential books of his day was Friedrich Nietzsche's *Thus Spake Zarathustra,* a kind of dreamy, outraged power-poem that contained descriptions of a character called the Übermensch, or over-man (what we call the Superman). The Übermensch was a figure which many Evangelicals worried about, in Oswald's time and into the present. The ideal it set forth—of a fully independent individual, a self-actualizing "will-power," who created his own values rather than deriving them from a system, a religion, or history—was extremely seductive. It appealed strongly to a generation which felt itself hemmed in on all sides by the vast, impersonal forces governing modernity: by the industrial forces that had ripped them from their ancestral homes, sending them en masse into cities and factories, where they truly became lost in a crowd (London, Oswald's home as a teenager and again as an adult, swelled from 1 million inhabitants in 1800 to 6.7 million in 1900); by the oddly distant political system that had replaced the old one, breaking its bonds of kin and clan; by the economic system, capitalism, which seemed to make money the entire measure of the man. Capitalism had brought with it unprecedented wealth—more and more people were joining that comfortable rank known as the "middle class"—but it had also increased inequality, the effects of which were garishly on display in the city streets. In London, the wretched and downtrodden (to borrow the nineteenth-century vocabulary) mingled perversely with the more fortunate, who found themselves racked with a new kind of guilt.

All of these issues obsessed the citizens of the late nineteenth century, Oswald among them. He wrote mournfully of the "commercialization" of humanity and worried that the individual had been devoured by the machine (indeed, ideas of machines and mechanization filled both his youthful poetry and his later preaching). He was, in fact, sympathetic to Nietzsche's critiques of society, but because he was a Christian this sympathy was complicated. Nietzsche had denounced Christianity as a religion that enshrined weakness and subservience, robbing the individual of his independence and power; it was, in large part, against Christianity that his Übermensch rebelled. Oswald essentially agreed with Nietzsche's characterization of his religion. Nietzsche had been "diseased and wild," Oswald wrote, but he was this way only because he'd seen the truth of "things as they are," without grasping the right way out (this being, in Oswald's mind, the Cross). But even though Oswald *had* seen the right way out, still he was filled with distrust about his religion. His creeping suspicion that it was a fraud might have been related to his trouble with defining his individuality, with determining what it meant to be both an individual and a Christian in a modern age.

One way he dealt with his problem was to latch on to (slightly) less inflammatory writers. He became devoted to Ralph Waldo Emerson, the great American Transcendentalist. Emerson's "Self-Reliance" put forth a notion of the self as an entity which, if it was

fulfilling its own potential, was radically and conspicuously dif-
ferentiated from its society:

> A foolish consistency is the hobgoblin of little minds,
> adored by little statesmen and philosophers and divines.
> With consistency a great soul has simply nothing to do. He
> may as well concern himself with his shadow on the wall.
> Speak what you think now in hard words, and to-morrow
> speak what to-morrow thinks in hard words again, though
> it contradict every thing you said to-day.—"Ah, so you
> shall be sure to be misunderstood."—Is it so bad, then, to
> be misunderstood? Pythagoras was misunderstood, and
> Socrates, and Jesus, and Luther, and Copernicus, and Gal-
> ileo, and Newton, and every pure and wise spirit that ever
> took flesh. To be great is to be misunderstood.

Oswald recited the first line frequently enough at Dunoon
that more than one acquaintance recalled the habit decades later.
At times, he seemed to go out of his way to be eccentric. Shortly
after his arrival, he threw himself into the work of the eighteenth-
century Swedish scientist, mystic, and philosopher Emanuel Swedenborg and tried, unsuccessfully, to get his students to embrace
him, too. Swedenborg was tremendously popular in the later nineteenth century (indeed, there is hardly a major literary figure from
the period who failed to express strong sentiments about him, one
way or the other), but he was genuinely odd. A genius scientist
who had enjoyed much legitimate success in his day, Swedenborg
also claimed to have visited heaven on numerous occasions and to
have received there a new revelation from Jesus. Upon returning
from heaven, he'd mapped its geography and laid out a compli-

cated scheme of "correspondences," linking everything on earth to a heavenly counterpart. He'd also created a scheme for history, dividing it up into several dispensations, or ages, the last of which, the "New Church" age, was, he said, currently being ushered in (all the churches of the present age would meet their doom in the process).

Swedenborg's followers kept themselves busy teasing out his various schemes and systems, in which were embedded keen philosophical and scientific insights, and some of them had launched a Swedenborgian church, which they called the New Church. Oswald, though he did not join the church, was enough of a Swedenborgian that a talk he gave on the subject at the New Church headquarters in Glasgow, later reprinted in *The Dunoon Herald*, merited an angry letter to the editor of the paper. "Has Swedenborgianism obtained a foothold in Dunoon district?" it demanded, before listing Swedenborg's various heresies.

Had Oswald felt "great," in the Emersonian sense, when he was misunderstood in the press? If the rapidity with which he abandoned Swedenborg afterward is any indication, the answer is no. He certainly didn't feel great after the accusation made against him by the village woman, nor during the long period of public judgment that followed. Through these traumas, it seemed, the burden of self grew so heavy that Oswald saw just one solution: losing it. This was why he wrote of his desire to go one day soon to more "commodious premises." They were the only premises imaginable where the burden would be lifted forever.

∾

In the chambre, the hour had grown late, and, having reached a good stopping point in Oswald's story, I shut the biography and took a bottle of rosé out of the minifridge. I poured the wine into a glass and went to look out the window, though it was difficult to see anything at the moment: a scaffolding had gone up on the building a few days before, creating a shadow-space just beyond the frame. I hated scaffolding, but it had the benefit of focusing my mind on Oswald. Toward the end of his life, when he was living in the desert, he'd made a note in his diary. "Surely," he'd written, "all rational things such as civilisation, organisation, and Church-ianity are but temporal scaffolding of the Real, which is ever hid with Christ in God." It was strange, I thought, that his belief that religion was false and in need of smashing had never faded. More than twenty years had passed since he'd first written about taking a hammer to the "plate glass" of tradition, yet his position had remained unchanged. And this even though he'd been for many years a very successful preacher and teacher, a professional Christian, through and through.

Leaning farther out the window, I strained to see beyond the scaffolding, to the lights in the Thirteenth Arrondissement. I couldn't help but wonder what would have become of Oswald if he'd come here as a teenager. There was the briefest mention of it in the biography: his brother noted that Oswald had won a two-year scholarship to study at "the great art centres" abroad. The country wasn't specified, but at the time, the waning days of the nineteenth century, France was certainly an artistic hub. The great French modernists—Manet, Monet, Pissarro, Rodin, Renoir, Cézanne—were at various stages in their careers, and the culture they'd inspired in Paris was thriving. According to his brother, Oswald had declined the scholarship on moral grounds. He'd "seen men come back from their travels both moral and physi-cal wrecks. . . . 'Art for Art's sake' was a cry much in vogue at the time, and only those in art circles know the insidious temptations into which young students were frequently drawn." It was true that the modernist cry "Art for art's sake" was utterly in opposition to Oswald's Realist ideology—his was "Art for God's sake"—and it was also true that, as a Realist, he was by no means avant-garde (Courbet had made his big splash nearly fifty years before). But I still wondered at his refusal. Oswald had always been adamant, in *Utmost,* that a saint could thrive in any circumstances; also that he wasn't to hide himself from the world (God wasn't looking for "specimens to put in His museum," he wrote). I had no doubt that he would have been able to resist whatever lurid temptations Paris offered, particularly because he considered his art a divine mission. Would someone on such a mission really have refused the very thing that would have helped him to complete it, simply because the path was perilous? It seemed more likely that his father, and perhaps also his mother, had encouraged him to decline.

Yet I knew that Oswald's fear was probably justified in one respect: a trip to Paris would most definitely have altered him. Trips to Paris taken as a teenager changed a person, as I myself had learned.

The boulevard was quiet now, save for the occasional roar of a motorcycle, and I thought about getting ready for bed. But just as I began to close the window, I noticed something moving in the periphery of my vision, several feet away on the scaffolding. Turning, I saw a light, small and orange and bobbing. It grew still for a moment, and brighter, then dimmed, lowering slowly down. It was, I realized, the tip of a lit cigarette. I yelped, and jumped inside, shutting the window and the shade. A few moments later, I heard a knock on the door.

"*Oui?*" I said.

The answer came back in muffled French (I really did not understand French, despite all the lessons I'd had over the years) and

I asked again. This time, I discerned a single word—"Yascha"—and I went to open the door. It was the name of the acquaintance who had sublet the chambre to me.

Outside in the hallway, which was still dark, stood a young man, tall and skinny and disheveled in the French way. He apologized for frightening me, speaking English this time, and said again that he knew Yascha.

"Yes, right," I said—Yascha had told me he had a friend on the hall. "But you've been away, or . . ."

"In the mountains."

"And now you're climbing scaffolding?"

The young man smiled.

"Do you want to come up?"

"Where?"

"To the roof."

"Are you crazy?" I said.

The roof was a steeply slanted Haussmann affair, and we were six stories up—seven, in American measurements.

He rolled his eyes. "You Americans," he said. "You're always so afraid of things like this. I think it's because you don't have health care."

I laughed.

"What does health care have to do with falling seven stories to your death?" I said. "Or do you think the social safety net will catch you?"

"It's fine," the young man said. "People work on it all day. You can tell me why you're here."

"Is it legal?"

He shrugged.

I considered. It was hot in the chambre, and my concentration had broken. Sitting on a rooftop sounded nice.

"Okay," I said. "But it better be safe. I actually don't have health insurance."

The young man grinned, and I took the bottle of wine from where it stood on the desk. Then we climbed through the window and up to the roof.

❧

"It just means nothing to me, since God does not exist," the young man was saying. "It's like you're talking about the Easter Bunny."

Paris was spread out before us, glittering through the smog. I looked behind me as he spoke, so that I might see Sacré-Cœur, up on the hill. In the opposite direction were the glass towers of the library.

I held my tongue. It was very pleasant up on the roof, and the young man was nice. Instead, I said, "I guess none of your friends are religious?"

"No."

He stood and jumped onto one of the chimneys, teetering perilously on tiptoe, one leg lifted slightly in the air. It was, I thought, insane behavior. Insane, and very, very free.

"Tell me why you want to write about religion and why you are in Paris to write about it," he said.

"Well," I said, "I was reading the book I'm writing about the summer I first came here, when I was fifteen—but that's not really why I'm here."

I paused.

"At least, I don't think it is. I don't really know. Maybe I'm just getting some distance on everything."

"You are religious? You have been baptized?"

"Sort of."

"What's this 'sort of'?" he said. He jumped down from the chimney and came to sit next to me. Behind him, the blue, white, and red of the French flag waved gallantly from the gate of the Garde Républicaine, and the horses snored softly in their berths. The wind picked up the young man's hair, which was wild and brown and which fell, when the air was still, in large curls upon his forehead. "How can you be 'sort of' baptized?"

"I was baptized under duress," I said. "They don't baptize babies in my church—you're supposed to choose it when you're old enough."

"But you didn't choose."

"Not really."

It had happened, I said, one hot August night in the plains of East Texas, the summer I was thirteen. I was spending a week at church camp, where I was having a great time—camp was fun in America, I reassured him (the French seemed to believe that American childhood was tortured because of things like camp and church and peewee football leagues)—and not thinking at all about getting baptized. It wasn't that I didn't want to. In fact, I'd been looking forward to it my whole life. The baptism was a great moment in the Sunday service, when all the lights in the sanctuary would go down and two figures, both dressed in white robes, would wade out into a giant glass tank, lit by a single blue beam. I'd imagined myself up there, behind the glass, holy and perfect, several times. But I'd never actually gotten around to scheduling the event.

"It wasn't required for salvation," I explained. "For us to be saved, all we had to do was ask Jesus to come into our hearts, and even this was a formality. All we really had to do was believe. I thought I believed, and I constantly asked Jesus into my heart, just in case He wasn't getting the invitation, you know? But it was confusing, because I'd also been singing little songs about Him being there since I was two."

"Like what?" the young man asked, and I sang him a short one:

> *I am a C*
> *I am a C-H*
> *I am a C-H-R-I-S-T-I-A-N*
> *And I have C-H-R-I-S-T*
> *In my H-E-A-R-T*
> *And I will L-I-V-E E-T-E-R-N-A-L-L-Y*

"Like that," I said, and the young man smiled.

I continued the story. Though I'd wanted to be baptized, I hadn't gotten around to scheduling it, because I was a kid, and, like most kids, I'd had other things on my mind. Then one night at church camp, a counselor had given me an ultimatum: either I would agree to be baptized in the swimming pool with the other dawdlers, or I would make peace with the fact that I'd been choosing against Jesus my entire life, *and He knew it.* I hadn't heard logic like this expressed before, but it was effective, and on Saturday night, beneath steady stars and flickering neon lights, I was baptized. It was a stressful experience. In addition to finding myself in a swimsuit in public, something I hated, I'd slipped going down the steps, prompting the onlooking campers to start chanting that I was "tryin' to baptize myself." My family had been invited, but I could not see them through the crowd. I'd felt cheated—I really had wanted to do it in the beautiful sanctuary back home—and when I'd come up for air, I hadn't felt that I was really dead and buried, nor that I'd risen to walk in a new way of life, a sister, now, in the church family I'd always had.

"Uck," the young man said. "Religion."

I laughed. "I guess so, but it's funny—I wouldn't undo that experience, or any of my experiences from my childhood."

"And then you came to Paris."

"Yes, two summers later. But I'd already started to pull away from the church."

I looked out toward the river, remembering.

"So then why are you still religious if the church was so bad?" the young man asked. He'd slid his body partway down the roof, so that his head was high and tipped up, toward the stars.

I considered for a moment.

"I suppose a lot of it has to do with this guy I'm writing about, Oswald—his book. You know what his friends called him? The 'Apostle of the Haphazard.' He had these ideas about God that were so free, or freeing. He said that God worked through circumstance and that He worked through chaos—what felt like chaos to us. He called it 'haphazard order.' It's a kind of chaos-order that embraces all possibilities, good and awful—even the 'blackest facts.' I guess on some level it sounds trite. You could say his philosophy was just something like 'God moves in mysterious ways,' or 'God works everything together for good'—for the faithful, I mean, because that was a big part of it, this idea that we never needed to worry about the chaos because God was working it all out. When you study more what he's saying, you start to see why it's so freeing. When he talked about God's order embracing all possibilities, he didn't mean only things like natural disasters and historic events, he meant *people*. We, each of us, are unique possibilities, none of us predetermined, each of us necessary—have you heard the saying that it takes everything to make a world? It takes all of us to make God's world, or rather each of us. Oswald has this one sermon about how there's no such thing as 'humanity,' that God doesn't make groups or masses, He makes individuals, each one a 'single, solitary life.' That also might sound trite, but if you start thinking about yourself as this haphazard collection of circumstances, stretching back to the beginning of time, encompassing everything that conspired to bring this thing into being that is you, every event in every one of your ancestors' lives, up to the point they procreated, at least, every variation in their always-mutating DNA, you begin to understand that you're as vast as the universe, as incomprehensible and uncontainable as that. He said that personality was like the tip of an island in the sea: the true dimensions lie beneath the waves, too grand to be reckoned by anyone but God. It was important for me, because it meant that nothing in my immediate world had an ultimate claim over me. Those things had some claim, but not the *final* claim. There's only one authority, Oswald said, and that's Christ. Everything else— your tribe or society or family or a church—is just collections of individuals, each one the product of his or her own unique, chaotic set of circumstances, as indebted to the mystery as you are."

"Wow," the young man said. He sat up and poured more wine into the cups.

"Sorry," I said. "I've just been reading about him all night. All year."

"Does it work? This philosophy? You feel free?"

I smiled. He was maybe as clever as he looked.

"Sometimes," I said. "Not always. I think one reason Oswald protested so much about groups and cultures and religions is that he knew how powerful and eternal their grip on us was. He knew that on some very basic level we needed frameworks and authorities. He was about rebellion, not anarchy. But I've never been a very good rebel. I definitely don't feel free from the pull of everything I grew up with. I'm not sure what I'd be without it. Mostly, I feel guilty when I think about it. I feel guilty about not belonging to a Southern Baptist church and not living at home. I feel guilty that I like what I like, and not what my family wants me to like. I even still feel guilty about not enjoying my baptism. But I'm not sure that's the point."

"What's the point?"

I looked out in the direction of the Bastille, to catch a glimpse of the angel on top of the column. Or rather of the "spirit." An angel, I reminded myself, wouldn't have been welcome on that particular spot.

"I might not feel free," I said, "but I *am* free. Otherwise, I wouldn't be able to do the things I do. I mean, I don't *feel* free to be sitting up here on this roof, drinking wine with someone who thinks God is the Easter Bunny. And it's not just about religion. I don't feel free to be in Paris, like some libertine of yore, and not working hard in New York. I have degrees and a lease on an apartment and a résumé and a fantastic credit score that is rapidly being destroyed. I feel like I do belong to a system, that it owns me. My degrees and my credit score mean nothing outside of it, so why did I bother working for them, right? Sometimes in the morning, I jump out of bed and start getting ready for work. I feel like my cubicle in Times Square is actually waiting for me to come back. But here I am. It's not about feelings—that's what Oswald said. It's not about ideas. Life's too big and wild, and feelings and ideas are just these things that float over the surface, trying to make it make sense. Some are more successful than others, but none are entirely successful."

"What's a credit score?" the young man said.

"What?" I said, incredulous. I told him to remain in blissful ignorance as long as he could, and then I continued. "I mean, we make up these stories so that we can explain to ourselves what's happened, what the point is. You ask me why I'm in Paris and why I'm religious, and the answer is that a lot of crazy things happened. Things happened before I was born, and after I was born. Some things made me fall in love with my religion and with the idea of Paris, and other things made me wonder about them. The better question might be why I'm religious in the way that I'm religious, and not in another way. I had this teacher who was important to me, who took me to Paris when I was fifteen. And there were some theater people who kind of changed the way I thought. And Oswald, of course. But it's all a jumble."

"Tell me," the young man said. "I'll give you a cigarette if you do."

"Okay," I said. "I don't really smoke, but okay."

He pulled two papers from a packet, followed by some rolling tobacco, and I began to tell the stories as he worked, leaning back on the roof so that I might smoke looking up at the stars.

XIII

∾

Our Lord trusted no man; yet He was never suspicious,
never bitter, never in despair about any man.

—MAY 31

Somewhere over the Atlantic Ocean, 1995. What was amazing was that you couldn't feel a thing. The world was collapsing, split seams rejoining, and it felt like nothing. A bit of pressure in the ears at the start, that was all.

This was why they were all able to sleep so well, I thought. Now that they were fed, now that the movie was done and the lights dimmed, they'd all drifted off, placing the masks over their eyes, huddling beneath the viscose blankets. As if this were just another class trip to Nashville or Austin, as if we were just on the bus. But I'd kept watch as we passed the sun, entering out into a darkness as deep as it was high. A darkness that was black and wet below, black and broken above. A delirious darkness where the stars gathered, waiting. I'd seen them, pressing my face to the window. Now that I'd seen them, I would never feel the total dark sublime, no matter how much time I was given.

Across my lap, on a blue blanket, lay a copy of Auden's poems, though I was too excited, for the moment, to read. They were there just in case—in case, on his way to speak to one of the chaperones, Mr. Holamon passed by and looked down. If he did, he would notice and be impressed. I knew he would, since he noticed everything, and since he always gave credit where credit was due.

But he had not passed by yet. I glanced down at my wrist, at the watch I'd set to Paris time weeks earlier. There were only three more hours of flight left, three hours till real time harmonized with the time on my wrist. Soon, the breakfast cart would come; soon, we'd catch the sun. A different sun, gentler than the Texas sun, with rays colored Parisian pink. Something unfurled inside me as I thought about it, pink petals radiating out and down along the green stem—almost too much to bear. How had I been bearing it all these weeks?

But for the moment, time was running out: if I was to go, it would have to be now. I removed my book to the floor and unfastened my belt, climbing slowly over my sleeping companions. As I reached the aisle, the sound in the cabin shifted, and the notes of a conversation reached my ears: two voices, both familiar. The first was round and insistent, like a small bell set to ringing. The second was weightless, grave, and perfusive, like the smoke that often accompanied it. It was a voice that clung to you long after you'd gone from it, a voice that lingered like a scent inside your hair and your skin, a bit disgusting or a bit intoxicating, depending on your disposition. Many, maybe most, were disgusted, not by the voice but by its owner. He was gay, some students said, though there was no proof of this one way or the other. He was tall and thin—or rather he was narrow. He dressed well; he had a large brown mustache, a feature which accentuated the gauntness of his cheeks and the smoothness of his skull. He was often seen alone outside, smoking, leaning against the wall, one knee bent, his solid chest oddly concave, oddly inviting. That was enough to convince some of his persuasion. Or they said he was a sadist, happy to cause suffering in the students he did not like, and sometimes in the ones he did, though to them it was not suffering: they were happy to spend long hours after school perfecting a project with him—for him—to feel themselves being perfected. He was a true perfectionist, possessed of a certain vision, incapable of allowing his students to disrupt the vision. He'd been a blue-faced clown in the circus in younger days and had traveled the world, but the rumor was that he'd been born in the middle of nowhere Texas, far from civilization of any kind. He would admit nothing of his origins, nor did his accent place him, but he would often say to us— to some of us—"Leave. Leave this place, and never look back." To make escape seem really possible: that was why he took children to Paris in the summertime.

The row in which he was sitting now was a row of five seats, and they were all in darkness save for one. Inside a small column of light issuing from above, two strands of smoke rose steadily, intertwining their way up into the shadow region of the luggage rack. He had requested, of course, to be placed in the smoking row, as had Stefan—I thought of it jealously, since I never would have made such a request to my mother, would never have told her, even, that my teacher was a smoker, lest she form a picture of him that was a bit too close to the reality. Stefan was beside him now, on the aisle, the corner of his old black trench coat dusting the floor, the small diamond stud in his ear glinting. Their heads were bent together, Stefan's hair, thick and wiry as a terrier's, brushing the crescent of bare scalp that waxed in the light, and though I could not see what they were looking at, I knew that it was Stefan's sketchpad. He had the absorbed look he always got when he was drawing, as if he were inside the paper at the end of his pencil. The muscles in his face were utterly still, and his mouth, when it opened to take the cigarette or to speak, seemed to belong to a different field, disturbing nothing with its motions. He'd sketched me the year before, me sitting on the big black beanbag in his bedroom, looking up at posters of *A Clockwork Orange* and *Heathers*. Now, they were working on a project together—a large-scale poster for a play Holamon had directed. It was an adaptation of Alfred Jarry's *Ubu Roi*, translated into English, cut down by two-thirds, and reassembled into a nonsense that was total but kinetic: they'd performed it the year before, Stefan and the other players rushing around the stage on stilts and toe shoes, in fat suits and fake noses and mummy wrappings, shouting *"Merdre!"* all the time, each step, each word carefully orchestrated to cause maximum bewilderment in the audience. But I had not been among the players, had not yet known Holamon, had not yet known how fully, watching a rehearsal one afternoon, I would feel myself a part of it, though I was simply a spectator. After that, I'd snuck into rehearsals, hiding myself behind the railing on the balcony, and I'd gone to all the performances, sitting always in the front row, so that the sweat or the spit of the senior boys in the play (boys I'd never get that close to in real life) might fall on me. When, at the start of the following semester, I'd switched from Spanish to French in order to meet him—for Holamon also taught French—I'd claimed the desk closest to the lectern. But not two days into the semester, he'd announced his retirement from high school plays. I'd been too late. *Just* too late.

He raised his head as I approached, the two disks of his glasses round and blank in the light. A grin appeared below them, the lips spreading to reveal tobacco-stained teeth. *Mademoiselle,* I saw them say, though no sound came out. Then the grin was gone, vanishing upward in a puff of smoke, and I came to stand beside them, listening now to what Stefan was saying.

"And the polyhedron will be here, in Wenceslas's hand, and the title convex across the top, the two *U*'s inverted, like this, to emphasize the palindrome. With the grouping below, I think that will work."

"Brilliant, Stefan," Holamon said. "I think you've got it."

And with that, the pencil went limp in Stefan's hand, and his face reanimated. Now he looked up at me, and I smiled, as I always did when I looked into his eyes, soft brown and wild behind the heavy lashes. Two deer in a thicket.

"Hello," I said.

"Not sleeping, Solange?" Holamon inquired, using my French-class name (he required all of his students to select one on the first day). "You'll regret it, perhaps? No sleeping till nighttime."

"You're not sleeping, either," I said. "Neither of you."

Stefan reached out and took my hand, pulling me down as he pulled himself up.

"Sit," he said. "Smoke."

He reached inside his coat and fumbled to retrieve his eternal box of Camel Reds, shaking one out when he'd found them. I took it, so that I might stay, and he disappeared—to the bathroom, maybe, though I didn't see him go, bending my head to the flame that suddenly appeared in my teacher's hand.

"Stefan tells me you could do it."

"Sorry," I said. "Do what?"

Holamon leaned quickly into the light so that the beam reflected round the top of his head. Opening wide his eyes, he began to speak in a loud voice.

"Blood and money! Horn-belly! Madame Financier, haven't I ears to speak with and you a mouth to hear me? Or rather, no! You confuse me. You are the reason I am silly."

The old woman seated next to him raised her head, whispering "Hush," and he leaned back into the shadows.

"I'm sorry," I said again. "I don't understand."

"You're always sorry, Solange. I wonder whatever for?"

And as I shrugged he began to tell me, looking off into the distance. He'd retired from high school plays after *Ubu*, he said, as he knew I knew, but it had been for a specific purpose: he'd been writing music for a new adaptation. It was a long-standing dream. He'd fallen in love with the absurdist drama years before and had always wanted to make it into a musical. Now he'd finished writing the score, and he'd recorded much of it, too, using a synthesizer—he liked the artificial sound of it—and he was ready to add voices, to make a demo tape for potential producers. Stefan's artwork would serve as an album cover. And since the girl who had played Ma Ubu in the original production had graduated and moved far away, he was seeking a replacement.

"You, Solange," he said, turning his head on his seat to look at me. "You."

"Yes, yes," I said. "I'd love to!"

"The only trouble," he added, turning away once again, "is that we'll record at night. Sometimes on Wednesday night. Will that be a problem?"

Now I looked away, letting the ash of the cigarette drop to the floor. It was a pointed question, a reference to an incident that had taken place not long ago in his classroom.

Holamon's classroom was the nicest one in the school—how he'd won it was a mystery—a room with a front wall carved from oak, a floor laid with dark wooden slats, and a bay window looking out over the front lawn. It was one of only two rooms in the building that looked as if they could have belonged to a much finer institution than ours—most of the rooms had the plastic-and-laminate look common to inner-city public schools. But somehow Holamon's had retained the original character of the building, which was a beautiful Works Progress Administration building from the thirties. The other fine room was the auditorium—it was a real theater, complete with a curved balcony, brass railing, red-velvet curtains, an orchestra pit, and wings—and Holamon ruled it, too. In his classroom, where we were supposed to be learning the French language, the walls were decorated with posters of French films and the covers of records by French singers like Edith Piaf and Serge Gainsbourg, and the lessons had less to do with language than with culture. We watched films often, and we often heard of France's superiority to the United States—it was the land, he told us, of the artist and the student, of truth and rebellion, of idealism and love.

On the day in question, Holamon had entered the classroom and had written on the large blackboard behind the lectern,

Vendémiaire	*Germinal*
Brumaire	*Floréal*
Frimaire	*Prairial*
Nivôse	*Messidor*
Pluviôse	*Thermidor*
Ventôse	*Fructidor*

These were the names of the months, he'd begun by saying, of the calendar created by the First Republic, the government established during the revolution that brought an end to monarchy in France. This calendar had done away with all the trappings of the old order, all the religious and royal holy days that had once divided time and helped the human race to make sense of its predicament. The Republicans had reset the clock, banishing history (if Jesus could do it, why couldn't they?). The first Vendémiaire first was the first day of Year I. *Vendémiaire:* from the Occitan word for grape harvester, a fine representative of the sort of person the new order valued. The calendar, Holamon had explained, was a way of reifying certain other changes—most important, along with the end of monarchy, the end of religion. Religion, the Republicans knew, had no place in the enlightened, rational eighteenth-century world. To religion, there could be no concessions. In addition to being false (the basis of reality was matter, not mind, they'd discovered), religion was a tyrant, as deserving as all other tyrants of losing its head, and the calendar was one way of accomplishing this—together with the seizure of religious property, the destruction of crosses and bells, and the execution of priests who refused to swear allegiance to the new regime, as well as of anyone harboring such a priest, and the establishment of secular "replacement" religions, the Cult of Reason and the Cult of the Supreme Being. On the twentieth of Brumaire, Year II, the Republicans had held the first nationwide non-holy holy day, the Fête de la Raison.

At this point in the lecture, I'd raised my hand, to ask, with uncharacteristic boldness, how the French government had kept Christians from worshipping, and if they'd worshipped in secret, like they had in their earliest days, in the Roman Empire, drawing fishes in the sand with their sandaled feet, one arc rejoining its mate to form, again, the creature, two halves to remake the whole. You could banish history but not memory, I said. It was safeguarded in the feet; it was waiting in the sand, waiting to be etched. All Christians knew that; all religious people knew that.

Was that why, I'd asked, the experiment hadn't worked? Or did they still not have religion in France?

Holamon had been standing at the board, chalk ready in his hand. But now he dropped the chalk and walked back to his lectern, where he stood for a moment without saying anything, merely moving his gaze slowly over the room, his eyes dipping once, I thought, to my chest, to the large silver cross that always hung there.

"How many of you," he asked finally, "adhere to a religion which condemns people who do not believe as you do to an after-life of eternal pain and suffering?"

No one moved, no one dared even to breathe.

"Solange," Holamon said, after another moment, now locking his high gaze directly onto mine where I sat, trembling. "I am a nonbeliever. I do not believe in your God or your church. Do you think I am going to hell?"

"No, I—" I said, but I could not continue. His eyes were hard and black behind the glass.

"You what? You do not know the tenets of your religion, or you do not believe them?"

"No, no, I believe them. I believe them," I said. But didn't he know that I could say nothing else?

"Then," he snapped, "skipping ahead to the logical conclusion—you'll forgive me, we're short on time—your answer is yes, you do believe that I am destined for hell."

I struggled to formulate a response, muted by a rising panic, but he'd already turned back to the board, and, by the time I'd composed myself, the names of the months had vanished, and he had begun to write something else—the conjugation of the verb *aller*—something we'd learned months before.

So the incident had passed, never to be mentioned.

But now, on the plane, he was alluding to it, and I thought confusedly that it had been as significant to him as it was to me. Wednesday, as he well knew, was church night. Wednesday had been church night in America since forever. I always went with my family to a sermon and a supper on Wednesday nights, like many of his other students.

Many—though not all. I felt a hand on my shoulder and turned to see Stefan, hovering. They had much in common.

"It won't be a problem," I said, though I had no way of knowing whether my mother would let me go. I ground the cigarette into the armrest ashtray and stood, suddenly exhausted.

I made my way back to my seat and pulled the shade down on the window. Why, I wondered, was it always like this? For a while now, it had been like this. Complicated. Unfair. Unfair that it should be so complicated to love the things I loved.

The hush on the plane continued, and I closed my eyes, indifferent, now, to seeing the sunrise.

∾

XIV

*All noble things are difficult. The Christian life is
gloriously difficult, but the difficulty of it does not
make us faint and cave in, it rouses us up to overcome.
Do we so appreciate the marvelous salvation of Jesus
Christ that we are our utmost for His highest?*

—JULY 7

Dallas, 1993: "I don't know," my mother was saying. She darted her
eyes from the windshield to the rearview mirror. "It's clear downtown. And seven performances a week—that's a lot of driving. I
don't know if Nana and I can commit to that."

In the passenger seat, my grandmother turned, looking back at
me. She smiled brightly, her blue eyes vivid against the upholstery.

"I'd love to help drive Macy!" she exclaimed. "It sounds to me
like a wonderful opportunity. The arts are so important, that's
what I always say. Arts and education."

"I don't know, Mom," my mother said. "This isn't theater
camp. This is a professional production. I'm not sure I want her
downtown every day for the rest of the summer, hanging around
with a bunch of actors."

My grandmother considered.

Quickly, I said, "But it's a *children's* production, and it's *The Lion, the Witch, and the Wardrobe.* It's Christian."

"Well," said my mother. She raised an eyebrow in the mirror.

"And I'm sure I'll meet people who can give me a ride."

"I thought you were going back to church camp this summer," my mother said. "I thought you had a good time last year."

"I didn't."

My grandmother turned around again.

"Oh, yes, it was so nice last summer. Don't you remember your baptism?"

"No."

"Well I do," she said, patting my knee. "It was a beautiful, starry, starry night, out in the country, and you were in the swimming pool, and all your friends were gathered round."

"I don't want to talk about it," I said, looking hard out of the car window.

"Don't speak that way to your grandmother," my mother said, and I apologized.

"Please, Mama," I said. "I really want to do this. More than I ever wanted to do anything."

My mother turned the minivan onto Wabash Drive and came to a stop in front of the house.

"You say that about everything," she said, taking the key out of the ignition. But when she turned around, I saw excitement in her eyes. "But yes, okay. It does sound fantastic. I know how many times you've read that book."

"Like a million!" I threw my arms around the back of her seat, and around her neck.

"Oh, good," said my grandmother, smiling still. "I can't wait to see it. We're so proud of you, Macy dear."

"Thanks, Nana," I said, and I pulled back the sliding door.

☙

From the outside, it looked like nothing. An old tin-can ware-house with a parking lot all around, the kind of Texas-big lot that was everywhere in the city, fields of melted tar and tire capped with quivering waves of heat. It was the kind of lot you circled twenty times trying to find a good spot, just so you could avoid walking through it.

There was one nice thing, though, about having to walk across lots like these, and that was the deliverance you felt when you finally reached a building and stepped inside. *Deliverance:* that was the word I'd been saying to myself all summer—a word they'd been using in Sunday School, a word I liked—and I said it every time I stepped onto the street at the far end of the lot, which was where my mother or my grandmother dropped me each day, so that they could save time on the drive. "Deliverance," I would say, holding my hand above my eyes so I could see the traffic. "Deliverance," as I ran across the lot. And, finally, really, *"Deliverance,"* as I placed my hands on the great glass door that opened into the lobby, and pushed.

In the late afternoons, before the box office opened for the evening, the lobby was completely empty, and the only light was the light that fell through the door in a slanted block. The lobby was a large cube, with gray on the walls and exposed-pipe ceil-ings, and there was something about the quality of the air inside it, something to do with its scent, which was clean and sweet and static, and with the way it felt, ice-cold and embalming. It was like the air in a museum or a church, but there was also some-thing else, something that was present only in a theater. There was powder and perfume and sweat, and the peculiar smell of cos-tumes cleaned just once in seven performances, then left to hang overnight in a darkened hallway. These were backstage smells, but they traveled, from backstage to stage and then to the lobby, vanishing when the doors swung open to the outside. You could follow them from the moment you entered and they would lead you all the way through: through the double doors that led to the large black space where the shows took place, past the technicians' booth, down the long corridor the actors walked each time they prepared to make an entrance, onward to the gold-lighted dressing rooms, to the beautiful women in shimmering flesh-colored tights and practical brassieres, to the men in their shorts, combing pomade through their hair, to the girls, the little girls who played Lucy and Susan, and the older girls, like me, who played trees and nymphs and ghouls and train conductors. Extras, recruited from theater camp earlier in the summer. And you would find the boys there, too. Peter and Edmund and the eagle. The boys kept to themselves.

"Now be still," Britta Sang said to me one evening, her accent turning British. We were sitting in the common area of the dressing rooms on high stools, our faces pointed toward the yellow bulbs framing the mirror. "I'm going to make you truly frightening tonight. The children are going to *die.*"

And she tossed her head back to laugh, though with less effect than usual, since for the moment her wild long brown hair was tucked beneath a skullcap, and her mouth, normally painted black, was merely plum. But her skin was its usual paper-white, and she had not yet removed the little glass vial that always hung around her neck. "Blood," she'd told me, when I'd asked what was inside it, though I didn't believe her, and believed her even less when she'd explained that she was a vampire. Britta Sang, I'd decided, was not her real name, though she insisted that it was. There was no way of knowing for sure.

I never had Britta do my makeup for my first two roles in the show. One was the role of a ticket taker in the lobby, which was transformed into a train station at the start, so that the audience could take the journey the Pevensies had taken in the book. Walking among the audience with a little blue cap, I asked for tickets in an English accent, while whistles blew and a voice on a loudspeaker announced track information. When the voice called "All aboard!" two doors flew open, and the audience passed through them into a small room, empty except for a large wooden wardrobe. While they waited in this room, the room where the first part of the play was enacted, I ran backstage to change into my tree costume, taking my place for the moment when the wardrobe doors opened and Lucy came through, bidding the audience to follow her into Narnia. Then the audience took their seats, walking past trees in shimmering white body suits, trees which moved sometimes but otherwise ignored the humans as they climbed high into the bleachers that rose around the stage. The play continued. Tumnus came, then Edmund and the witch, then Susan and Peter. By the time they'd made it to Mr. and Mrs. Beaver's house, I was backstage, putting on my final costume, the ghoulish one I wore as a minion of the White Witch. It was for this role, a fearsome role in which I ran onstage screaming and clawing at the air, falling down and writhing in agony, like a figure (the director had explained) in a Hieronymus Bosch painting, a demon out of hell, that I always requested Britta's help. She'd volunteered to help all the ghouls with their makeup, since, as she said, she had a much stronger connection to the dark side than the rest of us.

"There," she said this evening, removing her hand. "All done."

I looked in the mirror.

"Ew!" I said. My fingers flew to my cheek. "It's too thick."

A large clump of brown Pan-Cake fell to the floor.

"Don't touch it," she said, slapping my hand away. "Claw it off onstage, then scream like your whole face is falling off. You look amazing."

"I look disgusting."

Britta lowered her head to mine and moved my shoulders until our faces were side by side in the mirror, hers perfect white and plum, mine brown and decaying. "Exactly," she said.

"You do look disgusting," said a voice.

We turned our heads. Britta let go of my shoulders.

"Peter," I said.

"Matthew," Peter said.

"Oh, right."

Then I said nothing, because Peter (I couldn't not think of him as Peter) was sixteen and because he was the *star* of the show, a real actor, who'd auditioned and was being paid for his work. He'd been getting paid to act since he was a little kid.

"Are you going to the party?" he asked.

"Who?" I said, turning to Britta. "Me?" But Peter nodded, gripping the hilt of his sword with his right hand, as he always did when he was in costume. It was the sword given to him by Aslan, the sword he would wield for decades and decades as king—one day, in another book, another play.

"The party on Friday at the White Witch's house?" I said.

"You do know there's a difference between actors and the roles they play, don't you?" he said. "But yes, that party."

"Are you going?" I asked Britta.

"Can't. Friday's *Rocky Horror* at the Casa Linda. I'm Magenta."

"I don't think so," I said to Peter. "It's out in Plano, and I don't have a car."

"I can give you a ride."

"I—" I said. Would my mother let me go?

"That sounds great," Britta said. "She'd love to. I'll give you her address. What's your address?"

I mumbled my address, while Peter looked on.

"I'll get a pen," Britta said, and she walked off, leaving us alone.

ᑭ

The White Witch's house was a tall white house in a subdivision filled with tall white houses. The sun had already begun to set by the time Peter and I found it, picking our way along the treeless streets, looking for signs of life. We had a map, but it wasn't any good: in the spot where the subdivision ought to have been was just a blank space, shaded green. Prairie land. Looking down from the elevated highway, we'd seen what was left of it—an empty expanse, still vast. But marching across it from the west was an army of houses, ten thousand strong. Nothing but houses, as far as the eye could see, and, in the opposite direction, nothing but nothing. What was odd was that when you drove from one to the other, as we did, exiting the highway in the prairie, nothing of any consequence seemed to have changed. They both felt exactly the same—or they did to me, anyway.

"This is awesome," Peter said, as we pulled up to the White Witch's house. "Sonya's husband must be loaded."

"Or Sonya," I said, but Peter rolled his eyes, and said she was his second wife, if I knew what he meant.

Another car arrived behind us, rattling for a minute before the engine shut. It was Mr. Beaver, in his brown Buick, a car we all made fun of. But I liked Mr. Beaver. He really was exactly like his character, which was the nicest character in the whole play—with the exception of Mrs. Beaver, of course. I was disappointed to see that they hadn't come together, even though I knew that she was married, and not to Mr. Beaver.

As I stepped out of the car, Mr. Beaver slammed his door, and waved hello, and then he turned around to slam the door again, cursing a little when it failed to shut.

"Mr. Beaver, do you need help?" I asked.

"Oh!" he exclaimed. He never corrected me when I called him Mr. Beaver. "How kind of you, dear. Yes, that would be wonderful. If you'll just place your hands here"—he pointed to a spot on the door—"and push with all your might, I do believe we'll manage it."

I placed my hands next to his, and on the count of three we pushed. The door slammed against the frame, sending up a cloud of dust but failing to shut, and by the time we'd tried again, a crowd had gathered on the front lawn to see what the matter was. A few crew members came over and tried pushing, and then there were a dozen people, all clustered around Mr. Beaver's car, giving advice.

"Yoo-hoo!" said a voice, much louder than the rest. Everyone turned.

Striding across the grass in a long black dress, holding high in her hands two glasses filled with electric-green slush, the White Witch approached the car. She looked very beautiful, I thought, as she always did, and even more tonight than in the play, since her hair, so long that it covered her hips, was down and her arms and feet were bare. As she walked, two Great Danes, big as ponies, galloped behind her, while the sun, fiery orange and hazy, slipped behind the house.

"Take this, take this, David," she cooed at Mr. Beaver, as the crowd dispersed. "I'll have Mike look at the door while you relax."

Mr. Beaver pressed a red bandanna to his scraggly brown beard and took one of the glasses.

"Oh, Sonya, thank you. A margarita. Exactly what I need," he said. "And perhaps just a bit of rope, for the drive home."

"Of course. We'll tie one on, David, don't you worry. And you!" she said, turning to me and Peter. "Little darlings. Follow me, follow me inside."

She turned and began to walk quickly, the dogs trotting next to her, and we followed.

"This is the *foyer*," she said as we entered the house, pronouncing it in the French way. "And over there's the living room, and the kitchen, and the bar—well, you get it, don't you! And you see, here's everyone, out on the terrace. Why don't you go out and find your friends? I'll bring you some drinks."

The White Witch's house was exactly as I imagined all the houses in the subdivision looking, filled with furniture from Weir's and Pottery Barn, scented with Glade, decorated with family pictures in frames. But it was not at all how I'd imagined *her* house, and I realized that Peter must have been right about it being her husband's money, that it must be her husband's house, or even his first wife's. Suddenly, I felt sorry for her—it was so nice to live inside a house decorated to one's own tastes, a house like my mother and grandmother's and mine.

Peter and I went to stand on the patio, and, a few minutes later, the White Witch returned, her hands filled once more, this time with red liquid instead of green. She extended a hand toward me—the liquid was inside a glass bottle—and I accepted her offering, studying the label: "Bartles & Jaymes Black Cherry."

"Now, I know you're young," she said. "But don't worry. These drinks are mostly sugar and water. Mike stocks them by the case, I don't know why. They're so eighties. Really, they're such childish drinks! Which is why it's so nice to have children here tonight. Not," she added, placing a hand on Peter's arm, "that you're a child, Matthew dear."

She turned and walked back inside, and Peter clinked his bottle to mine.

"Cheers," he said.

He leaned his head back, drinking deeply, and I watched as the red liquid bounced inside the glass, one bounce for every swallow, moving in time with his Adam's apple. Up and down, up and down, six times, until half the bottle was gone. Hesitantly, I raised mine to my lips, then lowered it.

"Drink," Peter said, and I took a sip. It was sweet and soft and bubbling and cold, but still disgusting. Peter grabbed my hand, leading me out onto the tight square lawn.

"Let's look at the stars," he said, sitting.

"There aren't any," I said. It was just dusk, just the start of twilight.

He shrugged and lay back on the grass, pulling me down with him. I lay very still, staring up at the empty sky, afraid to move. I had never been this close to a boy before, except Stefan, but that was just lying around during gym and choir, where everyone lay around on each other. This was different. The ground beneath me was hot, as hot as in the noontime sun; the grass was thick and rough, like a woolen blanket; and Peter's arm was a rock beneath my head.

A long time went by. I took another sip of my wine cooler, then let it spill out on the grass and watched as stars began to appear in the sky, faintly at first. Peter was talking, but I wasn't listening to the words, only to the sound of his voice, rugged and valiant. He was the wise one in the family, if not so wise as Susan, and it was easy to see why Aslan trusted him. His wild brown hair, his strong nose, his excellent diction and projection. There was no misunderstanding Peter. I'd had a feeling in my heart, as if I loved him, from the very first performance, when he'd run by me in his tweed jacket and his little English cap, brushing my branches, though he knew I could not move, bound as I was by the witch's spell and by the white beams of light shining from above, holding me—holding all of us—in the silence and stillness of the stage. That was the most perfect place on earth—I'd suspected it before, in the kiddie productions I'd done at school and at camp, but now I knew it for sure, and I never wanted to leave it. I wanted always to be standing in that light, branches frozen and outstretched, and for Peter always to be passing by. Passing and never stopping.

Suddenly, the patch of sky I'd been watching grew dark with Peter's face, and my head dropped to the ground. He said something I didn't hear, and my head rose again, weightless inside his hands. Then everything seemed to grow still, so still that I was certain we were back onstage, beneath the light. The stars grew brighter, pressing through the darkness, their circumferences widening and widening until they began to blur into one bright white light, filling the sky. Witnesses in a cloud of witnesses. They were the stars I'd prayed to—or not *to,* but toward—the summer before at camp, asking God to hear me, to spirit me, somehow, onto a stage, far away from that place, and to make me, somehow, unhideous to boys. All prayers were answered, my mother said. All the prayers of the faithful. But to have them answered so soon and so fully—it was overwhelming. I blinked, filled with love and charity, and was grateful for the sweat on my brow, for my eyes were hot as mouths and beginning to tear. I looked up again at the stars, so full now, and I sank farther into the ground, until I felt my heart begin to beat in time with the turning soil, the sprouting grass, the dancing worms.

"I think it's getting late," Peter said at last. His head dropped to his shoulder as he tried to lift it, and he laughed and stood, pulling me up beside him. It was a perfect night. A perfect night, I thought, as I tried to walk, swaying, though I'd drunk nothing.

"Uh-oh," Peter said, as we came into the light on the patio. "Your shirt."

"What?" I reached over my shoulder, straining to see.

In a wicker lounge chair, fully reclined, lay the White Witch. She was talking to one of the handymen from the show—we'd never seen her husband, I realized. A cigarette dangled at the end of her outstretched arm, and I watched the orange dot rise slowly as Peter called to her, waving her over.

"We have a problem," he said, turning me by my shoulders. "There."

"Heavens, the dogs!" she exclaimed. "Those beasts. How awful. Come with me."

And she took me by the hand, leading me through the kitchen and the living room to the staircase. She had a shirt I could borrow, she said, and she'd wash this one—she didn't want to hear any argument. I followed as best as I could through my mortification, saying nothing, not daring, even, to glance back to see if Peter was watching me. I could feel the tears returning to my eyes—now my shirt was the only thing I could smell. The smell seemed to fill the house. It was stronger, even, than the Glade PlugIns, stronger than the cigarette that still dangled in her hand. It was the worst thing I'd ever smelled. How had I not smelled it all that time?

"Whatever is the matter?" the White Witch asked, stopping for a moment on the stairs.

"Smell is linked to memory," I told her. "I just learned that."

We came to the end of the hallway, and she pushed open a door.

"Heavens!" she shrieked. "David, what are you doing?"

Inside the room, Mr. Beaver lay on the bed belly-down, three empty margarita glasses on the table beside him. His pants and shoes were scattered on the floor, together with his red bandanna.

"Mmm," he said.

The White Witch snuffed her cigarette out in a tray on the dresser. Then she opened a drawer, pulled out a shirt, and handed it to me. It was a short-sleeved white blouse, with two vertical lines of ruffles on either side of the buttons, which were shaped like daisies. It was nothing I would ever wear.

"There's a bathroom down there," she said, pointing. "Just leave your shirt in the sink, and I'll return it to you."

She kissed me twice strangely, one kiss on each cheek, and glanced behind her at the figure on the bed.

"And now you'll have to excuse me. I must deal with *this*."

I turned and walked to the bathroom, a feeling coming over me, one I didn't recognize. I switched on the light and looked in the mirror. What was it? I began to laugh, smiling at my face, at the way it was arranged, two blue eyes, a nose with freckles, a chin with a cleft, teeth with a gap, a widow's peak, and two new lips, bright red. I raised my lips to my nose and inhaled; I pressed my fingers to my face. Maybe it would make sense never to wash it again, I thought. That's what girls said, wasn't it? I laughed again, because I really didn't want to wash it. I took off my shirt and put on the witch's shirt, laughing at the little daisies blooming in the ruffles. Now I wasn't sad at all, I was just laughing, and that was the new feeling—a feeling of hilarity, like a pretty vase had smashed into a thousand pieces, and all the pieces were dancing, quivering with life where they lay on the floor.

"Thank you," I whispered, closing my eyes to the image in the mirror. "Thank you!"

∾

"How was it?" my mother asked me later that night, pulling up the blanket. "How was Peet-ah?" She always said his name in a British accent, like everyone did in the play. "Cute boy."

"Fine," I said.

"Where does he go to church?"

"Nowhere."

My mother was silent for a moment.

"And everyone else?"

"They were nice. And funny. They're all so funny."

She switched out the light, and I turned over onto my stomach and pulled my T-shirt up, so that she could scratch my back. The soft acrylic nails moved rhythmically, tracing figure eights.

"Well, they're all real characters, aren't they? That witch. And Britta! I pray for that girl."

"I love them."

"You'll be in high school now," my mother said after a while. "We'll have to talk about a real curfew in the fall, if you're going to be going out."

"Okay."

"I'm very proud of you, you know, how hard you've worked on this play—your commitment. And the way you've kept up with your summer reading on top of it."

I turned my face in to my pillow, drifting now to sleep.

"All noble things are difficult," I murmured.

"What? Where did you hear that?"

I reached an arm out and let it flop onto the bedside table, on top of my book.

The hand stopped its motion for a moment.

"Oh, *Utmost.* You're reading this?"

"Not really," I said.

My mother resumed scratching.

"I was going to say. It's a little difficult for a child."

"I'm not a child."

"No," she said. "No, you're not."

And she began to pray, whispering into the darkness, while the hand continued in its path.

XV

∾

There is only one answer: "O Lord, Thou knowest, I don't."

—JUNE 1

Paris, 1995. Inside the Jardin des Plantes, there was a museum and a zoo and dahlias in ten thousand colors—violet and lemon and zebra-striped; tangerine and chartreuse and magenta; crimson and coffee and mahogany; bronze and silver and sand—so bright against the white-rock dust coating the pathways that they narrowed the retinas to tiny points, splintering the light. In a dark corner, tucked behind a greenhouse and ancient pines, a walkway spiraled up a hillside, breaking, at last, into sunshine. A circle of benches, crowned by a silver belvedere, graced the summit. This was where we'd found each other again, Stefan and I. I'd made my way there from the market on the Rue Mouffetard, where I'd bought some cherries—a whole warm bag of them, scooped from a table laid with paper. *S'il vous plaît,* I'd said to the man, embarrassed that I didn't speak his language; nervous because, lacking boldness, I relied on precision, on being able always to find the right word, and here I didn't have any words. But he'd answered in English—"Cherries? A kilo?"—and I'd nodded, handing over a fistful of the funny money, shocked to see how big a kilo was.

Yet we'd eaten them all, sitting on the summit. I was looking out over the park, and Stefan was busy with his pencil and paper. He'd been desperate to begin drawing ever since we'd entered the train station at the airport. Even that had been astonishing to us, the grand gray tunnels, industrial but still artful, and the trains that arrived so mundanely, as if it were normal for people to travel by train. We'd exited at Saint-Michel, riding the escalators up from leagues below the Seine, noting the peculiar scent of the Métro station. How it was dusty and sweet and organic, living and dead at once, quite unlike anything we'd ever encountered. That had been in the early morning. By midmorning, after we'd dropped our bags at the hotel, we'd encountered it again, this time in the catacombs. We'd peered into the sockets of skulls emptied centuries before, unable even for a moment to comprehend what it was we were seeing. By lunchtime, we were falling asleep on our feet, but Holamon had forbidden us from dropping our heads onto the table at the restaurant and had made us raise our cups. Tiny cups, filled with kir royal—champagne made pink and sweet with cassis. To the first grand adventure of our lives, he'd said: may it be the first of many.

After lunch, we'd been given time to ourselves, and I'd returned to the hotel with Elodie. We'd closed the curtains, and I'd reached for a book, not Auden but rather *My Utmost for His Highest*, which had seemed somehow like a good book for traveling with, though I'd been reading it only on occasion and without understanding much.

It was still only two when we left the room, making our way along the Seine to the Sainte-Chapelle. We'd gone silent as we entered the upper chapel, holding our arms in front of us to study the kaleidoscope on our skin, looking up to the ceiling, at the gold fleurs-de-lys sparkling dimly against the blue. In the chairs along the wall, we'd bowed our heads to pray, taking each other by the hand.

Now, in the park, I'd found Stefan again, trading cherries for a cigarette. I was feeling holy, like even smoking was holy, in this place where everyone smoked, so elegantly fitting themselves into the frame. It was not true, the impression Holamon had given, of France being a godless place, a churchless place, a wild place. Everything here seemed sacred, as if every stone had been carved with the idea of God in mind, or with the voice of God whispering in the ear. Also, it felt like it had been made with the idea of humans in mind, since everything was designed to please the eye and to ease movement. Walking was revelation here, not a means to an end. Holamon had talked to us about the lines, the vistas, of Paris, the boulevards that connected one plaza, one monument, to another, so that you could lock your gaze on your destination and let the city shift around you as you went, each step revealing a different tableau. It was a nineteenth-century city, an Enlightenment city, the middle bit of it, anyway. You could pause in your walk to stop in at a church, as we had. There were beautiful churches everywhere, with bells that rang out each hour, and sometimes more, calling people to prayer, adding rhythm to their days and music to their walks. Maybe all the praying people were tourists, like Elodie and me, but what did that matter? There were always tourists in Paris.

And how I would pray, if I lived in a place like this! I thought, raising my face to the sun. Freely, with my heart and my mind, taking my friends by the hand. Here, where I didn't have to feel torn about my Southern Baptism, or guilty about how much I'd started to dislike it, its miserliness (I'd settled on that word for it), the way it condemned so much of what I loved—theater, movies, books, music, if those things weren't Evangelical—and all the people I loved, if those people weren't saved. The way it had made me condemn my beloved teacher, in class, in front of everyone. I didn't have to decide anything about it here, I realized, because by some miracle it did not exist here. In Paris, *southern* referred to a different place, and *Baptist* to a different people. There could be churches *like* my church in Dallas here, but never that church, the church my family sat in on Sundays. There could never be that pulpit—raised and red-velveted, set with thrones. Five wooden thrones, carved and royal, for five old men, white and business-suited. Thrones on a platform, facing out, so that the men could survey the congregation while we gazed up at them from below, the TV cameras rolling noiselessly over the faces in which resided all authority. Faces I'd always feared, and often loved, until I'd begun to see them in a new light. One of them was the laughing face of the man who'd baptized me, two summers earlier, in the swimming pool, the last summer I was a child.

But now all of Paris had slipped underwater, and Stefan placed a hand on my arm, asking if I was okay. His touch drew my eyes down, to the paper in his lap, to a drawing of rooftops beyond treetops, and I studied them until my fear had quieted. I was often afraid, now, of my own thoughts.

I dropped my head onto Stefan's shoulder, returning my mind to the Sainte-Chapelle. Would I have prayed there, I wondered, if my teacher had been there, and not just Elodie? And what did it mean if the answer was no?

There is only one answer: "O Lord, Thou Knowest, I don't."

I sat up in surprise as the words came to mind. I'd just read them, in the book my grandmother had given me. I would read them again tonight, I decided. The entry had been talking about other people's souls, whether it was right to despair over someone who seemed lost, whether it was possible to know that they were really lost. It wasn't, the book had said. It wasn't possible to know, it wasn't right to despair, it wasn't *permitted* to judge. Jesus had never despaired, and Jesus, if He'd known, had never *had* to know. It was faith, not knowledge, He'd embraced when it came to considering other people. Faith in God's character, God's wisdom, God's goodness. I despaired of others, the book said, because I forgot what had been done for me.

That was what I should have said that day in class, I realized now: that I didn't know.

I didn't know, I thought again and again, smiling. I didn't know, I didn't have to know, I couldn't know.

"You should add some color to this one," I said to Stefan. "Some gray and blue and green and pink."

"All the colors of the earth."

"All the colors of the earth."

The light brushed the needles of the pines. Down on the path, a pair of sandaled feet kicked at the dust, filling the air with fine white matter. Stefan leaned his head backward on the belvedere, lit another cigarette, and exhaled.

XVI

૦౭

An average view of the Christian life is that it means deliverance from trouble. It is deliverance in trouble, which is very different. "He that dwelleth in the secret place of the Most High . . . there shall no evil befall thee"—no plague can come nigh the place where you are at one with God.

—AUGUST 2

Paris, 2012. The view from my window this morning was of tree-tops nodding in a reluctant breeze, of rooftops, and of a gray sky. The city appeared much as it had three days before, but I was in a different world. For the past nights, I'd been telling my *Utmost* stories to my neighbor, whose interest (or whose patience) was apparently boundless. I'd been surprised at the course my memories had taken, how they'd led me into times when *Utmost*'s touch had been subtle at most. But perhaps that's how it was with any book that registered deeply—perhaps it was always there, in the background, shaping our understanding of events in ways we couldn't fully grasp or appreciate in the moment. The stories were a reminder to me, too, that the Christian life was, first and foremost, just a life, lived at times in great consciousness of its ideologies, at times simply in the fullness of experience, reveling in God's mysteries.

I'd always been glad when the day's reading in *Utmost* touched on this theme. It was one Oswald had felt strongly about: that God wanted us, simply, to be and to enjoy the life He'd given.

I'd also always considered it key to understanding Oswald's character. But in the months since I'd started piecing together his story, I'd found myself growing more and more perplexed. The night I'd climbed to the roof, Oswald had been in bad shape. Having failed to become a professional artist, he'd drifted into the career his father had chosen for him, which was also the one career he'd sincerely hoped to avoid. His life at the Bible college in Dunoon had been a success by some measures—his students had liked him, and he'd had the access to nature he craved—but he wasn't happy. Indeed, he was in the grips of a serious depression, one that had him convinced that his religion was "a downright fraud." Intellectually, he was scattered and reactionary: he was still swinging Ruskin's hammer of reality against the "plate glass" of phony civilization, but now he was doing it by embracing unorthodox thinkers like Swedenborg, frightening his congregations and boring his students in the process. For four years, he'd been trapped in "hell" and had written to his parents of wanting to die.

How, I wondered, could this be the Oswald who wrote so movingly of being lost in ecstatic experience? The day's *Utmost* entry spoke of being so fully in God's presence that "no plague could come nigh." But Oswald, for at least his first twenty-nine years, was more or less constantly plagued—by ambition and by the feelings of impotence and anger that often accompany ambition when it goes unfulfilled. The entire time I'd been reading about his life, I'd had the uneasy feeling that some cataclysm was approaching.

This feeling had perhaps been intensified by the talk I'd had months earlier with Larry Eskridge, the professor of history who'd met with me at Wheaton College. Eskridge had mentioned a "bomb"—some "big Pentecostalist thing" about Oswald that had been "swept under the rug." I'd been waiting ever since for the bomb to go off, and my forays through Oswald's biography had convinced me that when the explosion came, it was going to be big and messy and dismaying. Mainstream Evangelicals were decidedly not Pentecostalists, but the final split between the two hadn't come until Oswald was well into his career (Pentecostalism wasn't born properly as a movement until 1906), and the two traditions shared many qualities. So there was a chance that Oswald had embraced certain doctrines that had become problematic from the perspective of mainstream Evangelicalism, only at a later date, and that hadn't—for reasons that were as yet unclear to me— made their way into *Utmost*.

I should have expected that, Oswald being Oswald, the bomb would explode not so much with a bang as with a series of artfully concealed whimpers. There was, indeed, a bomb; this much was certain. Three days earlier, I'd seen the first reference to it: Oswald, who had been "born again as a lad," as he put it, was born again *again*, at the age of twenty-seven, in 1901, when a preacher named F. B. Meyer visited Dunoon and lectured on the necessity of being born from above by the Holy Spirit (presumably, Oswald's first born-again experience had involved asking only Christ, and not specifically the Spirit, to come into his heart and life). Four years passed without any change. Thinking that perhaps he hadn't done it properly, Oswald asked again. This time, it was a success, and from then on he considered himself "sanctified," filled and reborn by the Spirit, a new, supernatural being living inside a supernatural realm—what he called the "Kingdom." In the Kingdom, Oswald no longer suffered from weakness, failure, or doubt. Instead, he was filled with "power" and with "manly" strength.

The reason Oswald's sanctification was a "bomb" was that most mainstream Evangelical traditions rejected the notion of a second, Spiritual baptism, while most Pentecostalist traditions embraced a version of it. But why had Oswald?

Having learned by now that there was no getting to Oswald except through the books he'd read ("silent, wealthy, loyal lovers," he called them in a letter to his sister in 1907), I'd begun to make my way through his library. I was interested in the finer theological points of sanctification, but first I wanted to know how Oswald had understood it.

I picked up with his life shortly after where I'd left off: at the end of his time in Dunoon. After preaching around Scotland and England following the conclusion of his studies, Oswald embarked on his first big mission trip abroad. For roughly a year, starting in 1906, he traveled around the United States. In 1907, he sailed to Asia and then to the Middle East. He was thirty-three years old, and three years sanctified. His depression was gone, and now in his letters and diaries he sounded like the Oswald beloved by *Utmost* readers: inspiring, triumphant, childlike, and wise.

Now began the life story of the new Oswald Chambers.

∾

Oswald was lying in his berth, reading and watching the coast of Japan pass through the tiny window. He'd been traveling the world for more than a year and had relied on his books ("friends that are ever true and ever your own") to keep him company. He'd just finished Balzac's *The Wild Ass's Skin,* and before that he'd devoured

S. R. Crockett's novel *Kit Kennedy*, about a Scottish lad who must learn to battle his demons as he journeys into manhood. It was, Oswald thought, full of the "Scotch pulse," and one of its characters in particular pleased him, because he seemed "drawn from life, with scarcely an idealizing touch." He'd read Dillon Wallace's harrowing autobiographical survival tale *The Lure of the Labrador Wild*, about a group of fearless adventurers who'd journeyed deep into Quebec, some never to return. He'd read "The Strenuous Life," a speech by Teddy Roosevelt, delivered in 1899:

> I preach to you, then, my countrymen, that our country calls not for the life of ease but for the life of strenuous endeavor. The twentieth century looms before us big with the fate of many nations. If we stand idly by, if we seek merely swollen, slothful ease and ignoble peace, if we shrink from the hard contests where men must win at hazard of their lives and at the risk of all they hold dear, then the bolder and stronger peoples will pass us by, and will win for themselves the domination of the world. . . . For it is only through strife, through hard and dangerous endeavor, that we shall ultimately win the goal of true national greatness.

Roosevelt's rousing, manly sentiments were ones Oswald appreciated. He'd always loved stories with proper heroes—individuals who, overcoming weakness and self-doubt, rose above common sense and the binds of civilization in displays of willpower and strength to fight for righteousness. His favorite writer was George MacDonald, the Scottish preacher who had pioneered a genre: realist fantasy. *Phantastes*, his first entry in the genre, had appeared in 1858. It told the story of Anodos, an ordinary man who wakes one day to find that the walls of his bedroom have transformed into a forest, transporting him to a magical realm called Fairy Land.

In Fairy Land, Anodos embarks on an odyssey that will last twenty-one years. Along the way, he battles ogres and goblins and evil trees. He encounters false forms—"ideal" women, false prophets, fake religions—and cannot distinguish them, at first, from true ones. But by the end of the book, he has learned discernment: stumbling across a crowd of people gathered around a stone idol, Anodos rouses himself to a final act of heroism, destroying the idol and dying at the hands of the angry mob. After death, he wakes back in the earthly realm to find that hardly any time has passed. His challenge, he understands, is to keep the lessons learned in Fairy Land alive. For now he knows that earth is only a shadow of the higher, spiritual realm and that reality is twofold: it is earth and Fairy Land combined, as he is flesh and spirit.

How long ago had Oswald read *Phantastes*? It must have been when he was just a boy. Now here he was, a real-life Anodos, having finally found his way into the twofold reality. He'd marked down a poem by Elizabeth Barrett Browning on the topic:

> *And in this twofold sphere the twofold man*
> *(For still the artist is intensely a man)*
> *Holds firmly by the natural, to reach*
> *The spiritual beyond it,—fixes still*
> *The type with mortal vision, to pierce through,*
> *With eyes immortal, to the antetype*
> *Some call the ideal,—better called the real.*

As his ship traversed the Inland Sea, Oswald pondered the bizarre reality beyond his window. The junks and sailboats, he wrote in his diary, looked like "huge birds floating noiselessly away and down and across." On dry land, he was amazed by the customs of the Japanese. In the temples, people rubbed the hands of sick babies over the feet of stone idols: it was "unbearably pathetic" to see them, Oswald thought. And yet, the crowds who gathered to hear him preach seemed hungry for Christianity: they seemed to "simply swallow salvation wholesale."

It was a "mystery," but mysteries abounded here. Japan, he wrote to his brother, was a "fairy country," an "Alice in Wonderland place." He was not just an Anodos but an Alice, too. He'd tumbled out of a starched British world of tea and cake and custom into a "nonsense" that was closer to the true nature of the universe— and of God—than the realm of common sense could ever hope to be. That was the message Lewis Carroll, a close friend and aco- lyte of MacDonald's, had hoped to communicate in *Alice*, a book inspired by MacDonald's work. It was a message Oswald was busy applying to his own story, which was a true hero's journey.

Oswald was on a very specific mission. He'd come to colo- nize souls for Christ, to bring them fully into the land where he himself had dwelled for some years now: "the Kingdom." The Kingdom was a place of mysteries, wherein reigned a version of Carroll's "nonsense," what Oswald called "haphazard order." Oswald had come to Japan, bearing the Kingdom within him, in boldness and in strength, to rouse and to challenge. He'd come to preach a certain doctrine, the doctrine which revealed the path by which the Kingdom might be discovered and entered. The doc- trine was called by many names: Holiness, entire sanctification, the baptism of the Holy Spirit. It worked by forming Christ in the body, the mind, and the soul; by removing sin and enthron- ing God. The process of being remade was uncompromising, as terrible and demanding in its way as the Cross had been for Christ.

Oswald knew that his mission was not to coddle his listeners or sell them on an easy version of Christianity; it was to prepare heroes for the difficulties of the quest that lay ahead. It made him sick to discover that many of his fellow missionaries hadn't come in the same spirit. In his diary, he wrote,

> Today I met Mrs. Braithwaite, Mr. Paget Wilkes, Mr. Cuthbertson, Rev. Lichfield, a group of people I am not at all drawn to. There is the stamp of the effiminate [sic] and sanctimonious about them which is languid. They carry large Bibles and speak in extravagant terms of "such a lovely man," "a sweet man of God," dearly beloved brother so and so. To put it in rugged language, it is enough to make a fellow "puke." Lichfield gave a Bible reading on "the Lord for the body," mildly apologetic and very diffident—"Really, don't you know, it would be such a savour to the Lord Jesus if you were to be sanctified," this said with clasped hands and a sweet inoffensive smile. . . . Wilkes and his set are afraid of the Oriental Bible school and its strong advocacy of holiness, uncompromising and manly. . . . Had a very good talk with Mantle. What must he think? It is strange if he does not pity these unsexed namby pambyists.

Yet Oswald could perhaps remember, if he were to think back far enough, that such harsh things might have been said about him. The years of depression, dryness, and impotence—he could remember how badly he'd wanted power and how he'd been unable to get it, no matter what he'd tried. He'd wanted the power to stop sinning but also the power to start living a meaningful, productive life. He'd wanted to touch people with his painting, and then with his preaching, to no avail. He could remember hating his own religion.

But then, he still hated his own religion. Religion had no place in the Kingdom. There were no creeds or customs here, no priests or buildings, no rituals. After a long struggle, Oswald had finally reached a satisfying definition of Christianity:

> Behind Reality is God Himself, and the final authority is a personal relationship. Christianity is a personal relationship to a personal God.

To say that a relationship was the final authority meant that nothing else could be: the saint could "never rest in the Church, or in the Scriptures," Oswald wrote. "He needs living Reality."

But how had Oswald discovered this reality? The path, he would say later, had been long and tortuous, an exercise in "unlearning." He'd started by unlearning everything he thought he knew about religion, God, and the physical universe. It began with simple observation and proceeded through literature. God, he'd begun to notice, had made a universe that was always shifting, always evolving. Oswald had heard this radical, shifting, purposeful life calling to him, in the wind and rain and sun, in books like *Phantastes* and the many others that had followed in its footsteps.

If *Phantastes* was a new kind of fantasy novel, it was also a new kind of Christian novel, outfitted for the needs of the modern era. Oswald regarded its author as a great man of faith, one who recognized all the peculiar challenges posed to the religion by modernity. MacDonald had experienced firsthand the corruption of the churches. In younger days, he'd been a Congregationalist minister, until his rather liberal theological views had gotten him pushed from the pulpit. He knew, also, the strange pathways literature had gone down during the last century. Steeped, as a boy, in works of Romanticism, he'd become concerned about the creep of moral relativism and solipsism into the realm of the imagination. He'd been alarmed by the insidious notion, seized upon by certain Romantic writers, that one's own mind was the whole creator and standard of truth and reality. *"O Love!"* Byron wrote,

> *The mind hath made thee, as it peopled heaven,*
> *Even with its own desiring phantasy,*
> *And to a thought such shape and image given,*
> *As haunts the unquench'd soul—parch'd—wearied—*
> *wrung—and riven.*

> *Of its own beauty is the mind diseased,*
> *And fevers into false creation.*

In Fairy Land, MacDonald had reclaimed the imagination for God, colonizing the space of fantasy with Realist techniques, logic, and morality. "It is when we are most aware of the *factitude* of things that we are most aware of our need of God, and most able to trust in Him," he wrote. "The recognition of inexorable reality in any shape, or kind, or way, tends to rouse the soul to the yet more real, to its relations with higher and deeper existence. It is not the hysterical alone for whom the great dash of cold water is good. All who dream life instead of living it, require some similar shock." *Phantastes* was intended to administer a shock to the dreaming system.

MacDonald had also perceived the advance on spirituality from another side—the side of science and rationality. "Human science," he'd written, "is but the backward undoing of the tapestry-web of God's science, works with its back to Him, and is always leaving Him—His intent, that is, His perfected work—behind it." He feared the way science seemed to tear apart the world, atomizing it and calling the individual bits reality. He worried profoundly, as did Oswald, that magic would be drained out of existence, that there would be no more dreams, and no more reality.

James Denney, a Scottish theologian who was one of Oswald's favorite Evangelical realists, summed up a popular Evangelical view of science in his book *The Atonement and the Modern Mind:*

Every physical science seems to have a boundless ambition. It wants to reduce everything to its own level, to explain everything in the terms and by the categories with which it itself works. The physicist would like to reduce chemistry to physics; the chemist has an ambition to simplify biology into chemistry; the biologist in turn looks with suspicion on anything in man which cannot be interpreted biologically. He would like to give, and is sometimes ready to offer, a biological explanation of self-consciousness, of freedom, of religion, morality, sin. Now a biological explanation, when all is done, is a physical explanation, and a physical explanation of self-consciousness or the moral life is one in which the very essence of the thing to be explained is either ignored or explained away.

It was something like this way of thinking that had afflicted Oswald before his own sanctification and entry into the Kingdom. Even the Bible had become "the dullest, most uninteresting book in existence." People had begun to argue that it was a repository of "infallible" facts, facts meant to compete with the facts being

unearthed at an impressive rate by science. It had become cap-
tive to pseudoscientific schemes. Oswald was familiar with some
of these schemes—and there were plenty with which to be familiar. Among the more popular were Swedenborgianism, Christian
Socialism, Positivism, Evolutionary Progressivism, Christian Progressivism, Darby Dispensationalism, and British Israelism. (The
last was founded on the rather amazing theory that Great Britain
was the actual geographic location of the Israel of the Bible, that
Anglo-Saxons were the Chosen People, and that the British Royal
Family was descended from David.)

The schemes were part of a widespread nineteenth-century
project: that of using modern historical and scientific methods
to explain the strange course the human race had taken, and to
predict its future. Upset by the rapid changes wrought by modernity, Oswald's contemporaries had become deeply interested in
frameworks which might tie together the many various strands of
the human experience—strands drawn from history, art, science,
technology, religion, and politics—to create a coherent picture of
what it was all for and, more important, where it was all going.

Having considered some of these biblical-historical schemes,
Oswald came to a realization: schemes, like churches, like systematic readings of the Bible, didn't fully capture reality. All they
did was give people a false sense of control—over each other, the
future, God. Oswald realized that he didn't need to know more
about the future than he already did. God had made a promise
about final things: "I have overcome the world." It was a promise
that contained a command: "In the world ye shall have tribula-
tion: but be of good cheer; I have overcome the world." Oswald
expected to suffer, and he resolved to be cheerful, however little
he knew of what lay ahead. There were certain types of knowl-

edge, he thought, that were simply off-limits to humans. In his diary, he called himself a "complete agnostic mentally about God." He meant that he had no way of proving God's existence; that he could not know, in a scientific sense, that what the Bible said about God was true. What he observed of God's world told him that God was not predictable, that He worked through chaos as much as He did through order, that He worked through the haphazard.

Everything Oswald knew about God, he said, came not from the Bible but rather from his experience of the indwelling Christ. This was why he always called Christ a "living Reality," distinguishing Him from a deity at the center of a religion or a character in a book. Catholics, he wrote, often made an idol of their Church; Protestants of Scripture. Both approaches were fundamentally flawed. One couldn't limit a living person to a handful of practices, or of words and stories set down on a page. A living person was unpredictable. A person changed over time. A person had force. The verse 1 Corinthians 4:20 was important in shaping his understanding: "The kingdom of God is not in word, but in power." It was *power* that Oswald wanted now.

By the time he sailed for Japan, Oswald had figured out a satisfying way of approaching the Bible. "It is not a question of the infallibility of the Bible, that is a side issue." he wrote, "but of the finality of the Bible. The Bible is a whole library of literature giving us the final interpretation of the Truth." Truth, not fact, was the measure. Big, shaggy, shifting, living, uncontainable Truth. To get at it, he thought, one had to have the "liberal" viewpoint. Just that year, another of his favorite Evangelical thinkers, P. T. Forsyth, a native Scot and the principal of Hackney College, in London, had delivered an address at Yale, in which he'd described the Bible in fantastically slippery terms:

It is not a history of Israel, but it is a history of redemption. It is not the history of an idea, but of a long divine act. Its unity is a dramatic unity of action, rather than an aesthetic unity of structure. It is a living evolving unity, in a great historic crescendo. It does not exist like a library in detached departments. It has an organic and waxing continuity. It is after all a book. It is a library, but it is still more a canon. You may regard it from some points as the crown of literature, for it contains both the question and the answer on which all great literature turns. It is the book, as Christ is the person, where the seeking God meets and saves the seeking man.

The Bible, in this view, belonged to what James Denney called "the higher region of human experience." This was the level of reality where the soul lived, where explanations for such things as guilt and love lived, where "revealed" facts like the Atonement had their reality. It was a wilder realm, a magical realm. The higher region was not entirely separate from the lower, physical realm. The relationship between the two spheres was like that of Fairy Land to Anodos's bedroom: it was "effaced but permanent," Oswald wrote, hidden but there. Only those who had the will and the desire to venture boldly into this other dimension, to fight and to find "deliverance *in* trouble," were able to discern the link between them.

∾

Why had it taken Oswald, steeped in fairy stories from his youth, so long to find his way into the higher realm? He would say, in later years, that it was because he'd been trying to get there all on his own. Alice had needed her rabbit to show her the way, and Oswald, though he'd been among Christians for as long as he could remember, had needed the *right* Christian.

He'd found him finally when F. B. Meyer, an English preacher and author, visited Dunoon. During this visit, Oswald heard Meyer deliver a talk on the necessity of receiving the power of the Holy Spirit. Oswald didn't record precisely what Meyer said that day, but the talk probably covered the basic tenets of entire sanctification—or the variety of entire sanctification Oswald would eventually embrace. These tenets held that it was necessary for the Christian to be "born into a totally new Kingdom" through "a second distinct act of grace." The act was "second" because it came after the first gracious gift, the gift of salvation, or "justification." In the first, the individual accepted Christ as Lord and secured his eternal place in heaven. In the second, he was "invaded" or baptized by the Holy Spirit, who began to form inside him the likeness of Christ. To have the likeness of Christ was to possess the ability to obey God completely and to stop sinning; to love God with all of one's heart, mind, and soul; and to do it all *now*. The immediacy was key: justification was about one's future life; sanctification was about this one.

The inspiration behind entire sanctification was a command Jesus had given his disciples: "Be ye therefore perfect, even as your Father which is in heaven is perfect." How were mere humans to meet such a lofty requirement? The answer, as generations of Holiness Evangelicals (beginning with John Wesley, in the mid-eighteenth century) had taught, was found in the first chapter of the book of Acts: "Ye shall receive power, after that the Holy Ghost is come upon you." The Holy Ghost was a special, historical phenomenon. It had not always been in existence on earth, nor would it always be here. It had been sent by God after Christ's ascension, to serve as Christ's presence until the Second Coming. Its purpose was to empower Christ's followers, and also to unite them into a single community. No longer would they belong to different clans or tribes; no longer would they have many different dedicated deities, as they had when they were pagans. Now, *one* spirit would dwell inside all of them, and this—the Spirit-Baptized collection of individuals—would be the Christian "church."

According to the Holiness tradition Meyer, and later Oswald, belonged to, the way a person received the Spirit was to ask God for it, citing in the request Luke 11:13: "If ye then, being evil, know how to give good gifts unto your children: how much more shall your heavenly Father give the Holy Spirit to them that ask Him?" Then one had to accept it by "faith apart from feeling": that is, one had to believe that it had been done, even if one felt nothing, either physically or emotionally.

Oswald's Spiritual baptism had proceeded strangely. He'd asked once and had been ushered into his "four years of hell on earth" (this, he'd later say, was the Spirit revealing his weakness and corruption to him). Then he'd asked again. He'd felt nothing— a good sign. But soon afterward, he'd had a strange experience. He'd just finished giving a sermon, when many members of the audience began coming forward to be saved. Oswald was not accustomed to winning souls with his preaching, and he couldn't think what had made the difference. Then, "like a flash, something happened inside me, and I saw that I had been wanting power in my own hand." Now he understood that the Spirit's power was its own, and that it was inside him, using him for its own purposes. What he needed to do was to accept this power and to consent to becoming a laborer on its behalf. The Spirit, as Oswald understood it, didn't let the Christian off the hook; it put him to work as never before, drawing him more and more into the company of people in need, so that he might labor for them. "We have to work out what God works in," he'd say often in the future. "We are sanctified for one purpose only, that we might sanctify our sanctification."

Or, applying the vocabulary from his old life to his new, he would explain it like this: "The Actual world of things and the Real world of Truth have to be made into one in personal experience."

◯◡

With his Spiritual baptism, a difficulty Oswald had been worrying over for some time had been resolved. It was the difficulty of being a Christian in an era that celebrated powerful individuals, enshrining Nietzsche's Superman, that character who represented such a rebuke to "namby-pamby" Christian apologists. Oswald had felt powerless before. Now, he'd been remade from the inside out by a rugged, manly Christ. The blood of this Christ coursed through his veins, the muscles of this Christ plumped his chest, the thoughts of this Christ moved the machinery of his mind.

The physicality of the Holy Spirit was something Oswald dwelled on quite a bit. The Holy Spirit, Oswald wrote, was a *person*. He was "not a substitute for Jesus, the Holy Spirit is all that Jesus was, and all that Jesus did. He makes Jesus Christ both present and real. He is the most real Being on earth, 'closer is He than breathing, and nearer than hands and feet'" (the last line was Tennyson's). He went on:

> The whole purpose of being born again and being identified with the death of the Lord Jesus is that His blood may flow through our mortal body; then the tempers and the

affections and the dispositions which were manifested in the life of the Lord will be manifested in us in some degree.

Through the baptism of the Spirit, Oswald wrote, "God alters every physical thing in a human being so that these bodies can be used now as slaves to the new disposition. We can make our eyes, and ears, and every one of our bodily organs express as slaves the altered disposition of our soul." Of the mind, he wrote: "To have the mind of Christ means that we are willing to obey the dictates of the Holy Spirit through the physical machines of our brains and bodies till our living bears a likeness to Jesus. Every Christian ought to be living in this intense, vigorous atmosphere, no sentimental weaknesses."

Oswald and his contemporaries had found a satisfying answer to the Superman. Maybe the Christian religion, as Nietzsche had claimed, did breed weaklings, but religion wasn't Christ. Christ was a full-blown personality. In Forsyth's words, He was the "chief creator" of personality, "no less concerned than Nietzsche that the personality should receive the fullest development of which it is capable, and be more and more of a power." Where they differed, Forsyth thought, was in the "moral method" they used to develop this personal power. Nietzsche wanted to assert the self, Christ wanted to lose it; Nietzsche wanted to please the self, Christ wanted to sacrifice it.

Which hero was more powerful? The Superman had his minions, but Christ had his spiritual army. He was a man with a movement: Muscular Christianity, a movement which influenced Oswald nearly as much as the Holiness Movement, entwining with it in his theology to form a particular idea of the indwelling Christ.

The Muscular Christians had come out swinging in the late

nineteenth century, advancing the bold idea that the best way for the churches to reach men was through their muscles—literally. They believed in the rousing spiritual effects of physical fitness and outdoor activity. (In America, they were responsible for the foundation of the modern scouting movement and the first inner-city "boys' clubs.") Teddy Roosevelt, whose speeches Oswald took with him on his trip to Japan, was poster boy and proponent. "I do not want to see Christianity professed only by weaklings; I want to see it a moving spirit among men of strength," Roosevelt had said in 1903. In the late nineteenth century, Dwight L. Moody, one of the most famous preachers in America—and also in Britain, thanks to the numerous preaching trips he'd taken there—helped to propagate the movement, and after him the wildly popular baseball player turned Evangelical superstar Billy Sunday. Sunday, preaching in Chicago and around the Midwest, shadowboxed the devil up on his preaching platform, denouncing "weak-willed intellectuals" and the "wishy-washy, sissified sort of galoot that lets everybody make a doormat out of him." He never minced words: "No man can be a man without being a Christian," he preached, "and no man is a man unless he is a Christian. Therefore, if you want to be a man, be a Christian; if you want to be less than a man, serve the devil and go to hell!"

Oswald was a natural, rugged man, and he'd declared total war on the devil. Yet he was also more than a man. Now, thanks to the Spirit, he belonged to an elite (but also lowly) cadre of Christian. He was, as his students and friends would write in their remembrances of him, a saint. When one looked at him, one didn't see only Oswald: one saw the face of Christ, piercing the façade. "It was," one wrote, "that inner man, at one with God and the Spiritual Kingdom, that blazed out the light of God at us."

And what did Saint Oswald see, from his perch inside the Kingdom? "Glory be to God," he wrote. "The last aching abyss of the human heart is filled to overflowing with the love of God. Love is the beginning, love is the middle and love is the end. After He comes in, all you see is 'Jesus only, Jesus ever.'"

XVII

ॐ

Get to the margin.

—AUGUST 22

Paris, 2012. Oswald's story posed some interesting interpretive challenges. I still saw him primarily as a Realist, one who had passed from trying to capture God on a canvas to becoming, himself, the work of art, his life a moving portrait, every step, every word, every thought realizing God. The Spirit made physical for Oswald something that had previously been theoretical; it made immediate something that had previously belonged to eternity. Now, the hours he'd put into perfecting his craft as a painter became hours of working out the Spirit. His devotional life, always intense, became measured and methodical, even as he opened himself up to wild new possibilities. The suffering he'd endured chasing his artistic dreams—the poverty and uncertainty, the opposition— became suffering for Christ. It was still poverty and uncertainty and opposition, but now he embraced the haphazard, becoming its "apostle." He was like Tennyson, as Thomas Carlyle had described the poet in a letter to Emerson: a man "carrying a bit of Chaos about him . . . which he is manufacturing into Cosmos!"

But there were many possible ways of viewing Oswald. As I'd proceeded through his story, one thought had crossed my mind repeatedly. This was that the editor of *Utmost* had done a fantastic job of leaving out anything that might have proved especially problematic in the future. There had been, for example, a few feminist revolutions between Oswald's time and mine, and, although their work was by no means complete, they had led to a less macho idea of Christ, as well as to a change in vocabulary. One wouldn't today have heard the words *effeminate* or *namby-pambyist* preached in most pulpits. Another good editorial choice was the omission of passages detailing the more extreme physical effects of an indwelling Spirit. These surely would have raised the eyebrows of mainstream Evangelicals, who, apart from a belief in the power of prayer to help heal the sick, were not mystical about the body. It was also important that Oswald's lack of concern over the issue of biblical infallibility had not been mentioned. This was an issue that was only beginning to gain momentum in his day. In the middle and later years of the twentieth century, it was *the* issue, the crux of the ongoing war against rationalism. A related matter was Oswald's disregard of futuristic or "End Times" schemes (related because the schemes had to do with biblical prophecy, and with whether it was "factual" or not), which would probably have posed a hurdle for more apocalyptic-minded readers.

But the biggest strike against Oswald would undoubtedly have been his ideas about entire sanctification, which were never explained fully in *Utmost*. This might have been due to the fact that, although the baptism of the Holy Spirit had utterly changed Oswald's life, he often preached afterward that the focus of all teaching was *not* to be Holiness or sanctification: it was to be, simply, Christ. He seemed to grow wary of the ways the doctrine was used and abused as he grew older, and much of his preaching began to center on correcting other people's views of it. Still, the concept clearly formed the backbone of his theology. Without the indwelling Spirit, Oswald thought, a man had no way of forming the likeness of Christ in himself, nor could he maintain a relationship with Christ. And outside of that relationship, there *was* no Christianity.

Had this been made explicit in *Utmost*, it would surely have proved a problem. For though it was true that there were still Evangelical traditions which espoused sanctification, the doctrine was also hotly contested and had been since the very birth of the Evangelical movement. In the mid-eighteenth century, around the time of the First Great Awakening, John Wesley, influenced by certain medieval mystics and Moravian Pietists, had preached entire sanctification—or "Christian Perfection," as he'd called it—after which it spread quickly on both sides of the Atlantic. But he'd also been obliged to spend decades defending it. Sanctification was never a precise doctrine, and Wesley was often content with vagueness. For instance: to those who argued that sin in the sanctified soul was not "destroyed" but merely "suspended," Wesley advised, "Call it which you please." To the question of whether sanctification was gradual or instantaneous, he answered, "both." The Holy Spirit came in, he said, at the moment of justification and began the *process* of ridding the soul of sin, but a person was only entirely sanctified in the *instant* the last drop of sin was removed. To those who argued that the Spiritual doctrine had been much abused, Wesley retorted: "So has that of justification by faith. But that is no reason for giving up either this or any other scriptural doctrine. 'When you wash your child,' as one speaks, 'throw away the water; but do not throw away the child.'"

Most telling of all was Wesley's definition of "Christian perfection." It did not mean, he said, absolute perfection. It did not mean freedom from foible or infirmity; it did not imply perfect knowledge. It meant an ability to avoid "conscious" or "voluntary" sin, and it meant an ability to obey the two commandments Christ had identified as the highest: to love God with all one's heart, mind, and soul; and to love one's neighbor as oneself. This, for Wesley, was the ultimate mark of a saint: he was "perfected in love."

Wesley never did manage to sway Evangelicals from the Reformed, or Calvinist, tradition, to his side. They didn't like the notion that sin could be eradicated during this lifetime (perfection, they thought, was reached only in death), and they thought that the emphasis the doctrine of sanctification placed on human effort and action detracted from God's grace. Also troubling was Wesley's suggestion that a person was free to refuse the Spiritual gift, which he said worked by "allure," not coercion, a violation of the Calvinists' belief in "irresistible grace." Moreover, sanctification seemed to suggest that there were two classes of Christians, an idea that struck many as both dangerous—a good way of creating spiritual snobs and dictators—and nonsensical, for why would God turn someone into a Christian by saving her, but not into a *full* Christian? Another common complaint was that sanctification seemed to promote an isolated, individualized spirituality, over and above a corporate one. Finally, many thought that the doctrine was the result of a basic error in biblical interpretation. Criswell, my childhood preacher, who called himself a Calvinist (and who usually sounded like one), had taught that the word *sanctify* simply meant "to consecrate," or "to set apart for God." When Christ said, "For their sakes, I sanctify myself," He hadn't meant that He'd invaded His own body; He'd simply meant that He'd dedicated all His thoughts, words, and actions to God.

Whenever I'd seen the word *sanctification* in *Utmost,* this is the definition I'd had in mind. (In other words, I'd been misreading it from the start.)

In some of the wilder reaches of the Internet (personal blogs by militant Calvinists, chat rooms devoted to rooting out heresy among Evangelicals), it was easy to come across denunciations of Oswald as "dangerous" or "inappropriate." It was generally his Holiness that got him into trouble. Yet critics also often mentioned that his theology wasn't obvious in *Utmost* and that most people who read the book did so without knowing they were reading a Holiness text. Attempts at pinning Oswald down generally failed: "He was a sort of proto-Pentecostal mystic, and Wesleyan in his theology," wrote an anonymous commenter on Puritanboard .com. That was probably as close to correct as one was likely to get, but it still wasn't entirely correct. Oswald was clearly influenced by Wesley, and, like Wesley, he enjoyed reading medieval mystics. But he had numerous other influences, among them his immediate Holiness tradition, Keswick (the Holiness tradition which would eventually make its way to America, spreading rapidly to Evangelical churches across the country). And he wasn't a Pentecostalist, not even a prototype of one.

Keswick was a conference that had begun meeting annually in England in the 1870s, following a revivalist campaign there led by the American Evangelist Dwight L. Moody. The convention welcomed (and still welcomes) speakers from many different denominational backgrounds, making it theologically diverse. But one important hallmark of its Holiness teaching was its attempt to accommodate Reformed positions and to make sanctification generally more accessible. Sin, in the Keswick model, was merely counteracted, not totally annihilated; the rational mind was never disturbed by the Spirit, nor was the individual personality or identity threatened. "To be possessed by the Holy Spirit does not mean that we lose our individuality," wrote the Keswick historian J. C. Pollock. "The tyrant state of iniquity turns its citizens into machines. It is only as the Holy Spirit permeates our personality that it discovers itself and rises to a clear and holy subsistence."

This protectiveness about the self distanced Keswick, and Oswald, from Pentecostalism, a late arrival on the Holiness scene. The most important genesis point of the Pentecostalist movement was at a revival meeting in Los Angeles in 1906 (the Azusa Street Revival), during which people suddenly gained an ability to speak in "tongues," a Spiritual language that sounded to most ears like unintelligible babbling. At the time of this revival, Oswald was working for an organization called the Pentecostal League of Prayer, which had been founded in England in 1891. Its name would prove unfortunate, for it was unrelated to the burgeoning charismatic movement (eventually, it would drop the *Pentecostal*). The league was named for the traditional Jewish feast day of Pentecost. On that day, according to the book of Acts, the Holy Spirit had first swept down upon a group of Christ's followers, granting them power to preach the Gospel. They'd begun to speak, and, miraculously, everyone in the crowd around them, which contained people from every nation on earth, heard his *own* language being spoken, as the Spirit effortlessly translated.

Confusing matters were other mentions of "tongues" in the New Testament, which described it as an incoherent Spiritual language. In Paul's first letter to the Corinthians, "tongues" was listed as one of the Spiritual gifts. Trying to clarify some of the more novel aspects of the religion, like the notion of a single, unifying, indwelling Spirit, Paul asked the Corinthians to accept the mystery of division within unity. There was one body, he said, but it had many parts, and it needed all of them in order to be whole. So it was with the Spirit: there was just one Spirit, but there were many gifts, and they were distributed among God's people. One person might be given the gift of wisdom, another of knowledge; one of faith, another of healing; one of miraculous powers, another of prophecy; one of speaking in tongues, another of interpreting those tongues; one of teaching, another of distinguishing among spirits. All the different gifts were necessary to complete the body, for what was the babbler in tongues without his interpreter?

Modern Pentecostals seized on this idea of different Spiritual gifts, but Oswald and the League of Prayer thought they misinterpreted it. In an article Oswald wrote for the league's journal, *Tongues of Fire* (another unfortunate naming choice), he explained how the two groups differed. The purpose of the league, he said, was simply to pray. Its members prayed "for the filling of the Holy Spirit for all believers, for the revival of the Churches, and for the spread of scriptural holiness." The league, he continued, was not a sect or denomination or church. It existed alongside the churches, and it welcomed people of all denominations to attend its meetings. It did not preach sinless perfection, or an ecstatic moment of Spiritual baptism that could result in the sudden acquisition of a physical gift. It abhorred overtly emotional displays, and anything else that seemed to shut out the light of reason in favor of a "pure" Spiritual experience. The choice between reason and Spirit was a false one, Oswald wrote. "The work of God in us transcends reason, but never contradicts it." In a later work, he elaborated his position:

In dealing with the Corinthians, Paul tells them to form a spiritual *nous*, an understanding whereby the spirit can be expressed. When a soul is first introduced to the heavenly domain by the Spirit of God, there is a tremendous bursting up of new life in the soul and there is no language for it. Paul urges the Corinthians to form a spiritual nous as soon as they can, to come to the point of understanding whereby the spirit can be expressed. "If you don't watch what you are doing, this will produce disgraceful mockery among the nations. If they come into your meetings and see you jabbering, you will give an occasion to the enemy to blaspheme" (see 1 Corinthians 14:23). In the modern Tongues movement the responsibility is with the teachers. May God have mercy on them!

It was around the time that my notes on Oswald's theological influences reached their twentieth page that I knew I'd have to abandon the idea of describing them fully in my book. If one wanted to nitpick Oswald's theology, tracing back every idea inside his collected works to some defined tradition—to Calvinism or Wesleyanism, to medieval mysticism or Muscular Christianity— one could surely do so. But one would very quickly begin to encounter contradictions and confusions, and, when the time came to place that volume in a certain section of the theological bookshelf, one would be hard-pressed to decide where it ought to go. Like Forsyth's Bible, the collected works didn't "exist like a library in detached departments." It had "an organic and waxing continuity," which at times felt curiously discontinuous. This slipperiness was perhaps intentional. Writing in the journal *Theology* in 1941, the Bishop of Salisbury, a great fan of Oswald's, noted that he'd "left behind him no coherent and consistently worked out theological system. That is the last thing he would have desired." Consistency, as Oswald liked to recite to his students, was the hobgoblin of *little* minds.

A word Oswald sometimes used to describe the kind of spiritual mindset he liked was *liberal*. It was a word already being used disparagingly by some Christians, to indicate a moral or philosophical relativism, but Oswald thought this a misuse. He praised those who embraced "the larger, the more liberal views," the people who were "open-minded" and "not afraid to think." It was, for him, a matter of embracing the true nature of the universe, of reality, and of God. Oswald was not a relativist about morality, which he equated with obedience. He wouldn't drink or smoke or play cards; he embraced a life of voluntary poverty. He even followed God's commandment to "give to all who ask," emptying his pockets whenever he passed a beggar in the street. Yet his friends remembered that he could happily pass an evening in the company of men playing cards, and laugh and talk with them without uttering a word about their activities—that is, without judging. "He was the most irreverent Reverend I had ever met," one recalled.

Toward the end of his life, Oswald wrote in his diary that he wished there would be a new revival among Christians. He wished that those who professed to have a passion for winning and caring for souls would learn to be more ethical in their dealings, by embracing a "natural and holy life":

I mean by the last phrase, a recognition that the big, natural constitutions of cosmic nature and human relationships and "open-air-ness" are of God and not of the enemy.

Spiritual leaders, he said, should learn to keep their "hands off" the souls they counseled and to "let life grow . . . under the care of God." This was the way in which Oswald was liberal: he believed in teaching people, helping people, guiding people, but not in controlling them. He wanted people left to God; he trusted

God to take care of His people. Being Christian, for Oswald, didn't mean conforming to someone else's ideas. It meant having a personal relationship with Christ.

To help his students cultivate this relationship, he always insisted that they do their own thinking. "Treat the Bible," he told them, "as new territory needing to be colonized." His own Bible, which I'd glimpsed at Wheaton the previous winter, was in fact several Bibles, cut up and pasted into the margins of another: a fully colonized gospel according to Oswald. He rejoiced when one of his former students told him that she'd had her own experience of "revelation," quite distinct from the one he'd taught her about. "It means," he wrote, "she is gaining her own as the result of thinking and not of any propagandist teaching." As he grew older, he became more and more open-minded when it came to being taught by others: "I begin to notice with astonishment," he wrote in the last year of his life, "that I do not read in order to notice what I disagree with, as many people seem to do. The author's conclusions are of very little moment to me, what is of moment is a living mind competently expressed, that to me is a deep joy."

∾

To read without a view to conclusions, purely for the joy of experiencing a writer's mind at work, seemed to me to represent a gold standard of reading. It also seemed to hint at how Oswald's own work might be best approached. If one approached it with a dogmatic mindset, expecting it to fit tidily into one tradition or another, one would inevitably be disappointed. But it was easy to delight in Oswald—in his language and in many of his ideas—if one approached him with an open mind. I mean "open mind" as he would have defined it: a mind stayed on Christ, closed on that one point, and radically open to everything else. It was in this sense that Oswald was a relativist. "Once we think with God," he wrote, "all the rest is far and sinks to a relative place."

If one did read Oswald with an open mind, one began to notice the stunning variety of his influences, and to understand why he'd held such appeal for so many. I'd been thinking anew about why I'd read him over the years. It wasn't in order to be convinced—not after the first few years. It was, rather, to be reminded of essential truths, and to be filled with a certain feeling. The feeling I got from *Utmost*—focused, calm, powerful, full of hope, full of purpose, ready for action—was a feeling that was difficult to come by in literature. When I opened the book, I felt as though I were on a different plane, and also that I might carry that feeling back into the world with me.

How had Oswald managed to capture and convey this feeling? I thought it was another effect of his liberalism, of his free and voracious approach to reading and ideas. He'd read constantly throughout his life, and he'd never limited himself to the Bible or to works of biblical interpretation. He'd not confined himself to Evangelical authors. This mattered a great deal when it came to *Utmost*, for the book was shot through with the influence of poetry and fiction, those breeds of literature that traffic as heavily in mood as they do in ideas.

The mood captured in *Utmost* helped to explain its lasting appeal. Most other works of late-nineteenth-century Evangelicalism had long ago drifted into obsolescence, but *Utmost* seemed ageless, even though its language and many of its ideas clearly belonged to an earlier era.

How had the feeling produced in *Utmost* remained so recognizable? Perhaps through its partaking in another genre that had stood the test of time. Consider this ode to George MacDonald, written by C. S. Lewis in 1946. Lewis had first read *Phantastes* thirty years before and had found himself enchanted:

> A few hours later I knew that I had crossed a great frontier. . . .
>
> The quality which had enchanted me in his imaginative works turned out to be the quality of the real universe, the divine, magical, terrifying and ecstatic reality in which we all live. I should have been shocked in my 'teens if anyone had told me that what I learned to love in *Phantastes* was goodness. But now that I know, I see there was no deception. The deception is all the other way round—in that prosaic moralism which confines goodness to the region of Law and Duty.

Lewis was responding, I thought, to MacDonald's very modern themes: the romantic individual, struggling against the prosaic realm of law and duty and common sense, hungry for a realer reality than the one humans were continually manufacturing. They were still the themes of our late-modern lives. If we were to trace the iterations of Fairy Land from MacDonald's time to the present day, the journey would take us through Carroll's Wonderland, J. M. Barrie's Neverland, E. Nesbit's Magic City, Charles Kingsley's water world, L. Frank Baum's Oz, Lewis's Narnia, J. R. R. Tolkien's Middle Earth, Madeleine L'Engle's Uriel, Maurice Sendak's Wild Things bedroom-forest, and numerous others, on into the new millennium, with J. K. Rowling's sharply realized, eminently recognizable magical world in the Harry Potter series. Even Neo's journey into reality in the Matrix films fits nicely into the genre.

These works weren't identical to one another: some of the later writers had beaten MacDonald at his own game, taking his "dream Realism"—as the poet W. H. Auden (another MacDonald fan) termed it—to thrilling new heights. And not all of the entries were "Christian," not even in the implicit way *Phantastes* was. But they all shared some very important qualities. They all offered their heroes an escape from the dull meaninglessness of present realities, as well as a chance to act out their moral convictions—to fight and to find "deliverance *in* trouble," as Oswald put it. The version of heroism they offered wasn't isolated but chummy. These heroes never accomplished their goals on their own. The friendships, the loves, they made along the way often took on the quality of a higher cause. Selfishness was overcome through these relationships. The self the heroes hated at the beginning of their journeys was lost; the self they hadn't known they had—the *true* self, open to and embracing of others—they discovered. It was a self with full knowledge of its own powers, which always seemed to come along with a humble and righteous sense of how those powers ought to be used.

So it was with the hero of *Utmost:* the devoted reader eager to realize Christ in her daily life. That was the mood the book established, and even a reader like me (I had a twenty-first-century wariness about heroism as an ideology) was susceptible to it—particularly, perhaps, because it was so good at connecting the private life to the social life, personal expression to a higher, common good. *Utmost,* though it was a private devotional object, was ultimately about other people. On the Internet, Oswald was accused of portraying the ideal Christian as an "isolated self-made spiritual giant." "The Christian faith he taught is privatized and individualistic," wrote a Canadian pastor named Johan Tangelder on the site Reformed Reflections. "It lacks joy and some even term it 'morbid.'" This didn't square with the Oswald I knew. It was true that he was concerned with protecting the individual from institutional and tyrannical forces, but he was also concerned with protecting relationships between individuals. "God does not contradict our social instincts," he wrote. "Beware of isolation. Beware of the idea that you have to develop a holy life alone. It is impossible to develop a holy life alone; you will develop into an oddity and a peculiarism, into something utterly unlike what God wants you to be":

> "And hath raised us up together, and made us sit together in heavenly places in Christ Jesus" (Ephesians 2:6). We are not raised up alone, but together. All through the social instinct is God-given. From the Bible standpoint, whenever a man gets alone, it is always in order to fit him for society. . . . It is contact with one another that keeps us full-orbed and well-balanced, not only naturally but spiritually.

There were many perspectives from which to view Oswald Chambers, but only one, I thought, was really necessary: the perspective of relationship. First, the relationship he'd had with Christ; then the relationship he'd had with his fellow men and women. Relationship existed, for him, in a free space, outside the rigid bars of civilization. This, I suspected, was how Oswald would have read the story of his own life. "Get to the margin," he'd said. It was in the margin that Christ lived, and where one could begin, finally, to "watch with Him."

༄

XVIII

A river touches places of which its source knows nothing.

—SEPTEMBER 6

Paris, 2012. "What are you doing?" the mountaineer asked.

On the boulevard, the sun had reached its late-afternoon position, slipping behind our building toward the river. It sank to illuminate the red conical swirls of Le Week-End, a tabac-brasserie which, despite its name, was open only for a few hours on Saturdays and not at all on Sundays; and, farther away, the top of the July Column, in the center of the Place de la Bastille. Above this column soared the Génie de la Liberté—this was what I was looking at this afternoon. The figure was a monument to the 1830 Revolution and to the triumph of spirit over stone, the stone of the prison that had formerly occupied the spot. It was a unique figure, a statue of liberty for a heroic age, a powerful, romantic age. It was a figure Oswald would have liked. In France, representations of liberty were nearly always female (she was *la* Liberté). They wore softly drooping robes on their gently slouching bodies and floppy

Phrygian caps on their heads. But there was nothing soft about the génie—or spirit—of the Bastille. He was thoroughly male, entirely nude, and tautly muscled. He was leaved so brightly in gold that every rippling contour caught the light; even the feathers in his wings began to flex and quiver when gazed at too long. He was perched on the toes of one foot, and from his head, the mass of curls that shone so brightly above the trees, a single star blazed forth.

I'd grown quite attached to the spirit over the past few weeks, but now the scaffolding had come down from our building, trapping us inside. From the window of my room, if I leaned far out over the black iron railing, I could just make out the tips of his wings.

"Thinking," I said. I turned from the window.

"About what?"

"About where I was this time last year."

"Probably with your previous boyfriend."

He laughed, and I smiled.

"With my grandmother," I said. "In her kitchen in Texas, drinking coffee."

"Do you miss Texas?" he asked.

I turned back toward the window, resting my chin on the railing. It was his way of asking what my plans were.

The time had come for making certain long-delayed decisions. My visa was now well and truly expired, and, despite the fact that friends in Paris had told me repeatedly that the French state turned a blind eye to Americans who stayed on vacation a bit too long, I was getting nervous. I'd also recently received a call from the friend who owned the apartment I rented in Queens. She was going to have a baby, she'd said, and she needed the extra space— I would have to move out by the end of October.

But where would I go? New York seemed very far away at the moment, and the idea of searching for a new apartment from abroad, of trying to secure one without proof of employment or a steady income, of asking my mother (yet again) to cosign a lease I could ill afford, filled me with dread. I could begin to search for another job, but my book about Oswald wasn't done yet—it wasn't even begun—and starting a full-time position would delay it even more. Friends had advised me to go to Texas, where I could live with my parents and finish writing without any financial pressures. It was an idea my mother had voiced as well, on more than one occasion: If I wasn't to live in New York, wouldn't I come home? But I was thirty-three years old and accustomed to my freedom. Freedom was something I had in abundance in Paris.

But to *move* here? Life was so enjoyable here that it was almost easy to forget. To forget all the plans I'd made, all the work I'd done to get myself into a certain life I'd wanted, a life which had always and only been set in New York. I had no intention of vacating my accomplishments. Paris was a dream, but, as the summer had begun to fade and my fellow expat Americans had headed back to their real lives, I'd begun to appreciate how very decontextualized I was here. I lacked a language. I lacked connections. I lacked degrees from the schools which might help me one day to find suitable work. Most of all, I lacked that crucial, nearly indefinable thing that made a person *belong* to a place. How to describe it? Maybe it was a sense that her problems were one and the same as the problems of the land she lived in. I felt America's problems in my bones. I suffered them and worried over their solutions. I hoped that they might be solved, or at least alleviated, and I had a sense that I could play a part, however small, in the drama.

But France? I'd read about France in books and papers; I'd dreamed about it and walked its streets. But I didn't fully understand it, neither its promise nor its troubles. I didn't *feel* it. And this, I knew, was one of the main reasons life here was so romantic: I was still a tourist.

"I think I'll take a walk," I said to the mountaineer. His head was bent, as it often was, over a medical textbook. "It seems like a good time to take a walk."

"Have fun," he said.

I slipped on my shoes and started down the servants' staircase, as gray and dim as the normal-people staircase was gilded and light. I was headed to the terrace at the Institut du Monde Arabe, where there was a view over the city and where one could observe the génie of the Bastille in all his muscled glory. It was an excellent spot for thinking and praying, for trying to get the proper perspective.

I was in real need of perspective at the moment, not only for my life but for my book. A river touched places of which its source knew nothing, but I felt like I'd traveled quite far from my source material. I'd always felt very certain of *Utmost,* and very confident in my understanding of it. When it came to making decisions, for instance, the passage I'd always kept in mind was from January 29: "Has the voice of God come to you directly? If it has, you cannot mistake the intimate insistence with which it has spoken to you in the language you know best, not through your ears, but through your circumstances." Circumstance was God's language, the way His order reached us, through the haphazard details of our lives.

I'd always found circumstance an eerily exact guide. Even in the current moment, the answer, circumstantially, was plain. I could not afford to move back to New York, and even if I'd been able to, the life I'd led there no longer existed. My job was no longer mine; my last boyfriend was no longer mine; my apartment would shortly cease to be mine. My two best friends had also recently moved away—one for an academic job down South, one to Istanbul, to work as a journalist. Could my life in the city be rebuilt? Some version of it, perhaps, but not right now. Writing a book, as I was discovering, was a sufficiently complex endeavor, and not one I could perform to any satisfaction while trying, once again, to tackle New York.

In Paris, in contrast, everything was falling into place without any effort on my part. The friend I'd rented the chambre from was leaving, and I could take it over from him if I wanted to. It was cheap enough that I could afford it, so long as I did little jobs on the side. I could get a yearlong visitor's visa without much trouble, and the pace of the city was conducive to writing. And, of course, there was the mountaineer.

This person, who'd appeared outside my window like a gift or apparition, had significantly deepened the rosy tint of the glass. I'd seen him in action now on numerous occasions, floating up lampposts, scaling walls, dangling his feet over the side of the quai, studying medicine late into the night, undaunted and fleet in all endeavors. I'd heard his stories—of summer jobs herding cattle in the Alps, scooping ice cream in Lyon, keeping the graveyard shift at the front desk of a hotel. His mind was sensitive. He could recall with wistful precision the faces and personalities of his favorite cows—their spots, their nostrils, the tenor of their lowing. One night, after I'd locked myself out of my chambre, he climbed a ladder to a skylight in the hallway and, looping a rope around a chimney on the rooftop, dropped himself down the side of the building and through an open window. The first book he gave me was *Humboldt's Gift*. Together, we read Bellow's description of Demmie Vonghel, the "Fundamentalist princess who liked to drink." We laughed at its accuracy (was Bellow ever off even a jot in his characterizations?). "Fundamentalist Demmie became an

Episcopalian in New York," he wrote. "She had fitted herself into New York. The miraculous survival of goodness was the theme of her life." Demmie read a daily devotional called *The Upper Room.* We laughed at everything.

The mountaineer was a compelling circumstance. But lately, having dug so deeply into Oswald's work, I found my old methods of deciding threatened. Now, my thoughts were haunted by passages like one from August 13: "The voice of the Spirit is as gentle as a zephyr, so gentle that unless you are living in perfect communion with God, you never hear it." Before, I would have skimmed this passage, reading it simply as a variation on a theme. The Trinity, as I'd always understood it, was very sticky: to speak of God was to speak of the Spirit, and saying that the Spirit had a gentle voice was another way of saying that God spoke through circumstance. Now, I understood that, for Oswald, the Spirit was a very specific entity. I further understood that, according to Oswald's logic, I'd never been in *perfect* communion with God, however close I'd felt to Him at times. Such a thing, in Oswald's view, was possible only for the sanctified.

To say that this was a letdown was an understatement. The reason I'd started on this journey was to find out whether I was real by Oswald's standards. Now I knew for certain: I wasn't. Only the sanctified were real, only saints were real.

Could I become "real" in this way? It was an idea which seemed to belong to an entirely different tradition from my own. I would sooner pray to Saint Francis than I'd pray to God to be invaded by the Holy Spirit. I couldn't say exactly why this was, except I knew it had to do with circumstance. Oswald had been drawn into an entire *world* of Holiness before he'd accepted its premises; I'd always lived in a different world. I'd been raised thinking that Christ was already in my heart. If He wasn't, after all those years of asking, and if He wasn't the same as the Holy Spirit, what was the point?

I also didn't like where the ideas behind entire sanctification could lead. Oswald, like John Wesley before him, had wedded the notion of an indwelling Spirit very strongly to an idea of humility and also of action: they'd both led disciplined, methodical lives. They'd also both been avid readers and deep thinkers. Without these balancing qualities—humility, discipline, and learning—it seemed to me that a culture which embraced entire sanctification would inevitably create spiritual snobs and dictators. I suspected that it lay behind the language of "reality" that had existed at my church when I was a girl. The doctrine of sanctification may have been officially rejected, but the language and the basic ideas had wound their way through history, mutating along the way, to wreak havoc on my childhood. At my church, they'd been used precisely for the purpose of setting some Christians—generally those who were less intellectual and more emotional—in a higher spiritual sphere than others, to the extent that everyone (myself included) was eager to have a certain kind of experience.

I wasn't totally done with Oswald, though. Even as I followed the message of entire sanctification to its logical end, understanding, finally, the full implication of his idealistic language—all the *perfects* and *bests* and *utmosts* and *highests* he'd thrown around—I heard his voice telling me to calm down. I heard him saying, in a thick Scots accent, that I ought to do my own thinking. Because however certain he'd been about the need for sanctification, he'd also written quite a bit about the ultimate flimsiness of theories and doctrines, even if he sometimes found them useful. If we allowed them to become our standards of belief, he'd said, we were bound to suffer: "When we become advocates of a creed, something dies; we do not believe God, we only believe our belief about Him." We turned tough and mean, not only toward others but toward ourselves. Where we were "soft," Oswald said. That was where God had looked at us and where we'd looked back at God.

I'd arrived at the institute to find it crowded with tourists: Americans. I found a spot along the railing on the Bastille axis and listened to them speaking. I listened to their accents, plain and pleasing. Each word was a house, as spacious as that, with many rooms, many meanings, and I shut my eyes, feeling my way through them. French was still something else. It was a wall— a pretty wall, to be sure, papered in Brunschwig & Fils, but just something one sat beside as one ate dinner, admiring and ignoring at the same time.

Down the street, the spirit of the Bastille arched his back, lifting one leg elegantly in the air. In his left hand he held a chain, broken into two pieces, and in his right the liberty torch. His curls seemed to fall over his eyes, and I watched intently as the wings lifted and settled, as if weary from flight.

A feather broke free from the wings, floating brightly toward the sun, and I followed it, letting my thoughts carry me away from sanctification to a more pleasant line, one which was actually helping me in my current dilemma. I hadn't fully appreciated Oswald's ideas about relationship before, but they were ones I liked. What did he mean when he said that Christianity was a relationship? He meant, somewhat surprisingly, that one had developed the correct perspective. Oswald was extremely concerned with perspective— what he called "watching with God." To watch with God was to be "rightly related" to Him, and to be rightly related to God was to be rightly related to everyone and everything in one's life. To participate in the relationship of Christianity was to hone one's vision, bringing it into accord with Christ's.

The question to be asked about Christ's vision was not what Christ saw but rather what He *chose* to see (when there was a choice), and also *how* He went about seeing. What Christ chose to see was God. For Oswald, this meant "soaking" in Scripture, and also in nature, in which there was "a real coming of God to us." Art, too, could be a portal into the eyes of God, as well as literature.

How did God see? Just like an artist: "If you are being trained as an art student," Oswald wrote, "you will first of all be taught to see things as a whole, in mass outline, and then in detail. The meaning of perspective is that we keep the view of the whole whilst paying attention to the detail." For God, the whole picture was, of course, visible reality together with invisible reality. In human terms, this meant learning to see every small thing as infused or indwelled with divinity. "Can I see the Invisible One in the thing that is nearest to me—my food, my clothes, my money, my friendships? Can I see these in the light of God?" Once a person began to recognize God's order in the "passing moments," he began to see that "nothing was unimportant."

That was the first lesson: to see what wasn't (visibly) there. The second was more challenging. It was about learning to see what *was* there. It was about learning to see past what you thought you saw when you looked too quickly, or when you relied on past knowledge or hearsay. Oswald called this developing the "innocence of sight" (it was a term he borrowed from Ruskin). He used as an example a tree with a red light shining on it: the innocent eye would record that the tree was brown, but it would struggle against the mind, which would constantly suggest that the tree was, in fact, green.

The stakes were low with the tree, but they were high in other instances, namely, when we looked at other people. What did we see? Did we see types? Members of a group? A race or a gender or a religion? "Many of the cruel things in life spring from the fact that we suffer from illusions," Oswald wrote. "We are not true to one another as *facts;* we are true only to our *ideas* of one another." In Oswald's view, types did not actually exist. "I do not believe in the type hunt," he wrote in his diary. "Every human being is his own type, therefore take him as a fact, not as an illustration of a prejudice."

To watch with God was to look fiercely for the individuality of every person one came into contact with. It was extremely challenging, because our minds developed a kind of shorthand over time—a system for cataloguing people based on past experience that allowed our attention to move on to other matters. In other words, our minds, as they became "smarter," also became less precise and a bit lazy, lumping people into groups that poorly mapped onto reality. We were further hampered by the narratives that swirled around us—reports of this or that religion, race, nation, trend. Never having encountered the subjects of these reports ourselves, we took the stories as truth, allowing them to shape our ideas of masses of people.

But God didn't work in the mass, and He didn't view His creations as ideas. He only made individuals, and when He looked upon them, He looked upon *each* of them. If we didn't learn to look with God in this way, we were unlikely to develop in love as He'd commanded: "Love your neighbors as yourselves." We couldn't love in the abstract, and we couldn't know someone in the abstract. Oswald wrote,

> We must never think of men and women in the mass. We talk about "the struggling mass of humanity"—there is no such thing, the mass is made up of separate individu-

als. The danger of thinking of people in the mass is that you forget they are human beings, each one an absolutely solitary life.

Oswald's insistence on placing observable facts over ideas was drawn from Enlightenment philosophies, but it was also drawn from a more recent scientific mode of "seeing": that of seeing variation rather than similarity. Uncovering the truth of variety was a great achievement of the mid-nineteenth century, and for a time there had been Christian thinkers who, like Oswald, thought it expressed something essential about the religion. Apart from Christ (an individual person, a variation on the theme of humanity), Oswald wrote, God was "nothing but . . . abstraction." Only by relating to an individual Christ was the individual Christian fulfilled; only in that fulfillment could Christianity as a religion be said to exist. It existed in many souls, not just in one, and its character—varied, living, evolving, adaptable, as full of heretics as it was of saints—reflected this fact.

Why had the idea of variety fallen out of conservative Evangelicalism? One reason was that its most eloquent formulator was Charles Darwin, whom many Evangelicals loathed and feared nearly as much as they loathed and feared Nietzsche, thinking him dangerously unsettling for religion. He had been unsettling for religion, but in a way truth seekers could only celebrate (as Oswald put it, many people found God only *after* they'd lost their religion). Oswald hadn't considered Darwin's theory complete or final (all scientific theories and schemes were destined to change, he wrote, calling his era the "age of the evolution of Evolution"). But he hadn't simply dismissed him, either, recognizing that Darwin had possessed an enviable innocence of sight. He'd been able to see, as the historian Louis Menand put it, that "difference goes all the way down." When Darwin studied the finches on the islands of Galápagos, for instance, he'd seen that each bird was not *like* the others of its species, but rather *not-like*. Every attribute of every bird, from the tip of its tiny beak to the final tuft in its tail, was unique, the way that every human face or fingerprint was different from all others. Each bird was a collection not of similarities but of variations, and the truth of the finch was that there was merely the "idea" of finch, an idea that was very useful (to humans) in "naming groups of interacting individuals." Darwin was a visionary who'd seen through the surface sheen of similarity which our *minds* draped over the world. It was partly because of him that Oswald could admonish his listeners, half a century later, to be true to each other "as facts," and not merely as "ideas."

This, in essence, was the lesson of perspective Oswald was trying to teach: to look at the whole as infused with God; to look at the detail as it really was; to account for the activity of one's mind and ideas in shaping one's perceptions; and, finally, to bring the perspective in line with Christ's.

Over the past week, I'd been trying my hand at it and had begun to understand just how challenging it was. It was one reason I'd come to the terrace this evening, to keep the génie in view. I wanted to see him there, solitary, shining, and unique; I wanted to see *only* him, forgetting all the other iterations of the statue I'd encountered over the course of my life. The spirit had been copied numerous times. I'd seen a likeness of him in the Louvre, and another on top of a bridge outside of London. For a long time, his likeness had graced the ten-franc piece (until the French currency had gone defunct), and I remembered spending him, and also tossing him, one evening, into the Seine.

Despite my best efforts, I found that it was this last image of the génie that kept returning to mind, even while I looked at the statue in the distance. The coin toss had taken place during my high school trip to Paris, nearly twenty years earlier. I'd been walking with my classmates along the river late at night as we made our way back from dinner, when our teacher had suggested we stop off on the Pont Marie. We'd gone to the middle of the bridge, and he'd made a little speech. If we ever wanted to come back to Paris, he'd said, we should toss a franc into the river. We'd stood in a long line—ten of us, perhaps—holding our coins with fisted hands. Then we'd kissed them and let go, watching as they fell. Ten coins, turning their way down, the gold catching and releasing the light, before disappearing into the black water. I'd thrown in ten times more than the required amount, so serious was I about coming back.

Standing on the terrace this evening, I found that I could recall the night perfectly. I could recall the weight of the coins and the flicker of gold, the smell of the river and the face of my French teacher as he'd watched. My eyes had been alert, and I'd seen everything clearly.

But really, I knew now, I'd seen nothing.

A few months earlier, I'd received word that my French teacher had died. We'd fallen out of touch over the years, thanks entirely to my negligence in replying to emails and Facebook messages. He'd been good about keeping up with his former students. But I'd let us drift apart, holding on to some old grudge, wary of the inevitable complications which would arise, should we continue to be friends. Yet I'd also been plotting something, in my daydreams—a reunion at which I'd revive our old dispute. I'd fight with him again about religion, I thought, this time armed with adult intelligence and experience. I'd show him that he couldn't talk to me as he used to. This time, I'd imagined, I would win.

I'd been planning on dropping him a note to tell him I was

back in France, that the wish on the bridge had worked. Maybe, I'd say, our paths would cross.

On Facebook, amid the expressions of grief flooding his news feed—tributaries swelling a river that had already run dry—someone had posted a photograph. It was a photograph almost entirely filled with ocean and sky, and, in the foreground, a solitary figure making its way out to the horizon, walking with certainty above the water along a pier. "Uncle Philip," the caption read:

> I picture him saying goodbye & crossing over to Heaven this way.
> See you soon!

❧

I dropped my chin onto my hands, resting on the railing. What had I really known about my French teacher and his beliefs? His relationship with Christianity? With God? I had to admit that I'd known very little and that, knowing little, I'd supposed a lot. I'd put distance between us because of my suppositions, a distance which was now permanent. Somehow, I'd allowed an idea to triumph over a person.

I could do nothing about it now, only determine that, since my own eyes were still shining, they would strive to develop better perspective in the future. The stakes were too high, and life was too short, to continue going through it viewing friends and loved ones as fixed types. How much love had I already lost in this way?

I watched the génie until he fell into shadow and the electric lights at his feet came on. Then, the terrace having closed, I made my way home, a bit closer now to making my decision.

XIX

ॐ

*Never look at yourself from the standpoint of—Who
am I? In the history of God's work you will nearly
always find that it has started from the obscure, the
unknown, the ignored, but the steadfastly true to
Jesus Christ.*

—SEPTEMBER 7

Paris, 2012. In September, the Paris of August redeemed itself.
The temperature fell to a perfect seventy-seven degrees, the shops
reopened, and the ranks of the tourists thinned considerably. One
out of every two seemed to have suddenly disappeared, as if rap-
tured back to a lesser paradise. The mosquitoes, too, had received
their home call.

In order to make the most of it, and of our remaining time
together (that morning, I'd bought a ticket for a flight to New York,
departing in two weeks), the mountaineer and I had taken to pic-
nicking on the tip of the Île Saint-Louis, whenever our schedules
allowed. Our picnic consisted of what I imagined Parisian pic-
nics had consisted of for at least a century: baguette, pâté, cheese,
cornichon, wine, and fruit. Or else it was falafel, a newer Parisian
staple, carried to the river from the Rue des Rosiers.

Tonight, the tip of the island was crowded, as it generally was, with young couples. We found a spot among them, and soon we were sharing our wine, our cheese, our corkscrew, our cigarettes, our *feu*. On one of our first dates, while we were riding the Métro back from a farmers' market, the mountaineer had bet me that he could hand off the mostly drunk bottle of wine we had with us to a well-heeled young man sitting across the aisle. In France, he'd said, young people shared everything, without suspicion. I'd lost that bet (wager: one bottle of champagne), watching in amazement as the man, hardly looking up from his book, had finished off the bottle, sipping as politely as if we'd all been at a dinner party together. And I'd seen more evidence that what the mountaineer said was true. One weekend, we'd hitchhiked our way from the center of Marseille to a nearby beach and back. Both times, we'd been picked up by women of around my age, both driving Peugeots (the French were loyal to their cars), one of whom had had her little daughter with her. I couldn't pinpoint the cause of this strange behavior, whether it was that the French were unusually trusting or rather that they were so polite—for they were extraordinarily polite—that the instinct to self-protect was overridden by a compulsion to uphold the customs governing social interaction. Perhaps it was simply that, within the confines of an agreed-upon structure, it was easier to move about freely, to be free to be good. Whatever the cause, the result was a marvel.

This evening, as the mountaineer struck up a conversation with the couple next to us, I lay back, half-following what they were saying and studying the branches of the plane trees overhead. I was feeling quite happy to be one-half of a couple, even if it was only temporary. It was the privilege of having a person in your life who filled the foreground. It allowed you special access to the details, the variations that set one individual apart from all others.

It allowed you to appreciate for a moment God's guiding hand, the mystery of two people relating to each other as they related to no one else. And it allowed you to begin to see how two people, brought into close contact in this way, could begin to reshape each other and, eventually, the world around them. Partnerships were not static and self-contained. They were generative and wide-reaching; they revealed the true dimensions of the individuals involved. "Personality," Oswald wrote, "is like an island":

An island may be easily explored, yet how amazed we are when we realise that it is the top of a mountain, whose greater part is hidden under the waves of the sea and goes sheer down to deeper depths than we can fathom. The little island represents our conscious personality. The part of ourselves of which we are conscious is a very tiny part, there is a greater part underneath about which we know nothing.

It took another person to plumb those depths: "Personality merges, and you only reach your real identity when you are merged with another person. . . . Love is the out-pouring of one personality in fellowship with another personality."

I'd often wondered about Oswald's visions of love, and now I was beginning to understand. I'd spent the day reading about his relationship with his wife, Biddy Chambers, née Gertrude Hobbs. She was a late arrival on Oswald's scene, this Gertrude, or Gertie, as she was called. He was already thirty-three, several years into his sainthood, and a year into his life as an international man of ministry. But it wasn't until he began his relationship with Biddy that Oswald became his "true" self—the self expressed in *Utmost* and his other books. Since he was already quite settled in his ways when they met, the process of change was a bit turbulent. For Biddy, it was perhaps less of a shock: she was just twenty-four and, on the day their romance began, embarking upon the first big adventure of her life.

I'd been looking forward to meeting Biddy. She'd been an intriguing figure throughout the years I'd been reading *Utmost*, thanks to the rumor that she, and not Oswald, was the book's true author. Now, having read through thousands of pages of his work, including articles he'd published pre-Gertie, I could say that this was definitely not the case: Oswald's voice was his own. And yet, the rumor wasn't entirely without foundation, though to see how this was true one was forced to read between the lines. There was always more to a relationship than was apparent to the casual observer, and in the matter of Biddy and Oswald, it was difficult to be more than a casual observer. As their daughter, Kathleen, had said in her interviews with Oswald's biographer David McCasland, many of her mother's personal papers, including the letters she'd written to Oswald, had been destroyed. Biddy had been an extremely private person and had taken great care, even during the years she was busy transforming Oswald from an unknown preacher into a global phenomenon, to hide herself away. In the brief introduction she'd written for *Utmost*, which she'd typed in the basement of the student boardinghouse she ran in Oxford in the 1920s and '30s, she'd signed herself, simply, "B.C." She'd selected a quote for that introduction, from the Scottish preacher Robert Murray M'Cheyne: "Men return again and again to the few who have mastered the spiritual secret, whose life has been hid with Christ in

Oswald and Biddy in London, circa 1915

God." It was a quote she might better have applied to herself, for from the moment she met Oswald, Gertrude went into a kind of hiding, one from which she never totally emerged.

It began with the name. On May 28, 1908, in Liverpool harbor, Gertrude Hobbs boarded the SS *Baltic*, a ship in the White Star Line; on June 6, Biddy soon-to-be-Chambers disembarked in New York. She'd come to the city seeking secretarial work, but Biddy was not "just" a secretary. She was a very ambitious secretary, and a very good one. Trained in Pitman shorthand, she could record 250 words per minute. It was a skill she'd learned at home, via correspondence course, having suffered as a girl recurring bouts of bronchitis that kept her out of school. Determined that they would not keep her out of life, she'd set a lofty goal: she would become the personal secretary to the prime minister of Great Britain. To that end, she'd gone to work for an officer at a munitions factory outside of London, then for a solicitor at a law office inside the city. New York represented adventure, but it was also another jewel for her résumé.

Biddy's romance with Oswald began on the *Baltic*. But in fact, they'd met on occasion before, in England, at a church where Oswald's brother Arthur was minister. Biddy's mother, catching word that Oswald would be embarking on his second big mission trip on the same ship, had sent him a note asking him to look after her daughter on the crossing. In the end, they'd looked after each other, falling in love swiftly and permanently. They'd begun a correspondence after the ship docked, Biddy writing from New York and Oswald from Ohio, Massachusetts, and Maine, where his preaching and teaching schedule had taken him. By November, she'd given up on America entirely, returning to England to be with Oswald. They married a year and a half later, in May 1910, at a Methodist church in a suburb of London.

Why did Oswald change Gertrude's name to Biddy? According to his friends, he'd had a habit of giving everyone close to him a nickname; he could not stand on formality. That was one possible answer, though it couldn't account for why Biddy took the nickname as a proper name: once she adopted "Biddy," Kathleen recalled, she never again allowed people to call her Gertrude.

I thought the answer lay in the particular circumstances of Oswald's life at the time of their Atlantic journey and in the philosophy of religion they came to share. Oswald, when he met Gertie on the ship, was not a free man. In his own words, he was a "bond-slave of Jesus Christ." Having felt, before his sanctification, like a slave to himself—to his "bad-motiveness" and his selfish desires—Oswald had arrived at an all-or-nothing proposition: either sin would die in him or Christ would. He'd come to a definition of sin as "my right to myself." Hence, to give up sin was to give up selfishness, and to give himself to Christ was to give himself entirely—body, mind, soul, pocketbook. For those who wished to be abandoned to God, Oswald wrote, there could be no "competing relationships." It wasn't the life for everyone, he conceded. Even Christ, when questioned about marriage, had said that there were those for whom celibacy—and the footloose life of a disciple— wasn't possible. But if a man wanted to be "one over whom Jesus writes the word 'Mine,'" he had to be ready and at liberty to obey the whims of the Spirit, whenever they might call and wherever they might lead. The Spirit's territory was the entire world, and the Spirit's character, according to Christ, was supremely unpredictable: "The wind bloweth where it listeth, and thou hearest the sound thereof, but canst not tell whence it cometh, and whither it goeth: so is every one that is born of the Spirit."

This was another example of what Oswald meant by "Apostle of the Haphazard." Having been born again by the Spirit, he had become Spirit (for "that which is born of the flesh is flesh" and "that which is born of the Spirit is Spirit"). To be Spirit wasn't always easy; it wasn't always pleasant. To go out "not knowing whither" demanded the great leap of faith, taken again and again and again. "Faith is the heroic effort of your life. You fling yourself in reckless confidence on God." The saint was "overruled, overmastered, held as in a vice by the love of Christ." There was no way of loosening the grasp, no way of reaching a compromise. A saint couldn't simply give up the missionary life for a church position. "Professional Christianity is a religion of possessions devoted to God," Oswald wrote. "What we possess often possesses us." Possessed only by Christ, the saint didn't even know, necessarily, where he'd find his next meal or where he'd sleep at night. His "only provision" lay in God.

This had all been well and good before Oswald met Gertie. On his first mission trip, the one he'd made to America and Japan in 1907, he'd sent off a blithe letter to his mother, thanking her for not being clingy, like the mothers of other missionaries he knew. But Hannah had a husband and seven other children to keep her company. A wife could never have been so understanding, nor would anyone of the time have expected her to be. Oswald's job was inappropriate for a man with practical concerns, and a wife—together with the children she might one day bear—was the ultimate practical concern. She was also, potentially, the ultimate distraction for a man who'd decided to lock his gaze on "Jesus only, Jesus ever."

Oswald was aware of all of this when he found Gertie on the boat. Indeed, over the coming months, as he began to understand the full magnitude of what marriage would mean, he started to fret. He'd planned to be "a theological Ishmaelite for a dozen years, tramping the globe." Now, he decided that the only way for him and Biddy to be together was for her to abandon her own life and to embrace his. He warned her again and again of what it might mean, and he reminded her, again and again, that the only way a person could stand such an unhinged existence was if she belonged in love to Christ. Anxiously, he monitored the progression of her feelings—not for himself, but for Christ:

> How does your spirit develop in intimacy with Him? Nothing else is right if that goes not well. He has all the circumstances in His hand—in His hand my whole life and yours with me must be for Him and not for domestic bliss.

Months later, he was still at it:

> Let me tell you what I see in outline. All comforts and comrades and countries are held lightly, all at His command. Can you, out of your love to Him and me forego every other interest saving the interest of His Cross?
>
> Do you know how it costs to write this—by grace mine eyes have looked on Jesus. I dare not think of that. Oh I know you will rise to any height of self-sacrifice—but you understand how many misgivings I have in calling you to come with me.
>
> I cannot give you any other warned couple as a specimen of what it will mean. We will be the two sent out by Him. I need you to keep me strong in the way He calls.
>
> I have no home to offer you. I have no money to give you. I have the great wild world and His commission—Go and make disciples.

I am solemn with the awakening to the grandeur of
His call—follow me.
I see loyalty to Him and nothing else and you will
help me to be loyal to Him.

I'd spent the afternoon marveling at Oswald's letters. Really,
how could a girl resist such a tortured mixture of anxiety, deter-
rence, and more anxiety, especially when topped with a healthy
dose of surveillance? How to take the line about what his attachment was "costing" him? But Oswald was not always like this. His
more romantic letters to Biddy were lost, but one he'd sent to his
parents about her survived:

My dear Mother and Father,

I want to tell you that I am in love and it is quite such a new
experience that it opens up so many unknown things that
I do not know quite how to put it. I love plenty men and
women and am loved in return not slightly but grandly
and truly; yet this is quite different. It did not come
passionately or suddenly but all permeatingly and now I
have abruptly told you the fact. . . . I cannot yet conceive
what good I can be to any woman, but I never feared
until now, yet I am sure His hand leads. Of course I quite
understand the avalanche of common sense and wisdom
that my many kind friends will see fit to subject me to
and I'll try my best not to be overwhelmed or frozen. But
I want you to know from me and I find it awkward and
difficult to write about myself. My thoughts for seven years
past have never pictured me further on than 35 years of
age and if you remember I sometimes used to say I should

like to go to more commodious premises then—and now this comes and in amazement I took the cup more or less dazed and stupid and am very and unspeakably thankful.

Perhaps Oswald's worry toward Biddy was simply love in disguise, as worry often is. And perhaps he'd driven himself a bit mad, worrying about worrying. Anxiety was an emotion he'd known very well as a young man, but he'd sworn it off in his new life. Saints, he would say often in the future, *refused* to worry. "Let not your heart be troubled," Christ had commanded. Had Oswald imagined himself beyond such a petty emotion, simply because he was sanctified? As it turned out, his recent peaceful abandonment had much to do with circumstance and with the absence of competing claims on his affections. It was far easier, as he would preach in later years, to live up on the mountaintop than down among facts in the valley. The valley was the space of compromise, a place where there were no easy answers, where one's dearest beliefs and theories were tested.

Oswald and Biddy's romance was, I thought, strangely relatable for contemporary couples. Glancing around me at the young men and women on the promontory this evening, I saw a generation which had been forced to embrace its own version of the haphazard philosophy. We lived, as Oswald had, in a global, shifting world. His era had been the era of empire, mass migration, and world war; ours was the era of international industry, extreme commuting, weak economies, frequent career change, and the dreaded "two-body problem." This was a dilemma which arose when both partners had to work—out of desire or financial necessity or both—but couldn't find good jobs in the same place. It was too common these days, but maybe some version of it had always existed. Oswald and Biddy had certainly encountered it. He would have said that, in the beginning, they literally had a two-body problem, arising from the fact that, although his body belonged to the Holy Spirit, Biddy's still seemed to belong to her (this, I'm guessing, was the reason he kept telling her about keeping his eyes on Jesus).

I quite liked how Oswald and Biddy had gone about overcoming all their obstacles. They'd come up with a solution that was totally personal. At some point, Biddy's spirit presumably "developed in intimacy" with Christ's to Oswald's satisfaction, and they became one flesh in marriage. But they also came to share one body in Spirit: Christ's. It was an idea they extended to their love. Human love, Oswald wrote, was a frail emotion. It could easily be upset, since everyone was imperfect. To love with Christ's love was the thing. Unless both people were hidden with Christ, marriage was "apt to become either a degrading tragedy or a sordid monotony." Strictly speaking, Oswald did not love Biddy. Rather, Christ in Oswald loved Christ in Biddy. It was, perhaps, in order to keep this idea at the forefront of their minds that Biddy buried Gertrude forever. Her new name came from B.D., for "Beloved Disciple."

Given the intertwining of their bodies and souls, it was perhaps inevitable that their professional interests would merge. "It will be such a meagre home we will have, you and myself going heart and soul into literary and itinerating work for Him," Oswald wrote to Biddy, allowing himself a moment of excitement about their future together. "It will be hard and glorious and arduous. I want us to write and preach; if I could talk to you and you shorthand it down and then type it, what ground we could get over! I wonder if it kindles you as it does me!" Indeed, it did kindle Biddy: the "work of the books" would become their shared passion, and would remain so, even after Oswald's death. This was one sense in which Biddy "wrote" Oswald's books: she physically wrote them, first in shorthand, later on a typewriter. How involved was Oswald in the process? In 1917, shortly before he died, he wrote a letter to a friend that stated it quite succinctly: "Hope to send you a book on Job soon (at least Biddy does, I take no more responsibility after having spoken my mind)." Since he never made any notes of his own for his sermons, Biddy's is the only physical record of Oswald's preaching. There was no getting to him but through her, and if she altered anything at any stage along the way, there would be no way of knowing what it was. She lived for forty-nine years after he died, producing books from her notes nearly up to the end, always under her pen name, Oswald Chambers.

But Biddy's devotion wasn't one-sided. Oswald, despite all his misgivings and protestations, did let go of the haphazard life for her. Not five months after their courtship began, he sent a letter to her mother, who was worried over his situation, assuring her that he would soon take a permanent position. In 1911, after a few months of traveling together, he and Biddy opened, under the aegis of the League of Prayer, a college for the training of missionaries and preachers on the outskirts of London. He was principal, she was lady superintendent, and they were both happy.

Did it matter, I wondered, sitting up to take a cup of wine being offered to me, that their happiness had been hard won? Did they wish that everything had been perfectly organized for them from the start, that their parents and friends had simply endorsed the union, that the path had been clear?

I doubted it. Oswald never spoke about avoiding a fight, only about having something worth fighting for. That was the miraculous part. "God makes our own our own," he wrote in a letter to his brother. "He brings and removes friends." *God,* not we. Thanks to Biddy, Oswald learned once more something he'd long known about God's character: that God, retaining the right to work through the haphazard, and caring little for men's plans, even the plan of having no plans, still brought His purposes about in the end.

And how did one know if a person was one's own?

I held up my cup for a toast, looking off to Notre Dame. The mountaineer drank and smiled, and went back to his conversation.

The same way, I thought, one knew if something was real.

XX

∾

Where we are placed is a matter of indifference;
God engineers the goings.

—OCTOBER 14

Dallas, 2012. "What have you got there?" Nana asked.

My grandmother and I were sitting on the sofa in the family room. On the short oak table next to the back door, the television was playing the news: two talking heads, predicting a win for the Republicans in the upcoming presidential election. My sister had told me that Nana had been watching more and more television, as her hearing had worsened and interaction had become more difficult. On TV, the words were printed at the bottom of the screen, and the volume could be turned up so loud that no hearing aids were necessary. It was a beacon of clarity in a muddled and confusing world.

To me, the world beyond the TV appeared much as it always had. In the window next to the screen, the pecan tree shuddered under the weight of the cat, who had just leapt from the window-sill onto a low branch. It was a new cat—I didn't even know its name—but it was like the others who had come before. A black stray, with green eyes. I watched it for a moment, looking up from my work.

"A gift," I said, shouting to be heard over the news. "A diary, for the book I'm writing."

"You're writing a book?" My grandmother's eyes grew wide. She smiled, delighted. "I'm so proud of you, Macy dear. What's it about?"

"*My Utmost for His Highest*," I said. "And us."

"My what?" Nana asked.

I reached for her copy of the book, which I'd just placed at her elbow. It was the third time we'd had the conversation today.

"Do you remember reading this?" I said. "You used to like it."

My grandmother took the book and held it in her hand, as if feeling its weight. She studied the title, then placed it down, confused.

"Oh," she said, handing it back to me. Then she asked me again what I had in my lap.

It was, as I'd told her, a diary—or a photocopy of one—a gift from David McCasland, Oswald's biographer. It had come into his possession only after he'd finished his own research, and he'd not had time yet to get it into the archive at Wheaton. But it was an amazing thing: the journal Biddy had kept in the YMCA camp in Egypt, where she and Kathleen had accompanied Oswald during the First World War. She'd started keeping it on January 1, 1918, not two months after Oswald's death. The diary wasn't very long or detailed, but it was in her own hand and her own voice.

The year dawned very wonderfully with a watchnight service and the recalling of Oswald's words "God shall wipe away all tears" (and He has taken on a big job, he said) and also that God keeps them away too by the angel of His presence for in His presence is fulness of joy, and on the threshold of the year came the words My presence shall go with thee and they will give thee rest. The sense of being compassed about by the righteous was very real too in the love and sympathy of all here. . . .

One realizes more and more that the unseen world is the real. . . .

Now it is the beginning of another day and as the past is not ours nor is the future, this present one matters. Thou hast laid Thy hand upon me for this day and at its close I'm one day nearer being with mein geliebt. Oh may I be his helpmeet ever.

That was the first entry.

"My word," Nana said, studying the page on my lap. "That's messy."

"You have no idea," I said.

The diary was written in longhand, not shorthand, but Biddy's scrawl was nearly illegible. It made me nostalgic for traumatizing afternoons I'd spent in paleography classes at Cambridge, bent over twelfth-century animal skins. And those had been written in medieval Latin, a language which I never had managed to master.

"You're rewriting it?" Nana asked.

"Yes."

I was copying it out in the margins, in my own hand.

We had a party. Always at those times I feel God's presence for just then I always long for mein geliebt with all his life and joyousness to be the centre of it all.

The sun was beautiful and bright but tonight it's frosty

again. The class was quite good, but so sorely I miss mein geliebt . . . but God knows and he's faultless before His throne serving Him day and night. . . . God be blessed for Him and keep me stayed on Him. Then will I sound to God my exceeding joy. Why art thou cast down oh my soul put thou thy trust in God.

It was a good thing to write out other people's words, I thought. It made you feel close to them. I felt as though I were inside Biddy's days—or at least part of her days. Unfortunately, the part she'd liked to record tended to be rather dull. The YMCA camp at Zeitoun consisted of a series of tents, one of which had been designated for spiritual care. Oswald and Biddy had christened it the BTC, or Bible Training College, hut, imagining it as a continuation of the work they'd been doing in London. Oswald had made it homey and inviting, creating a "tea time," during which the men could come drink and chat and listen. When Oswald died, Biddy had begun to take over some of the lessons, and it is clear from her diary that she'd been very busy. There was plenty of work to be done maintaining a wartime camp in the middle of the desert. Kathleen had been among several children in the camp, which had given them their own play hut, as well as animals to play with. But little of this was described in Biddy's diary, which was mostly a rundown of who had come to tea, and who had come to dinner, and what the subject of the evening's lesson had been, followed by many protestations of faith in God. Occasionally, the entries contained a notable detail about life in the camp, such as how the children of the workers had passed their days:

Kathleen has been radiant all day and had a fine ride on her donkey.

But for the most part, Biddy kept her feelings and observations off the page, even her feelings about Oswald. After her first expressions of grief, she'd stopped recording them. It seemed that she, like Oswald, didn't like to complain before God. I'd been so ecstatic to receive the diary, but alas: Biddy only half-emerged from her hiding place in its pages.

Still, I was in a kind of rhythm. Each page I deciphered was giving me a real sense of accomplishment. And this, too, was connecting me to Biddy. In the interviews Kathleen had done with McCasland, she'd mentioned how much her mother had loved to type Oswald's sermons. After their return to England and their move to Oxford (where Biddy had family), Biddy had gone to her typewriter every morning, before fixing breakfast for her student boarders. I imagined that the typing was one of the main ways she'd kept Oswald so present in her life. "My mother always talked about my father as if he was in the next room," Kathleen said. "She would always talk about my father as if he'd only just gone upstairs."

I wondered when Biddy had gotten into the habit of typing in the mornings. Perhaps she'd begun during the first years she'd been with Oswald, while they were running the Bible college in London. It seemed that the bulk of her notes came from that period, which had been very busy for both of them. Oswald had taught; Biddy had tended to the students, the building, the shorthand, and, with the birth of Kathleen in 1913, the baby.

"But whose is it?" Nana asked.

"It's the diary of a wife who lost her husband at a very young age," I said. "When she was my age, actually."

My grandmother frowned, and I remembered, suddenly, that she'd never been able to speak about her own husband, my grandfather, without tearing up. He'd died when she was still in her forties. Once, when I'd asked if she'd ever thought about marrying again, she'd said, simply, "I'm already married." My grandmother, like Biddy, had never thought of herself as a widow.

"How did he die?" she asked now.

"The war," I said. "The first one."

"He was a soldier?"

"No. He was a chaplain."

"Then why did he die?"

It was a good question. I looked again at the cat outside the window, thinking how to answer it.

"A blood clot," I said, though this wasn't at all satisfactory. It was merely the official cause: a clot in the lung that had formed after an operation to remove his appendix. In fact, the doctors in Giza (he'd been at a Red Cross hospital there) had deemed the operation successful and had expected him to live. But it was wartime, and the beds were crowded with wounded soldiers, and it was the desert in October, hot and sandy and generally unpleasant. Oswald had been feeling ill for days but had put off going to the hospital, perhaps because he'd often felt ill in Egypt. He hated to complain, but at times he'd been unable to help himself. "The day is still so awful that I have just deliberately asked God to alter it, for no other reason than just the immense unpleasantness which renders usefulness and well-being impossible." The wind in Egypt "blew from the mouth of the devil. . . . We eat sand, drink sand, think sand and pray sand." He'd dreamed often of home. "Coming Home!" he'd written to his brother just before his death. "What a Day that will be, back to the cool and the cold, back to the mountains and the streams, back to the sea and the wee greatness of Britain."

The real question, I thought, was how Oswald had wound up in the desert in the first place, when he might have remained in the cool and cold, in the nice life he and Biddy had created—for them-selves and, more important, for their two-year-old daughter. The record of his time at the college makes clear that his domestic life in London before the war was peaceful and that his career was thriving. He was lecturing constantly, at the college and around the city at various churches and gatherings. The recollections of his students from the time revealed that his quest for saintliness had been successful. "The first impression of Oswald Chambers was that of spiritual reality," one wrote. "No man had a higher vision, but it was a vision with feet as well as wings. . . . Nor was this mere theorizing, for Oswald Chambers had the power, born of his own reality, of calling forth in others a like glad obedience and joyous faith." He was "at one with God and the Spiritual King-dom," said another. "He led us into the Inner Shrine." He'd even still been able to embrace the haphazard life. At times, the school had money only to remain open for a week, and Oswald would have to pray for funds to arrive. They always did, but there was a satisfying chaos to the system.

So why had he left? The answers I'd come across so far were surprising. According to his diary and correspondence, Oswald had gone to Egypt for two reasons. The first was that he'd heard God telling him to go, through Scripture and through his emotions. In two letters to his mother, written in mid-1915, he explained that certain Bible verses had come to him "as purely spiritual intima-tions" and not of his own seeking. These included 2 Timothy 4:6: "I am now ready to be offered." Emotionally, he was chomping at the bit: "Since the war began it has been a pressure on me all but unendurable to be here." It seems he'd never really given up wan-dering, telling his mother that although he'd thought of settling over the years, it was clear to him now that "His way for me is 'the world.'" Biddy, he wrote, was behind him, one hundred percent.

She would "never do anything but back me up, no matter what it costs her." They had not, he reassured his mother, forgotten about Kathleen: "I am not several kinds of fools in one, I am only one kind of fool—the kind that believes and obeys God."

Oswald's second reason for going was that, like a great many at the time, he welcomed war:

> Personally, I am more relieved than horrified that war has come, because to a large extent the hypocrisy of diplomatic veneer is removed, also the immediate result among men is that much irresponsible pleasure-seeking and frivolity is ended and real stern issues have begun, and men everywhere are more open to talk about God, the soul, and final issues than heretofore. The fact that 100,000 men are battered into eternity (as they surely will be again and again during these months) strikes with paralysing awfulness on our senses and minds, but then, better instant removal than staying to abide many living lives of corruption and spreading disease and wrong. Besides, human nature has depths of surprising mystery, and in the very moment of disaster God has many ways of saving men. God's ends will issue, no matter what the world, the flesh and the devil say or do. Don't misunderstand me, I am not inhuman, the ghastly crimes of war are unspeakable, but they certainly are no worse than *sin*, that is the crime of crimes.

During the first year he spent in Egypt, Oswald was extraordinarily happy. All the suspicion he'd had about "civilization, organization, and Churchianity," all the disgust he'd felt at creeds and doctrines, vanished in a cathartic bloodletting. He delighted in seeing men going ruggedly and heroically into battle, freed at last from their meaningless, mechanized, sinful lives. It was a version of something he'd been dreaming of for a very long time. On December 31, 1915, he wrote in his diary, "Here ends the most devilish and ruinous year that has ever been, yet in my personal experience one of the finest and mightiest years of my life, God be praised. Here I am all after the desire of my heart, in the centre of a great military encampment, and Biddy and Kathleen . . . here with me. Hallelujah!"

"Maybe he died," I said to my grandmother, shaking off my disgust, "because he thought that war was realer than real life. That death was realer than life."

My grandmother smiled, uncomprehending.

"No," I said. "I don't really understand, either."

I did understand Oswald's glee on a theoretical level, or rather as a well-documented historical phenomenon. Mine was the privilege of hindsight and historical analysis, two things denied Oswald. "It was not easy to be a man in 1914," wrote the historian Philipp Blom, in *Fracture*. Men were appalled at the weak lives they led in factories and in offices—"coffins of masculinity," as the Austrian feminist Rosa Mayreder called them. Over a hundred years after the start of the Industrial Revolution, they still didn't know what to make of factories and offices, or, for that matter, of feminism. The burgeoning feminist revolution seemed an echo of the Industrial Revolution, a rise of the women to follow the rise of the machines. Not all women were like Biddy: not all would back their men up "no matter what it cost them." "Many men," Blom wrote, "greeted the war as an opportunity to reconquer their questioned manliness, saber in hand, braving the firestorms to reemerge stronger and purified of the dross of weakness and complexity that characterized modern life." In the German trenches,

Nietzsche's *Thus Spake Zarathustra* was the most read book after the Bible.

In fact, Oswald had had a strong love of the "German mind" (it was presumably his Germanophilia which had led Biddy to nickname him *"mein geliebt,"* the German for "my beloved"). He'd been fluent in the language and deeply acquainted with its more macabre elements—the "Liebestod," or "love death," for instance, which Isolde sang at the end of Wagner's opera *Tristan und Isolde,* based on the idea, proliferated in numerous other modern German literary works, that love, viewed as a state of eternal longing, could be realized or fulfilled only in death. And he'd undoubtedly known young Werther, Goethe's sorrowful autobiographical hero, so passionate and individualistic, so at odds with modern society and its demands, that suicide is his only recourse, his only hope of reaching God. Oswald had embraced living self-sacrifice, self-sacrifice for Christ, rather than literal martyrdom, but his thinking was still inherently Romantic.

On this historical, literary level, I could understand Oswald's giddiness—which was, in fact, destined to be fleeting. His delight would fade as time wore on and as the war, far from offering men an escape from mechanized existence, instead transported them (via machine) to trenches, where an ability to outlive boredom and constant anxiety, not heroism or physical daring, was the required skill. In the trenches, men didn't fight; they simply waited for machines—tanks, planes, guns—to destroy them. But I didn't quite understand how the delight Oswald expressed in his private papers squared with the generally measured tone he adopted in his preaching. It was true that, as an artist, a Romantic, a Realist, Oswald had long been suspicious of civilization and eager for a Spiritual revolution. Sometimes, he'd expressed disdain for projects aimed at bettering society. He'd hated Socialism, calling it a utilitarian scheme that squashed the individual and ignored Christ. He'd raised an eyebrow at the Progressive Movement, and particularly at those Christians who thought they could usher in the Second Coming through holy living (many Progressive Christians hoped to literally establish the Kingdom on earth, thinking this prerequisite to Christ's return). But he'd never been an anarchist. "Social reform, political purity, progressive civilisation, is our work, not God's," he'd preached. "And we must do it. If we don't, it will never be done." He'd made that statement in a sermon explaining what, exactly, God did for His children. He saved them, Oswald said, and He sanctified them. He didn't do their work for them; He didn't ensure that their civilization wouldn't fall into ruin. It was *their* responsibility to make sure that didn't happen.

So why, then, had he been so delighted at the prospect of this war? Perhaps he'd believed, like many of his countrymen, that the war would be over relatively swiftly. Indeed, by the end of 1916, when he'd been in Egypt a little over a year, he'd begun to wonder at how his beliefs had misled him. "There is an interesting puzzle in my mind concerning the intuitions born in communion with God. For instance, I had such a joyous confidence that the war would end this year, but there is no apparent likelihood that it will. It is just another indication of how little we dare trust anything but Our Lord Himself. Again, there are intuitions born in the same way splendidly and wonderfully fulfilled. It makes it clear that the Holy Spirit must be recognized as the sagacious Ruler in all affairs, and not our astute common sense."

Here, Oswald sounded like the Oswald of *Utmost*, warning about believing one's beliefs about God—and yet there was something muddled and contradictory, for his view of himself as a sanctified individual had long included an idea of his mind as belonging to the Spirit. There was always this tension in his formulation of the Spiritual doctrine—the tension between his humanity and his Spirituality, between embracing humility and refusing "to be weak in God's strength." He'd never thought himself free from foible or infirmity, yet he'd come to place enormous faith in his feelings and in haphazard details, like Bible verses that suddenly jumped into his mind or his line of sight when he let that book fall open haphazardly (a trick called "Bibliomancy," employed by many Spiritualists), that seemed to instruct him to go to war. The puzzle between faith, which Oswald insisted was blind, and reason, which he insisted was a gift from God, was never solved in his own teaching, though he strived to solve it. In the army camp, one of Oswald's fellow workers had christened the tent he taught in the "Agnostic's Redoubt," because he'd begun to preach quite forcefully about the limits of human knowledge. He'd been struck by a conversation with a nineteen-year-old German prisoner of war who'd been brought to the camp. The boy had informed him that the Fatherland was destined to win and couldn't conceive of another end. Oswald, being of sensitive intellect, hadn't simply dismissed the statement as the lunatic ravings of an enemy, commenting only that we were often led astray by our own perspectives. Yet he couldn't let go of the notion that God was guiding his own thoughts and emotions.

"Some folks," my grandmother said suddenly. "Some folks, they'd just rather tear down than try and keep something going. Easier that way."

I thought for a moment of which part of the conversation she was referring to, and then, remembering, I said, "Amen, Nana."

On the television, the pundits had begun screaming. I asked if we might turn the volume down.

"Of course," my grandmother said, picking up the remote.

"Who are you going to vote for, Nana?" I asked.

My grandmother looked at me as if I'd asked her what color the sky was.

"I'm going to vote for righteousness, of course," she said.

And she turned back toward the TV.

∾

XXI

The responsibility must be left with the individual, you cannot act for him, it must be his own deliberate act, but the evangelical message ought always to lead a man to act.

—NOVEMBER 4

Dallas, 2012. Had the storied French bureaucratic apparatus not lived up to its reputation so fully, my visa application, which I'd been obliged to file in person at the consulate in Houston, might already have been processed before Election Day. A month had passed since I'd moved out of my apartment in New York, and more since I'd realized that I could not choose a life apart from the person I loved. So I was waiting. It was quite pleasant, actually, to be in Dallas with my family for an extended period of time. I'd not had much time with them, or with the city of my birth—a city which had grown considerably, in population and in fascination both—since I'd left for college. And yet, if I'd been told that I could depart the country immediately, I would have. Quite happily, I'd have passed the rest of my life without ever again experiencing the death throes of an American presidential campaign. To be at home at this moment was, to paraphrase Oswald, to be up against facts in the valley.

On this Sunday, the Sunday before the election, I'd decided to go to church. I'd gotten out of the habit when I was in Dallas, even though attending was nearly requisite for those enjoying my mother's hospitality, and even though I'd loved First Baptist as a child. The church had been, throughout my childhood, the most beautiful place I knew. It was one of the last nineteenth-century buildings in glass-and-steel Dallas, a simple red-brick structure dwarfed by the skyscrapers surrounding it. The interior was a work of art. Shaped like a seashell and two stories high, it was painted a bright, Baptist white—white as the soul in the moment after immersion. Its pulpit was an expansive platform awash in a red-velvet carpet that ran down the steps and stretched like a tide beneath the feet of the congregation. On either side of the platform, in two branches, the choir swept up to a balcony that wrapped the back of the room from end to end. Above the pulpit was the great brass organ, and below this the large glass box that was used for baptisms, set deep into the wall and filled with turquoise water, like an open-topped fish tank. The pews, carved from light brown wood, were covered with red-velvet cushions, as were the antique kneelers. There was stained glass in the windows, but, in keeping with Baptist tradition, there was no other decoration. It was a worshipful space, at once majestic and comfortable, grand and plain, instantly inspiring of awe. I'd spent countless hours there, my head dropped onto my mother's shoulder, my bottom sunk into the velvet, while Criswell's slow Southern cadences, which I'd liked so much, had lulled me into a state that was half sleep, half prayer.

But time had passed, the church had changed, and I'd changed, too. Criswell had gone to glory a decade before, taking with him the peculiar atmosphere that had always defined the sanctuary. It would not have been possible, any longer, to drop my head onto my mother's shoulder, ignorant of the deeper meaning of what was being said, nor would the space have been conducive to reverie. At some early point in the new millennium, the Apocalypse having failed to arrive, the church had invested in its future, which is to say in screens. Massive screens had been hung over the pulpit. Small screens had been suspended from the bottom of the balcony. These displayed the lyrics to the songs—there was no need for hymnals any longer—alternating the words with the face of the music director, a man in whom the Spirit was so strong that the soles of his feet seemed hardly to touch the floor as he bounded around the stage, pumping his arms, marshaling beads of sweat on his brow, thrusting the tips of his hair mightily heavenward. The choir remained large—fifty people at least—but the only voice one heard was that of the music leader, thanks to the microphone that was never far from his mouth. During the sermon, the screens filled with the talking head of the preacher, a TV adept (he often performed for news cameras), whose face and voice so dominated the space that now, when I thought of it, I thought only of him.

Yet such changes were not the reason I'd started avoiding the church. They were, after all, merely aesthetic—matters of personal taste—not important enough to merit displeasing my mother and, in some respect, myself, since I did not feel right if I did not go to church on Sundays. I'd started avoiding First Baptist because I'd started finding myself in disagreement with a certain message that was preached there, a message which was not entirely separate from the style in which it was preached, but which I would have found disturbing in any package. The message, which the preacher—a preacher referred to by many of his parishioners as a "prophet"—had gleaned from his own reading of Scripture, was the imminent downfall of American society and the leaders and groups who were currently bringing it about. A few groups in particular were targeted (homosexuals and Muslims chief among them), and denounced in violent language (homosexuality, in the preacher's vocabulary, was "unnatural," "filthy," "perverse," and "abnormal"). The message was sly: the preacher never advocated actual, physical violence. The offense was rather on the level of those pervasive intangibles—mindset, climate, culture, tacit acceptance, tone—which, it seemed to me, might easily *encourage* violence, which had too often encouraged violence in the South.

Then there was the end to which the message was put: politics. At times, the service at First Baptist felt less like a church service and more like a political rally for the Republican Party. The effect was of course most heightened during election season.

I'd decided to attend this Sunday because I was eager to keep the peace in the family during my stay in Dallas. In past elections, differences of opinion had led to prolonged moments of estrangement, particularly in 2000, when I'd committed the unspeakable crime of voting (in my first ever democratic act) for Ralph Nader and Winona LaDuke. Today, I'd woken up early, to find a suitable dress and to steel myself for what lay ahead. The campaign season had been rough for everyone, but particularly for the members of First Baptist. During the primaries, the preacher had caused a media dust-up when he'd announced to TV news cameras (he was out stumping for Rick Perry, the governor of Texas) that Mormonism, the religion of Mitt Romney, one of the Republican challengers, was a cult. Then Romney had won the nomination, leaving the congregation in a tough spot. For though Mitt Romney was a cult member and therefore something to be feared, Barack Obama, as the preacher had suggested on occasion, was a handmaiden of the Antichrist. He wasn't *the* Antichrist (if he were, the preacher said, he'd "have much higher poll numbers"). He was, rather, part of "a tide of evil rising up that is about to engulf our nation."

I expected the sermon this Sunday to touch on this recent drama, and I was not disappointed. I'd been sitting in the pew with my family for nearly half an hour, singing and watching television, when it began. It began oddly. Before the preacher took the stage, several large cardboard panels, carried by several men, were brought up and placed in a semicircular arrangement behind the space where the preacher was to stand. Two of them had been printed with the sentence "How Can I Know?" On the televisions overhead, the panels created a blue-screen effect, blotting out the sanctuary, making it look like the service was taking place in some corporate conference room or onstage at a TED Talk.

"They're selling the recordings of the service?" my mother guessed, when I asked what was going on.

I had no idea if she was right, but I did know that such stunts were not unusual at the moment, at First Baptist as well as at churches across the Dallas–Fort Worth metroplex, which were waging a kind of war for souls. Since I'd left, in 1997, the population of the area had swelled to nearly 7 million, and with it the number of megachurches. They'd bubbled up like black gold across the prairie, massive and glittering: churches with stadium seating and movie screens wrapped around the back of the pulpit; churches with Starbucks and bookstores and television-broadcast stations; churches with smaller, satellite churches that had live music but no preacher, only a video feed of the sermon being delivered in the host church. When I was growing up, First Baptist had been the greatest show in town. Now other churches had hotter pastors, cooler buildings. Out in Grapevine, next to the outlet malls, a pastor named Ed Young had put a bed on the roof of his church and climbed into it for twenty-four hours with his wife.

"It's time to bring God back in the bed and put the bed back in the church," he'd told the media. T. D. Jakes, the beloved pastor of the Potter's House, which boasted thirty thousand members, was chummy with Oprah and had been on her talk show. At Water-mark Community Church—my favorite—a hipstery congregation with a Zen-like building and deafening music, celestial clouds of dry ice rolled endlessly around the feet of the pastor as he spoke each Sunday, spilling out over the audience.

Now, First Baptist was playing catch-up, to which end it had recently announced plans to raise $130 million for a remodeling of its "campus" (it now owned several buildings, making it one of the largest landowners in downtown). The mayor of Dallas himself had endorsed the scheme, which involved tearing down some older buildings belonging to the church and erecting a three-thousand-seat stadium in their place. The old sanctuary would be shuttered, and with it the final curtain would fall on the religion I'd known. In the new stadium, which had already begun to rise across the courtyard, the entire pulpit would be backed by a massive flat-panel screen, like a Jumbotron at a football game. This was a comparison the church seemed eager to court. "If Jerry Jones can build a $1.3 billion temple to the god of sports," the preacher had said during a radio interview, referring to the owner of the Cowboys football team and its new stadium, "we can spend a tenth of that . . . to build a facility for the glory of the one and only God."

This was another reason I'd decided to attend the morning's service: it would be one of my last opportunities to sit in the sanctuary next to my mother. I tried to push from my mind some of the more noxious remarks made by the pastor over the years, lowering my expectations till they could sink no further. But my patience had already begun to ebb at the sight of the cardboard panels, and it was gone entirely by the time he'd finished his opening speech. That speech went like this:

> This past Wednesday, Thursday, and Friday, the American Family Association arranged for 285,000 pastors across America to receive a telephone call from Mike Huckabee, David Jeremiah, and myself, encouraging them to take a stand today to encourage their congregations to vote this coming Tuesday, and to vote not for a Democrat or for a Republican, but to make a choice between righteousness and unrighteousness. And as I was making those 285,000 calls—

The audience laughed.

> —no, they use a robocall to do that. But as I recorded that, I thought it would be kind of hypocritical to send that message to 285,000 pastors and not say anything in our own pulpit about what is happening this coming Tuesday. And so tonight I'm going to bring a special message from our series in Daniel about what I believe is a turning point in American history. I didn't arrange it this way. I'm preaching through Daniel as you know and just happened to come upon Daniel chapter seven, that talks about the coming reign of the Antichrist. And as I studied and studied this message, I saw something I've never seen in the years that I've studied the book of Daniel, and that is in Daniel chapter seven, we see how the stage is being set right now for what is going to happen under the reign of the Antichrist. It's not going to happen suddenly. What is

happening in America right now is setting the stage for the reign of the Antichrist.

At the word *robocall*, I'd begun to gather my things and, excusing myself, to make my way out into an adjoining hallway. There was, I remembered, a smaller chapel at the end of it, and I thought I'd finish out the Sunday there. A sign stood outside the entrance: "Contemporary Service." I pushed open the door, then stepped backward quickly, letting it swing shut. The contemporary service was just a screen of the main service, filled with the pastor's talking head.

I walked across a corridor to get a coffee. When I was a child, there had always been free coffee and donuts in the hallway outside Mrs. Criswell's Bible class, but now there was a pricey café. I bought the coffee and went to sit at a table next to a middle-aged man wearing an orange-and-brown-striped T-shirt, white tube socks, and black Velcro sneakers. I smiled at him, but he looked away, out of the window onto San Jacinto Street, and, as I watched him look, I became aware of the sound of the pastor's voice issuing from a speaker overhead. "The rich man died and went into Hades," the voice was saying. "Hades is a place of suffering. It's a place of torment. But it is a temporary location for unbelievers. One day, after the great white throne judgment in Revelation 20, all unbelievers will be cast into the lake of fire. Gehenna, which is also translated 'hell' in your Bibles, that is the eternal destination of the unsaved."

I stood, pitying the employees of the café—there was no escape for them—and pushed through the glass doors into the street, searching for a bit of curb to sit on. I found one between two cars and squatted down.

∾

One aspect of the problem, I thought, turning my face as a car passed by, was that my path, diverging at the end of childhood, had led me to develop a sense of reality, of what qualified as authentic and true, that was quite distant from this one. The church today seemed to me like a reality-TV-show version of a church. The massive new buildings and screens, the lights and speakers, the robocalls and media campaigns—they were instruments which, I supposed, were intended to conjure feelings of majesty, power, and true connection to the divine; to suggest the preacher's spiritual authenticity, as well as the congregation's. To me they felt uninspired—like the cheap tricks of the Wizard of Oz (however magnificently expensive they were to produce)—and served only to highlight the artificiality of the future-telling that went on in the sanctuary.

Lately, though, while examining certain parallels in Oswald's story, I'd begun to see another aspect of the problem, namely a gap in my historical learning. I'd often been asked, during my years in New York, how fundamentalist Christians could swallow arguments which seemed to strain both credulity and conscience. To many outside observers, people who bought into religious-political-apocalyptic ideologies were simply out of their minds. Either they'd been brainwashed—trained, through a lifetime of subjection to subpar reasoning in church and on the television, to accept what did not pass muster; taught to identify themselves so strongly with a certain ideology that it became the sole measurement of truth—or else they'd not had brains to begin with. (I thought of Tom, my quintessential New York friend, who'd boasted of growing a brain and losing his faith in one stroke.)

But it was too simple to dismiss the message preached at First

Baptist as "mindless" or "irrational." Perhaps the logic it employed was initially impenetrable to outsiders, but there was indeed logic behind it, as well as a hardy tradition. One merely had to lift the covers of the history books and to come across a quote like this, by the British theologian Charles Hodge, in his 1871 *Systematic Theology*—

> The Bible is to the theologian what nature is to the man of science. It is his storehouse of facts; and his method of ascertaining what the Bible teaches is the same as that which the natural philosopher adopts to ascertain what nature teaches.

—to understand that, when it came to biblical interpretation in the era of scientific proof or fact, there was something quite complex going on.

Take, for instance, the notion that the president of the United States was toiling for the Antichrist, a notion which the preacher of First Baptist planned to prove through a reading of the book of Daniel at the evening's service. This idea, which was by no means unique to this preacher, was rooted, first, in the idea that Obama's policies were socialist in nature, if not in name. Socialist political schemes were dangerous because, in addition to placing too much control over people's lives in the hands of governments, they were intended to progress the human race toward a perfect state *without God*, and with no thought of Christ. It was a complaint that had been around since the birth of the Socialist Movement (Oswald, along with numerous other Evangelicals of his era, had often issued a version of it). The basic premise was that, while Socialism's most essential ideals (placing the means of production, distribution, and exchange in the hands of the community, which redistributed wealth for the benefit of all) sounded lofty, the end result was to interfere with the individual's relationship with the divine. God wanted to have unmediated access to the individual soul, and it was the individual's inalienable right to have unmediated access to God. This meant turning to God first and last to meet his needs, and it also meant not being required to turn elsewhere if he didn't want to. Socialist leaders, in contrast, told people to put their hopes—and required them to put their money—in governments, rather than in God. They offered in exchange fleeting consolations like health care, thereby distracting people from what they actually needed: soul care.

But modern Evangelical prophets also had another reason for believing that Socialism was inherently unholy. In pitting the individual, the independent, the local, and the private against the federal, the communal, the distant, and the bureaucratic, Socialism not only dethroned God and denied the individual immediate access to what was rightfully his; it also supplied the *means by which* the Antichrist would one day take over the earth.

Understanding how this futuristic element entered into Evangelical thinking on Socialism required a certain kind of Bible study. Modern Evangelical prophets interpreted prophetic passages of Scripture, found primarily in the books of Daniel and Revelation, to foretell that the federalist government of the United States would eventually join together with despotic regimes that reigned abroad to become part of the so-called one-world government (this phrase, often used in Evangelical circles as a shorthand for coming disaster, didn't actually appear in the Bible. It was derived from a passage in Revelation which spoke of a coming beast who would have dominion over "all kindreds, and tongues, and nations"). This global government would sweep in and solidify the Antichrist's reign, which would be accompanied by many desolations and which would last, according to some calculations, 1,260 days. During this period, people would have a chance to repent and to find the light. The faithful, however, would not be around for these desolations, having been taken up into the air to meet Christ in a great "rapture." This was one reason it was so important for the true believers to spread the message of the coming apocalypse *now*, before the Antichrist reached full power: afterward, those who'd been left behind would be forced to fend for themselves and to suffer the foretold horrors.

At the end of the 1,260 days, Christ would return to earth with His saints, defeat the Antichrist, and establish His kingdom on the earth for a thousand wonderful years—the Millennium, these years were called. To those who believed that Christ would return *before* the Millennium (the Premillennialists), the events leading to the Antichrist's reign had already been set in motion. Premillennialists were distinguished from Postmillennialists, who believed that Christ would return to earth only *after* His Kingdom had been established on the earth for a thousand years. Postmillennialists believed that it was up to humanity to build the Kingdom, working together in pursuit of Christian ideals, which included spreading equality, peace, order, and, of course, Christianity itself. Postmillennialism had been in vogue among American Protestants in the late nineteenth century and had helped to shape the positive outlook and vigorous social policies of the Progressive era.

Premillennialism, in contrast, had no such rosy outlook, no desire to perfect society, and no belief that it lay within the scope of humanity's power to establish the Kingdom (only Christ could do this, they thought). For them, the End Times had already begun. Globalization, the rise of socialistic leaders in American government, the ongoing conflict in Israel, and the surge in terrorism were just a few of the many "signs of the Times" discerned by

Premillennialists. Among other things, their viewpoint helped to explain the focus on politics in their churches. Since the prophetic passages in the Bible concerned earthly leaders, it was *necessary* that politics form part of the Evangelical message.

And yet, this was just one explanation among many of why twenty-first-century American fundamentalist Evangelicalism looked the way it did. The problem with settling on a single narrative concerning the End Times, the Antichrist, Socialism, and so forth was, as ever, interpretation. I'd been making a study of various End Times schemes as I worked my way through Oswald's story—for they'd abounded in his time period, the superschematized nineteenth century—and I'd been amazed by their sheer variety. Historians told very interesting stories about how such schemes had made their way into American Evangelicalism, establishing apocalypticism, futurism, and politicism as defining features of the landscape. It was a fascinating story, for it had by no means been inevitable that such thinking should take hold in America (nor had it taken hold uniformly across all traditions).

Certainly Evangelicalism, "the heart religion," hadn't started this way. It had started, in the mid-eighteenth century, as a revitalizing movement, when Protestants on both sides of the Atlantic had begun to preach in the streets and in the open fields in an effort to energize their churches, and to lend the Gospel message intimacy and immediacy. It had been a quintessentially modern religion, emphasizing personal experience and belief, and had fit well with burgeoning democratic ideals, particularly in America, where impassioned preaching and rousing hymns helped to fill the silence of the frontier. The focus, particularly in the Holiness tradition established by John Wesley, had been on the here-and-now, on holy living, on building one's life and settling one's (new) homeland. It had been optimistic and joyous, stressing the concepts of grace, salvation, blessed assurance, and, above all, love.

Those concepts were still the anchor of American Evangelicalism, but they were often overshadowed, a fact which disturbed and puzzled many Evangelicals profoundly, myself included. Over the past month, I'd been rereading what was perhaps the best-known book on the subject, *The Scandal of the Evangelical Mind*, by the Evangelical historian (and historian of Evangelicalism) Mark Noll. *Scandal* had become seminal among Evangelicals in the years since it first appeared, in 1994, its popularity hinting at how fervently Evangelicals wished to understand the conservativism and xenophobia that had gripped certain strains of their religion (as perplexing as religious-political fundamentalism was to outsiders, it was more so to us, the dissenting insiders). Books like Noll's represented an effort to critique from within our own culture, and to weave a coherent narrative of a religious movement that had always been haphazard.

The story told in *Scandal* began with the birth of Evangelicalism. It was a tale of religion, but also, crucially, of science and politics—indeed, as Noll's book made clear, building on the work of other historians (notably, George Marsden, in his *Fundamentalism and American Culture*), it was impossible to understand Evangelicalism except as a product of all three spheres. Early Evangelicals in North America, Noll wrote, in addition to being good populists, had been modern scientific thinkers. They'd embraced modern logic and methods of uncovering truth about the world, in particular Francis Bacon's scientific method of induction, in which one began by gathering individual facts before arranging and interpreting them. Early Evangelicals were drawn to this new way of knowing: induction, the experimental method, and the emphasis on fact. For them, inducting facts about the physical world in an orderly manner seemed to reveal the hand of a grand designer. It seemed obvious that there was an intelligent mind behind it all. The method fit well with an idea of progress, so alluring to a young nation eager to prove itself a New Jerusalem. Adding fact to fact, one could progress in an orderly way into a bright future. The future was not a concern but rather a promise, something to be built with confidence, using a method which seemed divine.

Shortly, Evangelicals began applying the method to Bible reading, taking individual verses as facts, and adding them up methodically to reveal a "proven" message: no longer would Bible-reading be a messy, individualized undertaking, resulting in a chaos of personal interpretations and competing theologies. Now, religion could be harmonized with modern ways of thinking, the life of the spirit with the life of the mind. These early Evangelicals, proving themselves progressive, bold, and studious, encouraged the development of intellectual life in America. They populated and funded universities, and counted intellectuals in their ranks.

All this began to change in the second half of the nineteenth century, Noll argued. After the Civil War, after Darwin, historians, philosophers, and scientists began to revise their views of the world, reshaping religious thinking in the process. Now, when scientists looked at the universe, they didn't see something fixed and mechanized but rather something shifting and organic. They began to value thinkers who broke from a mechanized approach, who were unusual and innovative. Ideas of religion began to shift from, in Noll's words, "particularistic and theistic to universalistic and agnostic." Everything was opening up, becoming less certain. The universe, in the popular imagination, was becoming something grand and incomprehensible, something filled with weird varieties and plenty of monstrosities. Species, Darwin had shown, evolved out of each other; they hadn't arrived fully formed on earth, perfect copies of a blueprint in the divine imagination. They were born of brutal, bloody battles whose purpose, beyond basic survival, was unclear. Species didn't progress toward some perfect state; they mutated blindly, as a result of these battles, and, though they might become more suited to their environment over time, it was only a relative perfection. Species could easily fall out of existence, even after millions of years of "progress." Even humans, who imagined themselves as occupying the highest rung on the ladder, weren't immune to the haphazardness of it all. If the hand of a grand designer was behind this system, it was a designer with a strong sense of chaos.

Evangelicals, Noll wrote, found themselves unprepared to respond to the massive shift in scientific thinking, which arrived at a moment of great social and political unrest. Some did try to harmonize their religion with the new ideas, or at least to formulate a thoughtful Christian response to them. The Bible, these progressives argued, had an "organic and waxing unity" (to repeat P. T. Forsyth's phrase); it was an "interpretation of the Truth" (to repeat Oswald's). They wanted to move away from approaching the Bible as a repository of facts to be inducted into arguments about the physical world, feeling that a more flexible, inclusive approach to defining truth and reality would come closer to capturing the wild, shifting universe they now found themselves inside.

But conservative Evangelicals rejected this approach. They continued seeing order, plan, and trajectory in the universe; they continued seeing a world of classic types and genres, created, ordained, fixed by the Creator. Their aim, as the years progressed, would be to close off and define, to halt the tidal wave of "free" or "liberal" interpretation sweeping the churches.

Noll credited these conservatives with preserving a few crucial aspects of Evangelical Christianity: the supernatural effect of the Cross, the centrality of Christ's sacrifice, the role of grace in salvation. But he also pinpointed the later nineteenth century as the moment when Evangelical Christians began to opt out, when a strain of anti-intellectualism took root in parts of the community. It was a particularly American phenomenon, fueled by the Civil War. The proud South, humiliated by Northern aggression, by the imposition of a federal state where there might have been a republic, was eager to define and defend its special identity. The South found it, in part, in a rejection of "Northern" philosophies: rationalism, scientism, atheism, social liberalism, federalism. Increasingly, conservative Evangelicals began to preach "Bible-onlyism," the idea that there was a single, authoritative, "fundamental" source, one that could not be controlled, mediated, or interpreted by an outside element. They began to flee the major universities and to set up a parallel educational track. As the twentieth century progressed, bringing with it ever greater challenges—the wars, the Great Depression, the spread of liberal education throughout the nation—Evangelicals found they had few intellectual tools in their arsenal. Because, Noll wrote, they hadn't "worked very self-consciously at thinking about the best ways, consistent with the Bible itself, to push thinking from the Scripture to modern situations and back again," their community began to turn inward, as the intellectuals in their ranks fled to friendlier climes.

In this new, "fundamentalist" tradition, spiritualism and supernaturalism surged. Before, Evangelicals had taken pride in their engagement with the wider culture, with making themselves understandable to outsiders. Now, the message was that outsiders' minds had been gripped by un-Christian theories, methods, and agendas, and that they could not access the truth. The truth was reserved for those whose minds had been born again by the Spirit. In certain sects and traditions (like Oswald's), this meant entirely sanctified minds, but throughout the Evangelical world a notion of spiritual intelligence began to come to the fore. The idea of a clash between mind and spirit, human intelligence and divine, which had always been present in the religion, began to dominate. Preachers became prophets, mystical seers who, like the prophets of old, issued warnings to the powerful, foretelling the end of the world, using reasoning that was more or less unintelligible to outside minds.

Yet it wasn't proper to say that there was no rationality behind the Spiritual mindset. Remaining committed to Baconian ideals, conservative Evangelicals continued reading the Bible in a highly systematic, highly rational way. This was where End Times schemes came in. The schemes were called "dispensationalist" frameworks because they set forth the theory that God had divided all of human history up into different ages or dispensations, which mapped onto certain divisions in the Bible (how to properly discern these divisions was a matter of Spiritual knowledge). One of the most important and lasting schemes, Darby Dispensationalism, had strong ties to Dallas, and therefore to the rest of the Bible Belt (Dallas was sometimes called the "buckle" of the belt). It was the brainchild of an Irish preacher named John Nelson Darby, who was active in Britain and America for several decades beginning in the 1830s. Darby's scheme was complicated and difficult to parse, but it had found a popular translator in a man named C. I. Scofield, a preacher who'd worked in Dallas at the turn of the twentieth century. Scofield published a Bible in 1909 that incorporated Darby's scheme, breaking down each page into several textual fields, which allowed for easy cross-referencing between Old Testament and New, presenting side by side all the verses Darby had added up to reveal the future. Scofield's book had swiftly become popular in Texas, and remained so—my mother and I both had Scofields—but its reach was international: Biddy Chambers's Bible (as I'd noticed during my trip to Wheaton) was a Scofield Bible.

Darby and Scofield helped to move several concepts which had been peripheral to the religion into the foreground. The infallibility of the Bible, and of the prophecies it contained, was one of them. End Times schemes were concerned with the fact that many biblical prophecies hadn't come to pass with the alacrity the Old Testament prophets had suggested they would. Dividing up the Bible and rearranging it, Darby accounted for the time lapse by discerning a pause or "parenthesis" in history, after which all prophecies would be fulfilled. His focus was strongly on this future time, for the present moment was the parenthesis, a kind of non-time. Because prophecy concerned Israel and the Roman Empire, neither of which existed in Darby's day, he argued that the Jews would be returned to their homeland, reestablishing it. That the Roman Empire hadn't really fallen but had merely dwindled, before surging again under new names (the British Empire, the American Empire) was another important idea. Also key were the notions of an Antichrist and of a one-world government that would rise before Christ's Second Coming. Reading the "signs of the Times" became a pastime, as did fantasizing about the Apocalypse (in fact, much of the current Apocalyptic vocabulary came from Darby, who wrote also of a "rapture," a word not found in the Bible, and of non-Christians being "left behind"). Stalking powerful figures, like Napoleon III in Darby's day, or like Obama in ours, so as to rightly interpret the meaning of their ideas and actions, was an activity dispensationalists heartily embraced.

And that was the general backdrop for the election of 2012, as it was being interpreted at fundamentalist churches around the country. It was an election which was destined, if Nate Silver's prognostications in *The New York Times* were correct, to secure the continued reign of a handmaiden of the Antichrist, a destiny of which the faithful of First Baptist Dallas were in hopeful denial, having come to the conclusion that Mitt Romney was the better bet. In fact, he was no longer a member of a cult. Around the coffee table at the Tuesday morning ladies' Bible study (which I'd been attending all month with my mother), I'd heard it opined that Romney was best understood as a representative of "the first truly American religion."

∾

While I waited on the curb for the service to end, I thought about one of Oswald's nicknames, the "Apostle of the Haphazard." Mark Noll had written sadly about the fact that most late-nineteenth-century Evangelicals had simply given up trying to formulate a response to the wildness of modernity; maybe present-day Evangelicals, myself included, were still wanting in this regard, not having understood, in our faithful childhoods, the challenge that would face us as adults, as we ventured out from our bubbles. But Oswald had never given up. It was amazing to me how strenuously he'd tried to incorporate various contradictory ideas. Spiritualism was there, but also intellectualism. Active ideals of individualism and strength were there, but also passive ideals of "letting go and letting God." He'd embraced a methodical style of devotion but had also tried to live the haphazard life, adjusting his views of nature and of God to the new, shifting scientific vision. He'd been wary of pinning the Bible down to facts but also eager to protect the essence of the religion. The focal point of his preaching eventually became something simple: Christ's saving sacrifice, God's grace in sending His son. But there was so much around it.

Perhaps thinking like Oswald's, combining as it did so many disparate strands, and never combining them perfectly, had been too confusing, too much, for the wider movement to bear. It had brought Evangelicalism to what are sometimes called the "limits of liberalism," that space where one must master the art of holding on tight with an open hand, or else back down. One seldom encountered wild Evangelical thinkers like Oswald anymore—not in the mainstream.

And here a question which had been much on my mind since the beginning of my journey recurred. Why had wild, intellectual Oswald been embraced so heartily by fundamentalists? I knew that the answer had something to do with the editing of *Utmost*, with what had been left out of its pages. But what explained the choices Biddy had made?

At long last, the doors of the sanctuary opened, and people began to drift out onto the plaza, shaking hands and chatting about brunch. Thoughts of hell and Apocalypse had apparently vanished into thoughts of pancakes and into the sunshine, which fell in dazzling circles on the heads of the children as they ran. I raised myself from the curb, brushed off my dress, and went to find my family, eager to get home to Biddy and her diary.

∾

XXII

We come up to the truth of God, we confess we are wrong, but go back again; then we come up to it again, and go back; until we learn that we have no business to go back.

—NOVEMBER 4

Dallas, 2012. That afternoon, I walked to my grandmother's house, to sit again on the sofa as she watched the pundits, and to read. There was one very interesting note Biddy had made in her diary, from August 1919, written right after she'd returned to England with Kathleen (they'd stayed on in the army camp for more than a year following Oswald's death). "We had a talk on 'Fundamentals,'" Biddy wrote, "and I personally see more and more clearly what abandon to Jesus Christ means and how it is everything in a life." *The Fundamentals* was a collection of ninety essays, published between 1910 and 1915, which aimed to rein in an Evangelical movement run amok. It was the brainchild of two California businessmen, who also provided the funding, and its essays were contributed by more than sixty Protestant ministers from a wide array of denominations. *The Fundamentals* attacked Higher Criticism, liberalism, evolution, archaeology, Catholicism, spiritualism,

Mormonism, and Socialism, and gave the "appropriate" reading of basic Scriptural topics. Initially, the essays weren't for sale. More than 3 million volumes were mailed free of charge to ministers and para-church organizations (including the YMCA, for which Oswald and Biddy had worked during the war) in English-speaking nations all over the world. People often credited the essays with laying the groundwork for American fundamentalism, but perhaps it makes more sense to think of them as part of a general and ongoing assault on heterodoxy in the religion, which became rather appealing in the years leading up to the First World War, and immensely appealing in the unsettled years following it. "The assertion is often made," the conservative Princeton theologian J. Gresham Machen said in 1921, that "Christianity is a life, not a doctrine. . . . It is radically false." Doctrine, orthodoxy, simplification: these were the new (or rather the old) ideals.

One of the chief characteristics of *The Fundamentals* was the way it dealt with the notion of "truth" and "fact" as things which were not open to interpretation. In a chapter on the bodily resurrection of Christ, for instance, the author listed numerous proofs of its veracity, including four separate eyewitness accounts and the fact that people had martyred themselves to defend it. Notably for *Utmost,* the essays lacked any scheme of entire sanctification. Their concern, as the title suggested, was to get down to basics: the Virgin Birth, Christ's Deity, and the Living God were among the topics in the first volume. There was also an essay on the Holy Spirit, which set forth a proof for the claim that the Holy Spirit was a person, not a power or an influence. He was a "friend" who "walks by our side every day and hour." There was a hint of Holiness language: the Holy Spirit is in our hearts and is "ready to fill them and take complete possession of our lives," but there was nothing about perfection, nothing about a second baptism or distinct work of grace. *The Fundamentals* wished to guard against any notion that the human could possess mystical powers or forces. To believe that through some effort of one's own one could capture the Holy Spirit, the essay said, would make us act "as if we belonged to a superior order of Christians."

Was it significant that Biddy edited *Utmost* nearly a decade after reading *The Fundamentals*? Her one commentary on them was that they reminded her that "abandon to Jesus Christ" was "everything." Surely she'd been aware of the fact that, in the years after the war, the drift of conservative Evangelicalism was away from Holiness, away from mysticism, and away from experimentation—away, that is, from much that made Oswald Oswald. But it was true that he'd always had plenty to say about Jesus and the ultimate power of the Cross. Even if he didn't try to prove the factuality of the Resurrection, his focus on the very basic message of Christianity—that humans, being inherently sinful, required the redemption won by the Cross to restore their relationship with God—made him a natural ally of the new fundamentalists. The heroic note, the muscular tone that ran throughout his work, was a nice fit, too.

I looked at my grandmother as she watched the television. The world we'd lived in together was the post-*Fundamentals* world, the essays' influence traceable through our lives, touching them in ways both grand and personal. There had been ample time, from Biddy's day to ours, for the fruit of the fundamentalist revolution in America to blossom, time enough for all of us to see whether figs had come, or thistles; grapes, or thorns.

I thought back to an afternoon years earlier, when we'd been sitting precisely as we were now, watching a different election on

TV. It was 1994, and Ann Richards was running for reelection as the governor of Texas, against a newcomer named George W. Bush. Bush had had a personal vendetta against Richards, or rather against her wit. During the 1988 Democratic National Convention, Richards had given a speech making fun of his father. With her smoky twang, her Texas-big hair, and her Mary Kay face, she'd enraptured the audience. "Poor George, he can't help it," she'd drawled. "He was born with a silver foot in his mouth."

Richards had been in less fine form during the 1994 debate, though. The questions had been barbed, intending to snare. When a woman in the crowd had asked the candidates if they'd support lowering the age for the death penalty to thirteen, Richards had equivocated, saying she would have to discuss it with law officials. W., though, had known what he was about. He'd seriously consider it, he told the woman. The core of the crime problem in Texas, he felt, was the juvenile-justice system, which let gang members off easy just because they were children.

"Thirteen?" I remembered saying to my grandmother. "So I would go to the electric chair if I committed a crime?"

"Of course not," Nana had said. "It's not for children like you. And they use lethal injection now."

"But what about Preston?" I'd said, because that was around the time my brother had gotten mixed up with some unruly kids at school, had turned unruly himself, and had been sent to Agapé, a disciplinary Fundamentalist Bible school for boys in Missouri.

"Preston will be fine," my grandmother had said.

My brother had written me a letter from Agapé. The only movies they let the students watch were Disney movies, he'd reported, and they made them settle their disputes in the boxing ring. In science class, the teacher played sound recordings of terrible screeching and howling and told them that the recordings had been made by dropping a microphone down a deep hole in the earth, one that led straight to hell. He told them that there were still dinosaurs alive on earth today, hidden in the Congo, where humans could never find them.

This was before Preston had been sent to the high school at super-Fundamentalist Bob Jones University, in South Carolina, where he'd swiftly violated the school's honor code by standing too close to girls (it was while he was there that the school came under fire for its ban on interracial dating). He'd already racked up numerous "demerits," as the school called its penalties, when he performed a grand gesture.

He'd done it in the wintertime, when the grounds of the school were perfect and pristine and white. Near the main building, beneath an American flag brittle and frozen on the mast, someone had built a regulation snowman: three perfect white balls, a corncob pipe, a button nose. My brother had decided to complete it, to give it that which would make it, truly, a man. All morning long, he'd stood by his work, listening to the girls giggling as they walked by, until a teacher arrived and removed the offending specimen, kicking it off with a shiny oxford shoe, then smashing it into the ground. Then the universe, which did not contain within it a sufficient number of demerits to punish such a crime, had collapsed, or would have, had my brother not met with swift justice—hardier systems than Bob Jones's had been wrecked by fallen angels. He was placed on restriction and expelled the next semester after daring, once again, to say hello to a girl.

While my brother was enduring this unsentimental education down South, I'd headed north to receive an education of a very different sort, one which bore quite different fruits. I felt *extremely fortunate* to have been allowed to go to Barnard. Many Evangelical parents wouldn't have permitted it, but my mother and my grandmother had always respected my desires, and they'd wanted me to have the best education possible. Quite easily, they might have decided that nothing good could come of allowing their child to attend a liberal-arts college. In the conservative-Evangelical mind (or at least in its press), such institutions were frequently characterized as bastions of relativism, places which infected the minds of their students with the idea that all cultures, all truths were equal, that one way wasn't better than any other. Education was supposed to teach a child how to reason from a moral standpoint, but liberal universities, it seemed, taught that there *was* no moral standpoint.

This was a theory that had been popularized by Allan Bloom in *The Closing of the American Mind,* a book which had had conservative parents quaking since its release in 1987. Bloom, a professor at the University of Chicago (and an avowed atheist), had argued that liberal-arts colleges, gripped by modern liberal philosophies, particularly those which held that all truth was relative, inculcated students with one value—and one value only—that of openness, and that they posited openness as the only solution to what they viewed as the greatest evil, intolerance. Instead of teaching students how to reason morally, the university simply taught them what to avoid: sincere belief. At the university, Bloom wrote, "the real danger" had become "the true believer."

Bloom's book was now twenty-five years old, but the ideas behind it were still current in the conservative community; perhaps they'd even become more pronounced (they'd also been persistently misread and misapplied). I found Bloom compelling, but his ideas hadn't mapped onto my own experience. I'd arrived at Barnard a true believer, and I'd left as one four years later. To be sure, my college skewed liberal, and it was true that during my time there I did begin to question the *culture* or style of belief I'd been raised with. But this was not the same thing as questioning the essence of Christianity, which was in fact being taught to me in new and stunning ways by professors of religion and history. It was also true that, for a time, I'd been captivated by the idea that truth was relative, as had my friends. In college, we'd called ourselves "relativists" because, being virtually uneducated when we arrived, we were shocked to find ourselves in the midst of so many competing identities and ideologies, and, being ignorant of both history and philosophy, we'd been easily swayed by the very powerful idea, never before presented to us in full, that the view changed depending on where one was standing.

Were our professors total relativists? The simple answer to that was no, but also that they faced great challenges, namely having to oversee classrooms filled with students of different religious and antireligious mindsets. Our professors strived to communicate their viewpoints, which tended to be very strong and directed, while urging students to form their own opinions and to respect each other's during discussions. It was a grand exercise in pluralism, not in relativism.

In fact, the discipline I'd majored in, history, did not lend itself well to total relativity. History writing, as I'd been taught it, was primarily a creative undertaking rather than a deconstructive one. The historians who trained me liked to tell stories and to build arguments, not just gut those that had come before. In my historiography class, we were taught (using the handbook *Telling the Truth About History*, by Joyce Appleby, Lynn Hunt, and Margaret Jacob) to push *past* total relativism, which was viewed as the dead end of postmodernism. One could accept the premise that, when it came to writing history, no absolute truth was possible—that it was destined to be fragmentary, trapped as it was in the past, in a finite number of sources, and in our own minds—and still move forward. One could build an argument from carefully researched facts and try not to let one's own ideology predetermine the conclusion. One could attempt objectivity, even while recognizing one's unavoidable subjectivity. Never was it suggested that the method embraced when writing history should be extended to one's entire life. If, as a result of academic efforts at objectivity, one did become a bit more willing and able to communicate across boundaries, this didn't imply a total loss of identity, self, or moral viewpoint.

In fact, I'd been surprised to discover that many of the liberal intellectuals I encountered in college were profoundly moral, in a Christian sense: they were helpful toward others, humble, and nonjudgmental. They did not hush those with whom they disagreed or condemn their ideas—not even their religious ideas. It had been a jarring discovery. The explanation I was sometimes given, when I would protest about my new friends' morality during visits to Texas, was that morality wasn't the goal; obedience to the Bible was the goal. This had always struck me as a neat bit of sophistry. Perhaps it was possible, as Oswald said, to be good without God; and perhaps God was the most important thing. But considering how deeply concerned with conventional morality most Evangelical Christians were, it seemed to me that they owed other good and moral people their respect.

☙

As I thumbed through Biddy's diary, thinking these thoughts, I recalled a quote Oswald had written out in his own diary, by the Congregationalist minister John Henry Jowett:

Our religion becomes an extra piece of baggage which we have to carry instead of being an extra power to make our burden light. We are not like a sailing boat which has just been caught on the sweep of a friendly wind and is being borne along joyfully to its desired haven.

Oswald liked it because it reminded him of how he was "ever borne on by the Spirit," in his own experience. I'd quoted it to myself repeatedly on this trip, finding the rocky waters of politicians and preacher-prophet-pundits difficult to navigate, and wondering why such things grew more difficult, rather than less, as one grew older.

Perhaps it was because as one acquired more knowledge about the past, it became more difficult to hold unabashedly bright views of it—even the most golden of childhoods dulled with knowledge. I thought of Criswell, my childhood pastor, of his own fixations and of the fruit they'd borne. Convinced of the infallibility of the Bible, steeped in the kind of Southern hatred for the North that Noll had mentioned in his book, Criswell, who could rouse the Spirit to its highest heights with poetic, joyful sermonizing, had also, at times, committed the most evil kind of error. This had to do with the historical tradition he associated himself with. He'd loved calling forth the ghosts of preachers who'd found themselves, at one time or another, in the crosshairs of public opinion, those who'd been rebellious against "the mainstream." Billy Sunday, Dwight L. Moody, Charles Haddon Spurgeon, William Jennings Bryan: these were the names Criswell called the "bright, shining lights" of the faith. For Criswell, Spurgeon was first and foremost the instigator of the "Downgrade Controversy," an event that rocked London in 1887. (After Spurgeon lambasted his fellow preachers for "downgrading" the Bible by seeking to reconcile certain of its passages with evolutionary theories and rationalist phi-losophies, his church had been stripped of its Baptist affiliation.) Bryan was memorialized by Criswell for his role in the Scopes "Monkey" Trial of 1925, the case in which John Scopes, a high school teacher in Dayton, Tennessee, was found guilty of violating a law that forbade the teaching of evolution in public schools. The system won the case but lost the battle of public opinion. Bryan, who had been in former days a congressman and then secretary of state, was one of the most beloved public figures in America at the time. He'd been called to witness on behalf of the prosecu-tion, but he'd done poorly on the stand, stumbling when asked by the defense attorney, Clarence Darrow, about certain Scriptural passages.

"I'm old enough to remember that," Criswell had cried for-lornly from the pulpit, speaking of the humiliation suffered by the great man and, by extension, all Bible-believing Christians. The attorney had asked the hard questions, but he hadn't been half as offensive as the media, which from the start treated the trial as a circus. The most gleefully offensive reports were produced by H. L. Mencken, whose pen was so poisonous it might give today's cul-ture warriors pause. "The so-called religious organizations which now lead the war against the teaching of evolution," he wrote in a dispatch for the Baltimore *Evening Sun,*

are nothing more, at bottom, than conspiracies of the infe-rior man against his betters. They mirror very accurately his congenital hatred of knowledge, his bitter enmity to the man who knows more than he does, and so gets more out of life. Certainly it cannot have gone unnoticed that their membership is recruited, in the overwhelming main, from the lower orders—that no man of any education or other human dignity belongs to them. What they propose to do, at bottom and in brief, is to make the superior man infamous—by mere abuse if it is sufficient, and if it is not, then by law.

Evangelicals were shocked by their treatment during the trial. As George Marsden argued in *Fundamentalism and American Culture*, they'd been used to thinking of themselves as mainstream, in the sense of thoroughly American. Certainly, they'd thought they had the respect, and perhaps even the affection, of their fellow countrymen; that they were the natural leaders of their society (the days of Teddy Roosevelt weren't so far gone; he'd died just six years earlier).

Perhaps it was no wonder, then, that the trial helped to usher in the era of fundamentalist ascendancy in America. It was an era which began quietly. After the trial, Evangelicals started to retreat from the limelight, taking their culture with them. No longer would Evangelical books be published or distributed by "secular" or mainstream houses (most of which had formerly had religious divisions). No longer would Evangelicals be heard on radio channels that were not their own. No longer would they write for mainstream papers. Instead, they'd begun—quietly, in the shadow realm to which they'd been relegated—to build their spiritual armies. It was in the interwar years that the Fellowship of the Burning Heart (Henrietta Mears's organization) and the Washington, DC, Fellowship got their start. Focusing their energies, refining their message, getting back to basics, they'd worked toward making a reentry into the mainstream. Evangelicals did slip from public view after the Scopes Trial, but they never stopped dreaming of—and working toward—a return to center stage, which they finally won (according to Evangelical lore) with the election of Ronald Reagan to the presidency, in 1980.

Criswell was a major player during this era, hitting the pinnacle of his influence in the sixties and seventies. By then, he'd suffered his own humiliations in the press, most notably in the mid-fifties, when he'd been roundly criticized for opposing desegregation—as in the federal-government-enforced desegregation of the races, which he saw as an attack on the liberty, religious and political, of Christians and specifically of Southern Christians. First evolution, then integration; in Criswell's view, they'd both been imposed from the outside by tyrannous force, just as free biblical interpretation had been imposed on Spurgeon, just as Reconstruction had been imposed on the South. "Integration is a thing of idiocy and foolishness," he'd said in an address to the South Carolina Baptist Assembly. "Let them integrate. Let them sit up there in their dirty shirts and make all their fine speeches. But they are all a bunch of infidels, dying from the neck up." A decade later, he'd reversed his stance and apologized ("Never had I been so wrong"), but he never warmed to the press, nor to those "dirty-shirted" Northern intellectuals, whom he continued to denounce in colorful terms.

In other words, while members of any race were welcome in my church from the 1960s (though, it must be said, the congregation long persisted in its whiteness), intellectuals of the liberal variety remained personae non gratae.

Such was Criswell, spiritual guide of my childhood.

∞

Thank heavens, I thought, that Nana had given me a new guide to lead me into adulthood. Perhaps *Utmost* had been pared down to palatability for fundamentalists, but it had retained enough intellectual richness, enough weirdness, to make it compelling for the rest of us, too.

I reached over and placed my hand on my grandmother's, resting for a moment in the sensation of the skin, thin and soft and familiar, draped so delicately now over the bone. I remembered how, in earlier days, she'd reached into pots of boiling water to retrieve eggs and pulled cake pans out of the oven without a mitt. Now she turned, patting my hand where it lay on hers. I'd never once argued with her about politics or religion. It was unthinkable to me that she and I would fight these same stupid wars, picking up the mantles where the men had dropped them, carrying on for them their questionable legacies, fitting ourselves into their camps.

I meditated for a moment on our own fundamentals, how we would define them. There was a word Biddy used over and over again in her diary, whenever she wanted to describe something she'd found beautiful and lasting: "Memorable." "The mail brought me over 100 letters and it was a memorable time before God reading them all," she wrote, referencing the messages of condolence that had poured in after Oswald's death. "It's been a week full of the goodness of the Lord and His renewings and each day is memorable," she wrote, when she was on the mend from the tragedy. And, writing about Oswald's grave, in the British military cemetery in Cairo: "I went to Old Cairo with K . . . and the moments at the grave were memorable." But her most frequent observation was, simply, "It was a memorable day." I'd begun to think that maybe this was the main criterion she'd applied to *Utmost.* She'd selected what had been most memorable to her, her own fundamentals.

"Do you remember, Nana," I said, "when we used to practice

the piano? Every morning at six, every evening at five. Your hands and my hands, together on the keyboard."

My grandmother looked puzzled for a moment, and I repeated the question.

"Oh, yes," she said. "I do."

"That was very nice of you," I told her. "To do that for me."

"Of course, Macy dear," she said. "It was a pleasure."

And she went back to watching the TV.

XXIII

༁

To believe is to commit.

—NOVEMBER 6

Dallas, 2012. The day had arrived, and my mother, my sister, and I had bundled ourselves off, ahead of voting, to the Tuesday morning women's Bible study at the church. I was determined to use the day to continue my experiment in perspective, the perspective Oswald had talked about. I wanted to keep striving to see both the whole picture and the detail, to move between them, allowing new conclusions to displace those I'd formed before, however sure they'd seemed; to take in the full variety of what I encountered and not to jump to generalizations or easy answers. The church, I knew, wasn't synonymous with its pastor. It wasn't synonymous with my own memories of it. It didn't appear the same from the inside as from the outside, from the past as from the present. My own view of late had been obscured by screens—by the pastor's talking head on Fox News, the pastor's talking head during Sunday service. But if Oswald was correct, there was behind the screens a world crowded with individuals, each of them unique. To enter this teeming world was, in part, to lose one's bearings, for everything one encountered there would be the first and last of its kind. But I was determined to move past any unpleasant feelings being unmoored might produce. I wanted to begin to find my anchor in Christ, in His wide-open, all-embracing arms, His ability to hold within Himself every single detail of every single human being who ever was or would be, every being who might have been but wasn't. It was this, His universalism, His ability to love all comers, which defined His character, this that most taught us the need we had of Him in this lifetime. We could hate and fear without help from anyone. To love, as Oswald had said, with Christ's love, not with our own: that was the thing. To love and not to hate; to love and not to fear.

In theory, the Tuesday morning Bible study presented a fine opportunity for exploring the diverse underbelly of the church. It was attended by around a hundred women, and the first part of it took place in a large conference room. Generally, the morning began with coffee and lively chatter, but today as we entered we found the lights dimmed and a video playing on the large screen that hung at the front of the room. As my mother, my sister, and I hunted for a table, I strained to make out the images, which were obscured for the moment by a podium. I could hear "God Bless America" being played faintly in the background, and I could see, in the corner of the screen, a waving American flag.

Finally, we found a spot and sat, and an image flashed onto the screen. It was the head of Ronald Reagan, talking. "I realize," it was saying,

it's fashionable in some circles to believe that no one in government should encourage others to read the Bible,

that we're told that we'll violate the constitutional separation of church and state established by the founding
fathers in the First Amendment. The First Amendment
was not written to protect people and their laws from religious values. It was written to protect those values from
government tyranny.

Reagan went on like this for some time, and I looked around
the room. The women were praying and a few were chatting, but for
the most part an uneasy hush filled the room. Even the president's
voice, echoing out of the past, couldn't break it. I imagined the
question had become, in their minds: What if the religious values of
those in government were no longer Christian, if the holy book
they encouraged others to read wasn't the Bible? It was a question
the nation had been asking and answering for generations, and
would continue asking and answering for generations to come.

I cast my eyes down at the floor, determined not to look again
at the screen, and waited calmly until the video was done.

∞

When the lights came up and the screen went dark, the veil lifted,
and I began to see. To see the faces of the women, the different fash-
ions they wore, the variety of ages and races they represented; then
to look beyond age and race and fashion, taking in each feature:
a nose, an eye, a freckle; then to peer even further beyond, looking for the human soul and personality, which rose up, somehow,
from the inside, wrapping each person, emanating outward. It was
amazing to me how, after only a few moments of this directed
effort, a strong feeling of love and sympathy rose up inside me, a
feeling of interest, of wanting to get to know a stranger.

I'd been attending the Bible study with my mother since my arrival in Dallas a month before and had been surprised at how much I enjoyed it. I enjoyed, first, how serious it was. It was a three-hour, multipart event. The first hour was taken up by a lecture delivered by one of several learned and eloquent female teachers, the second was filled with small-group discussions, and the third with lunch. The members of the study were smart and (to borrow their own word) real. By this I mean that they were concerned with the daily lives of the women in the church and that they worked toward finding practical solutions to the very pressing problems faced by those women, which were much the same as the problems faced by women everywhere: work, money, children, absent men, present men. When, for instance, my younger sister, who was a single mother, had needed new furniture after a fire in her apartment, the women of the Bible study had come to her aid.

The teaching this semester was focused on women in the Bible, and the discussions that followed were personal. That is, they dealt in specifics as well as abstractions, in the quotidian as well as the epic. They aimed to bring understanding and peace rather than the anxiety that arises from being handed a problem as vast, ill-defined, and out of one's own hands as the possibly near end of the world. Whether or not the end was coming, babies needed to be fed—they needed to be fed right up to the moment of their rapture. Apocalypse was fine for Sundays; Tuesdays didn't have time.

I viewed the women of First Baptist as warriors. It was true that women were still not allowed to speak in the sanctuary, and that there was still a deep interest in upholding "traditional values," particularly when it came to gender roles. But things at the church had changed in certain regards. For instance, you'd never hear a sermon like one Criswell had given, in 1986, on the topic of teen suicide, in which he declared that

> the most tragic development in modern life is the working mother. I can understand why she goes to work. I can understand why she has to work. I'm not decrying the mother who gives herself to some kind of a paying job; most of the time she is forced into it. I'm just saying that one of the tragedies that is overwhelming modern life is that working mother.

You wouldn't have heard it for many reasons, among them the fact that there were now many more working mothers in the congregation, and alienating them by suggesting they might kill their children wouldn't have been good for business. There was still much anxiety expressed over the crisis of masculinity among Christian men, just as there had been in my childhood, just as there had been in Oswald's day. The difference today, as far as women were concerned, was that the man hoping to assert himself over his wife—claiming as his justification a Bible passage instructing wives to "submit" to their husbands—might face open rebellion, the wife having assembled an arsenal of her own at Bible study.

The lesson this morning was a case in point. It concerned Abigail, whose story was given in the first book of Samuel. Abigail had been married to a man, Nabal, who was described as treating his servants "harshly." The teacher, who introduced herself as an ob-gyn nurse, had studied ancient Hebrew. In the Hebrew, she informed us, the word *harsh* meant "abusive," and from its use, the teacher said, we could infer that Nabal had been abusive to his wife. The drama concerned the arrival on Nabal's lands of David, who was passing through with an army of four hundred men. David had sent a greeting to Nabal, and had requested food and water for his men, but Nabal had refused him. David, becoming enraged, had told his men to draw their swords and prepare to kill everyone in Nabal's house who "pisseth against the wall," i.e., every male.

When Nabal's servants learned of the plan, they ran to the house to tell Abigail. It was up to her to do something, they said, because her husband was so hard that "a man cannot speak to him." Abigail sprang into action. She put food for David's men onto the back of a donkey and went to deliver it. The moment David came into view, she "fell onto her face" and begged him not to commit the massacre. He was in the right, she said, but she knew he was a holy man. See how the Lord had sent her to stop him? She would not want him, in the future, while he was trying to enjoy being king, to have his mind weighed down with regret at having "shed blood causeless."

David was won over. Blessed be the Lord, he said, for sending her to him; and "blessed be thy advice, and blessed be thou, which hast kept me this day from coming to shed blood." He sent her back to Nabal in peace.

That night, Nabal threw a wild party and got drunk. Abigail waited until it was over, then confessed what she had done. The shock of the news sent him into a kind of coma: "When the wine was gone out of Nabal, and his wife had told him these things . . . his heart died within him, and he became as a stone." Ten days later, he was entirely dead, and Abigail became David's wife (or rather one of his wives) and rode away with him.

The message our teacher took from Abigail's story was this: a woman should not be passive. Abigail, she said, had been faced with two "very powerful and fearsome men." She'd been abused by one of them. Yet, she didn't "cower in fear" or "sit by passively." She hatched a plan, executed it, and found her voice. Her speech, the teacher said, was one "of masterful rhetoric. It's one of the longest speeches in the Bible, and it's given by a woman."

Then the teacher made the implications of her message explicit: "Ladies," she said, "if you are in a marriage that is abusive, physically or even verbally, or if your children are in danger because of an abusive parent, God does not call you to be passive. Being submissive does not mean enabling sin. Please do not leave this place today until you've talked to our director and learned how we can help you."

Later, in our small-group discussion, the women, who were all, save me, of my mother's generation, reflected on how times had changed. Now, they said, even the pastor himself taught that men were to love their wives as Christ loved the church—to serve them, to be willing to die for them.

"I remember," said one woman,

how it used to be. Now there are options, but before . . . I've seen it, several times, people in ministry, members of this church, women who had husbands who beat them over the heads with their Bibles, saying, "Submit, submit, submit." One woman, I bought her underwear one time. He wouldn't buy her underwear. She sewed and made things, and sold them, so that she could have some money of her own, but he would take her money. Or he would badger her until she gave it to him. And this is a man in ministry. It happens a lot in ministry.

So it still happened: they acknowledged that. From an outsider's perspective, the fact that it still happened, that men still used

Scripture to justify abuse, no doubt appeared damning of the culture as a whole. But, as I'd learned in my adventures in the wider world, there were men in every culture who justified taking advantage of women, sometimes while professing (and perhaps believing) themselves to be great feminists. Today, I'd been afforded a view from within, and the view from within this particular culture was, to me, encouraging. Now, the women here were able to seek recourse *inside* their religious community. Now, they could interpret the Bible as an instrument for fighting back against oppression, as a justification for speaking out. The women's reading of Scripture had not stood still over the years. It had evolved alongside their shifting status in society. *They* had altered it. And they'd gone further still. Wedding action to idea, they'd built a ministry that helped women financially, legally, and emotionally.

It was more, I realized this morning, than I'd ever done in my lifetime. As the discussion drew to a close, a new thought crossed my mind. I thought about what I might have been a part of if I'd stayed in Dallas, if I hadn't fled all those years before. Perhaps I might have helped to build something useful, to work out what God had worked in in a concrete, purposeful way. Or, not staying, I might have found a way of pursuing such work in New York. As Oswald said, it was necessary to be of use where you were, for you certainly couldn't be of use where you weren't.

∽

My vision had cleared during the lesson and the discussion, but as we made our way to lunch, it began to cloud again. I found myself in step with Cynthia, a woman in her fifties. She was gripping her Bible against her chest, and, when I said hello, I saw that she had tears in her eyes.

"I'm just so worried," she said. "My husband thinks it's all over—the country. It's done. There's no way out."

"Really?" I said. "Because of health care?"

"Because of everything," she said.

I nodded, uncertain of how to reply. I had a few facts in my mind, as I was sure she had in hers, but I also thought that any debate we might have on the subject would be mostly fruitless. I still didn't know how to argue across the divide, so I simply took Cynthia's hand and told her I was sorry she was feeling so sad.

"Are you really moving to France?" Cynthia asked, and I told her that I was.

"Maybe," she said, dabbing her nose with a Kleenex, "you can straighten them out. They hate us, you know."

We came to the lunchroom, where I was surprised to see a man on the stage, holding a microphone. He'd come, he was saying, to lead the prayers for the day, since it was a special day. It was Election Day. After we were all seated, he asked us to bow our heads and close our eyes, and then he said his prayer:

Father, help us to remember that no man, no political party, no structure, can circumvent Your will or operate around what You have already decided. Father, help us to know that You're in control, that You love us, that You have provided a way for us through Jesus Christ. . . . Father, we know that that's where the real hope comes from, that's where real change comes from. So, Father, help us to be an influence this day, to influence other people at polling stations. Father, help them to see something different in us, not by the words we speak, but by our countenance, by the way that we exude who You are through our eyes, Father, help us to truly be people who honor You through our lives. Father, we pray for the lost among us. We pray for all those who are going to encounter with their friends and neighbors and family those people who do not know You, who don't have the hope that we possess, their hope lies in a vote, in a ballot box, and, Father, we know that that is so fleeting.

The prayer continued, and I looked up at the man, confused. It was a prayer I myself might have said (minus the bit about influencing people at the ballot box). It was confusing, because I would have said it for the people surrounding me at that very moment. If the church's hope wasn't in the ballot box, what was all the fuss about? I bowed my head to darken the room, looking in. That wasn't the question. The question was: What was all *my* fuss about?

The problem, I reflected, was that we were all so profoundly averse to change—when it was in a direction we didn't like. We were all unwilling to fling ourselves into the river, to lose ourselves in God's rapids. We were frightened of the giant, shifting, shrinking globe, the ever-expanding universe. We had not thought deeply about what the nature of reality was or what it was saying to us; what God was saying to us, bringing us always into contact with new, unfathomed cultures and peoples, new ideas. We imagined that He was telling us to throw up walls or to go on the offensive. We easily forgot His instruction to turn the other cheek, to love our neighbors as ourselves, to refuse to worry.

And we looked backward. We longed for Reagan, or for screen-free churches; we longed for a simpler time in the religion, or for a more complex one. We entrenched ourselves, and this, as Oswald (and his entire generation) had learned the hard way, was always a losing proposition. "Whenever the reminiscent is made the appeal," he wrote, "spontaneous originality goes and it is a battle against time to maintain a monument."

Just then, my mother reached over and took my hand, squeezing it, as she'd always done before we'd started a meal.

"Lunch," she said.

The prayer had ended. We raised our heads and began to eat.

XXIV

༄

Restate to yourself what you believe,
then do away with as much of it as possible.

—NOVEMBER 25

Dallas, 2012. In the afternoon, I took my daily walk down the block to my grandmother's house. My *visa de long séjour* had finally arrived from the French embassy, and I'd bought a ticket to Paris, for a flight departing in a week. I was still nervous—how difficult would it be to begin life over again?—but also, ultimately, convinced that I could make no other choice. A line of Whitman's had been running through my mind all week: "Only what nobody denies is so." There was this to say for love (the love one person felt for another): nobody could deny that it was so. Did I know the ultimate purpose of the love I felt? Did I know God's plan for drawing me into certain company? I did not. All I knew was that, for me, for now, only France was so.

I was interested in fundamental things at the moment, in that which persisted once the rest had been stripped away. I'd reached the final chapter of Oswald's story, and I wanted to get down to its essentials, having piled so much on during the course of my journey. Indeed, I'd learned so much about *Utmost* that I had to admit I'd not known it at all before. Or rather that I'd known it, used it, in a different way. It still framed my days, still filled me with a sense of urgency, but one that was quite removed from the one I'd felt before. For so long, it had been a river offering to sweep me into a dazzling future reality. Now, it was a challenge to remain rooted in the present, and to begin watching and acting inside this present moment from a higher perspective. "How are we going to have the love," Oswald asked, that has "no self-interest, no sensitiveness to 'pokes,' the love that is not provoked, that thinketh no evil, is always kind?" How were we to learn not to worry, not to fear? We had to get the viewpoint, not the one that was "near the highest" but the one that was "*the* highest." It was a lifelong process, he wrote, to be pursued "every day, bit by bit."

I felt myself ready to begin again with Oswald, but not before I'd finished my present task. What was the essential *Utmost*? Who was its author? The answers lay, I thought, somewhere between where Oswald left off and Biddy began, between how I'd read the book in the past and how I read it now.

I arrived at my grandmother's house and knocked on the door but received no response. I decided to wait, and went to sit beneath the big pecan tree in the yard, where I leaned back, turning my thoughts first to Biddy and the question of her authorship.

❧

Biddy Chambers had begun her new life's work shortly after Oswald's death, typing up notes of his sermons for newsletters and pamphlets while she was still living in Egypt. After her return to England, she'd continued typing and mailing out sermons in the Bible Training College newsletter, which she and Oswald had started in London years before. Soon, a committed group of friends and advisers had formed around her, and by the 1930s they were meeting regularly to discuss printing, distribution, and translation. The group, whose members rotated slowly as the years passed, was incorporated in London in 1942 as the Oswald Chambers Publications Association. The official minutes of its meetings stretched back to 1934, the year before *Utmost* appeared in the United States. At a meeting held that year, a letter "from New York asking for permission to print the books in USA" was read aloud:

Mr. Griffin suggested that a letter should be sent informing them that the matter of printing in USA was under consideration in the meantime offering them 530 copies of a paper edition of Sermon on the Mount at 8 *d* each + postage. The books to be despatched on receipt of the remittance.
Unanimously agreed.

A few quirks defined the OCPA from the beginning. The first was Biddy's insistence that the author of Oswald's work was the Holy Spirit. It wasn't really Oswald, and it certainly wasn't her. All proceeds from sales were to be poured back into printing and distributing more books, in keeping with Oswald's desire not to profit financially from the Spirit's work. In Egypt, where he'd sometimes had booklets of his sermons and lessons printed, he'd determined to let God raise funds as He would. "I have decided not to sell the booklet or any of my other booklets," he wrote in his diary.

Eager to honor Oswald's wishes fully, Biddy, for years after his death, worked second jobs to support herself and Kathleen. Even after the books had become best sellers, she drew only a very small salary (so small, in fact, that Kathleen was obliged to borrow funds for Biddy's hospital bills when her mother reached old age). She also insisted that no money ever be invested, feeling that profiting from interest was completely against the principles set forth in the books. In a similar vein, the books were never to be advertised, or marketed to any group in particular. In 1963, three years before her death, the minutes revealed that her stance on the final point was unwavering. A suggestion was made that year that "in order to meet the ideas of the younger generation, our Publications should be modernised in format, revised in language and condensed into four volumes; also that a change in our methods of printing, publishing and distributing should be considered":

The feeling of the meeting was most strongly AGAINST any such radical alterations. Mrs Chambers stated that it was contrary to Mr Chambers' views to divide people into categories and expressed the wish that NO "editing" of the existing texts should be made.

But that was while Biddy was still alive. In the seventies, the secretary recorded a slump in sales, as well as the fact that many titles had begun to fall out of print. In the eighties, as Evangelicalism began to make its return to center stage in the United States, and as the economy began to pick up, very un-Biddy-like ideas began to surface in the minutes. Her notion had always been that "God as Sovereign would watch over the books as He had done through the years." Now, machinations were in place. From 1982:

The Chairman suggested that Council members give thought to the fact that by 1992 any existing copyright of MY UTMOST FOR HIS HIGHEST would run out.

Therefore some kind of revision or up-dating needs to be undertaken, in order to retain copyright.

In fact, the minutes had much to say about copyright, beginning in 1967, when it was realized that fifty years had already passed since Oswald's death. In the nineties, the association had consulted a lawyer, informing him of how the books had been produced. The lawyer had drafted an opinion, arguing that it was in fact Biddy who'd written them, despite her refusal over the years ever to have another name appear beside Oswald's on the books. At the very least, this lawyer thought, she was the joint author, and at the very, very least, she was Oswald's legal representative, and thus the copyright holder. But really (he went on), it was the OCPA who was the owner, since Biddy had "intended in equity that at all times that rights vest in the Association." Here, then, was another way in which Biddy was the "author" of *Utmost:* she was legally the author, or at least the person who'd signed over Oswald's life's work to an association.

The 1992 expiration date derived from complicated arrangements the OCPA had made over the years with various American publishing houses, particularly Dodd, Mead & Company, before Discovery House agreed to take over. In a 1989 proposal, Discovery House detailed their goals:

Our plan for Utmost:
Immediately issue a news release advising the Christian world, in general, and the Christian publishing community in particular, of the protected copyright status of Utmost, of DHP's posture as the U.S. representative of the Oswald Chambers Publishing Association, and as the successor to Dodd Mead as the U.S. publisher of Utmost. . . .

Begin developing, in cooperation with the Association, a new updated and revised edition to be issued in
1992, incorporating the NKJV text, with new copyright
protection, and endorsed as the "new authorized edition."

Possibly gift and large print editions of the "original"
in 1990 and an audio edition in 1990 or 1991. . . .

A major marketing strategy to develop the book club,
direct mail and "audio book" markets for Utmost.

It did indeed come to pass that a revised edition was put out
in 1992—an edition which would remain under copyright much
longer than anything Oswald or Biddy ever touched. In addition
to Oswald's name, the name of the editor, James Reimann, was
printed on the cover. The OCPA, assuming a watchdog role, did
continue operating as a nonprofit, its volunteers faithfully distributing the group's cut of sales to publishing endeavors in the developing world, and as grants to writers and educational institutions.
But, for the most part, Biddy's original intentions for the books—
that they be distributed as freely as possible, with no advertising, marketing, or change to the original text—hadn't stood the
test of time. There were many editions now, with many different
names attached to them, all under the control of Discovery House,
which had acquired "global" distribution rights. In 1970, David W.
Lambert, a longtime member of the OCPA, had put out a kind of
sequel to *Utmost* called *Still Higher for the Highest.* After the death,
in 2003, of David Bloom, an NBC reporter and *Utmost* devotee, a
special "commemorative edition" had been issued in his name. A
"teen" edition from 2002 involved truncated entries and "bullet
points to enable the reader to remember what he or she had read."

Were developments like these just the cost of doing business
in the modern literary climate? Was something similar bound

to happen to any book with a long shelf life? Perhaps no written work could hope to survive its own time without some kind of reinterpretation.

From the OCPA minutes, it was clear that the group had always struggled to address such issues, given Biddy's determination to keep Oswald's work unchanged. One sensed that there had always been a bit of defensiveness over the books, a wariness of who got to own them, control them, and bestow upon others the right of using them. The OCPA had imagined itself as a safeguard from its very beginnings. "The O.C. Publications Committee must be kept intact. It will not do to rely on religious Publishers to keep the O.C. books in circulation as it takes their fancy or suits their business interests," an early entry read. Worry over the quality of foreign translations was common, as was worry over licensing. In 1988, a proposal by a Pentecostalist organization in Florida to put out their own editions of some of the books was rebuffed. The committee "did not feel free to publish our books . . . under a charismatic umbrella," but wanted "to remain 'neutral' so that our books are acceptable to all kinds of people and in all camps." There was a mention of the difficulty of controlling copyright after the dawn of the Internet (among other things, people tweeted Oswald very frequently), and a decision that writers would have to pay to quote for commercial projects.

I'd met the board of the OCPA on occasion, as well as editors from Discovery House. They knew what a hot property they had in *Utmost*—the daily reading was the most visited page on the publisher's website—and they were proud that their devotion to the text had helped to keep it alive. Still, several members of the OCPA expressed a feeling that things had veered a bit too far from Biddy's wishes ("You can buy Oswald Chambers tea towels,"

Rob Wykes, a longtime board member, had said, half-joking, half-lamenting), as well as a feeling that there was little they could do about it, now that they'd licensed the rights to Discovery House. Yet neither did Discovery House have a sense of total control: on one occasion, an editor there opined to me that the OCPA probably wouldn't give me permission to use the words "my utmost for his highest" in the subtitle of my own book, after I'd mentioned that I was thinking of using it.

I was confused, since I knew that titles weren't protected by copyright law, but I didn't press the issue. Some time later, while looking up something about Oswald online, I noticed in the search results a symbol next to the phrase "My Utmost for His Highest": ®. Then, I realized: titles can't be copyrighted, but brands can be trademarked. A quick search through the US trademark database revealed that in 2004 "My Utmost for His Highest" had been trademarked for use on "pre-recorded CDs, DVDs, audio tapes and video tapes featuring religious and inspirational material; [computer screensaver software;] and computer software for use in communicating religious material [and decorative magnets]. . . . Calendars, daily planners, decorative seals for paper or stationery; [bookmarks, postcards,] and stationery."

I wondered what Oswald and Biddy would have made of it. Biddy had declared Oswald's work to be the property of the Spirit alone (following Oswald's wishes). And they'd both been extremely free when it came to borrowing and recycling others' words. Indeed, the phrase in question, "My Utmost for His Highest," wasn't really original to Oswald. His phrase was a twist on "my utmost for the highest," the motto of the Victorian symbolist painter G. F. Watts. ("Watts is . . . always true to his noble aspiration, 'My utmost for the highest,'" a contemporary wrote.) Oswald had quoted Watts in a sermon, elsewhere putting his own spin on the phrase, and Biddy had apparently thought it would make a good title. It was the watchword of one artist appropriated by two others. It was a phrase which perfectly elided Oswald's old life as a painter and his new life as a saint, Biddy's old life as a secretary and her new life as an author. It was a phrase that moved through history, through minds, through canvases, through books. What it wasn't was a phrase that belonged to a twenty-first-century institution—except, of course, that it did.

Most of Oswald's books were still institutionalized, but that was destined to change. Already, digital copies floated around the Web, free to all, and they would eventually enter the public domain. But I wondered how much of *Utmost*'s success could be chalked up to the fact that for so long it hadn't been free, that it had always been closely protected. Few books had had so much attention lavished upon them for so long; few had been so propped up by devoted institutions. I might never have come across it without their efforts. In the end, I found it difficult to fault editors and publishers for being proprietary about Oswald's words, and even more difficult to fault them for monkeying around with his text, against Biddy's wishes. This was precisely what she herself had done, to the benefit of all.

∾

So that was the essential *Utmost:* a collaboration, more than a century old, of writers, editors, publishers, and Spirit. Now my thoughts turned to Oswald, to identifying *his* essential message, the one which would represent his thinking best. I thought it was one he'd developed only very late in life, toward the end of the war. At the start of the war, Oswald had been happy to see people yanked from their lives of "pleasure-seeking and frivolity." Having been through his own, private hell in his twenties, and considering the experience fundamental to the development of Christ in his soul, he thought the suffering caused by war would benefit those who hadn't yet undergone such a trial. Perhaps he also believed himself to be inoculated against any nightmares lurking in the desert. Certainly, he did not place himself in the same category as those who needed "instant removal" to eternity. He thought of himself as already dwelling inside the eternal kingdom, where Christ-in-him lived sin-free.

But after he'd been in the desert for a year, Oswald increasingly found himself struggling alongside the men he was charged with guiding. His work was difficult: counseling soldiers headed to their deaths, trying to explain to them why God allowed such barbarism, trying to account for a war which struck many as absurd. In late 1916, hungry for new answers, he began to make a study of the book of Job. It reminded him of Ibsen's plays, he wrote in his diary, for its "clear-sightedness." In it, tragedy was allowed to swell to its full dimensions, to become a blackness which no light penetrated, from which there seemed to be no escape. It was the book, he thought, which most spoke to the conditions of war and to the character of the God who allowed them.

It was in this wartime study of Job that Oswald truly came into his Realism. He'd never preached much about social issues; he'd never tackled economic or racial or gender inequality, the cruelty of men to men. Shining light into the dark corners of his civilization hadn't interested him. He'd focused instead on the corruption of the whole civilizing project, viewing all men equally—as sinners in need of redemption. Now, he was confronted with a strong dividing line, between "us" and "them," "heroes" and "villains." He was confronted with a God who didn't always grant victory to the home team, a God who seemed at times to be immoral.

Oswald began to lecture on Job in a series of talks which would eventually become a book called *Baffled to Fight Better,* after a line of Robert Browning's (the proofs were at the printer's when Oswald died). God, Oswald said in these lectures, was a God of order and morality but also of "permissive will": He permitted His children to suffer. God was not synonymous with His blessings, and, though He was good, He didn't always spare the faithful. Humans of all stripes were in the same boat. God didn't care about national allegiances. In His eyes, there was no "us" and "them." It wasn't "rational that Christian nations should be at war," Oswald said, but "if God began to punish the nations for their sins there would be no nation left on the face of the earth." The basis of things wasn't rational but rather wild and tragic. This was true in both the natural world (it was "Nature, red in tooth and claw," Oswald wrote, quoting Tennyson) and the human character, which was inherently sinful and corrupt. Unless a person could look these facts, the blackest facts of life, full in the face and not doubt God— following Job's example—he did not know God. It was necessary to face them, Oswald said, and to think on them; horror didn't excuse a man from the burden of trying to make rational sense of things.

What did this mean for the soldiers? It meant first, Oswald said, that they didn't need to be blindly positive or optimistic about the situation they found themselves in. They didn't need to apologize or argue for God, or accept the platitudes forced upon them by "priggish" ministers. The thinking man's reaction to tragedy would always be despair, and "God never blames a man for despair." "Let the day perish wherein I was born," Job cried. "My days are swifter than a weaver's shuttle, and are spent without hope. . . . Therefore I will not refrain my mouth; I will speak in the anguish of my spirit; I will complain in the bitterness of my soul."

But Realism of this kind didn't mean that a person was *required* to set aside belief in God, merely to leave behind former beliefs about who God was. The reason men lost faith, Oswald thought, was that they found it impossible to swallow the absurd, unthinking versions of God preached in most pulpits. Throw away the pulpit, Oswald advised. Who was God? God was He Who Would Ultimately Triumph. Everything before this ultimate triumph was subject to chaos; everything tested faith. Yet faith often remained—faith seemed to *want* to remain. The believer's greatest fear wasn't his own demise, Oswald said, but rather that "his Hero won't get through, that God will not be able to clear His character." What the book of Job demonstrated was that God always eventually cleared His character and that it was okay to keep believing He would, even when it was impossible to believe anything else. Job hadn't seen any way out of his predicament or his suffering. His rational mind, following the logic conveyed to him by his very rational friends, had led him to despair, yet he'd kept the faith. "Nothing is *taught* in the Book of Job," Oswald said. "But there is a deep, measured sense of Someone understanding."

What was this sense? It was, Oswald thought, grace. Gracious God had, in fact, provided a way out, whether we felt it or knew it or not. To Job, who'd lived in the world of the Old Testament, God had offered reparations; to those living in the New, He offered redemption. The Cross came from the outside, breaking into the chaos, creating a highway to heaven that ran the length of its beams. This was reality: everything stripped away, only blackness remaining, and there, within it, the truth that one wasn't alone, that there was something beyond. Through faith, we were allowed to grasp it, but it wasn't enacted by or dependent upon our faith. It was a gift. What was the attitude and tone of the believer who knew that it was only through grace that he believed? It was gratitude and humility of the most profound sort. It was a stunned realization that he had no right to stand in judgment of anyone else.

It was in these lectures that Oswald gave his fullest account of what could be stripped away without harming God: tradition, authority, ritual, nation, church, family, creed, and, finally, mind itself. Oswald's vision of religion was so stripped down that it might properly be called postmodern, were it not for the single, luminous object providing the way out of the cul-de-sac. We were "not saved by believing," Oswald said. We were saved by the Cross.

∾

I'd come to the conclusion that this idea was Oswald's most important while I was nearing the end of Biddy's story. With this message—the message that God transcended everything, even our own minds and their beliefs about Him—Oswald had reached out to Biddy from the grave, offering her a reassurance in her final days which might otherwise have eluded her.

The story of Biddy's final days came through her daughter, Kathleen. In her mother's old age, Kathleen recalled, Biddy ceased to be in her right mind and began to believe herself separated from God. She had an "inexplicable" illness, Kathleen said. "She wasn't senile, she didn't have Alzheimer's disease, she was mentally ill. Mentally obsessed with guilt and separation from God." It was an extreme enough condition that Kathleen was unable to care for

Biddy by herself: "she became completely unmanageable." It was shocking, because Biddy had always "been somebody who had never for half a second questioned what God allowed to happen, ever." Kathleen's guess about the illness was that it was something the devil had brought, to try to obstruct the work that the books were doing. "I think the value to God of the books was the measure of my mother's real, appalling illness."

Bitterly, Kathleen recalled fighting with the board of the OCPA for funds to pay for Biddy's treatment. Eventually, they'd given them to her, but only, she said, "in incredibly bad grace," one of the members telling her that it would "be the end of the books." Kathleen had retorted that if that happened, it would be God's will, and that she couldn't imagine Oswald would have wanted the money used in any other way but for her mother's care.

Stays in institutions and bouts of electroshock therapy provided only temporary relief. For brief periods of time, Biddy had gone to live with two members of the OCPA board, Eric and Mary Pearson. Mary, whom I'd met in London the previous year, described Biddy's stays in harrowing terms. "To give Kathleen a break, we had [Biddy] staying with us for a few weeks toward the end. But we had to watch her all the time, because she would just go. Out the door. And a couple of times, she was going out with practically nothing on. And I said, 'You'll get cold.' Fortunately, I saw her, and I managed to get her back home again. But she just said to me, 'I am so unworthy.'"

There was one light in the darkness. In Biddy's very last years, after she'd come home for good, Kathleen read the Bible to her regularly. Biddy "found something in Isaiah which she cottoned on to and held on to for such a long time. It was a verse she didn't know that was in Isaiah." Isaiah 32:17: "The effect of righteousness shall be quietness and assurance for ever." Did it matter that quietness and assurance had fled from her, as her mind deteriorated? Did it mean that her righteousness had been called into question by God? That her salvation was at stake? It did not, said Oswald. As Kathleen had suggested, it was simply the work of the devil, doing his worst to one of the best, before her final release.

∾

Here, I'd come to the final piece of the *Utmost* puzzle: Kathleen. The jolly, skeptical, sharp-tongued woman who'd transmitted so much of Oswald's story was destined to remain as much of an enigma as her mother. Kathleen had led an unusual life. She'd never married, nor had she ever lived apart from Biddy, save for a period in adolescence when she went away to boarding school. She'd detested traveling and seldom left Britain. After training to become a nurse, she'd worked in the medical field for a time, caring for soldiers during the Second World War. Later, she'd joined the family business, tending to the publication of the books, and even helping to edit one herself: *Run Today's Race,* a collection of quotes, one for each day of the year, which Biddy had begun before falling ill.

It was evident to me, reading through the statements Kathleen had made in interviews, that she'd been proud of her parents' legacy and eager to carry it on. But she'd also wanted it noted that her unique position—as the daughter of two intensely spiritual people, people who'd helped to redefine Christianity in the twentieth century—was not without its challenges. "It's very difficult to be the daughter of people like that," she said in 1991. "In one way it's quite a handicap, because for a long time I didn't realize that I only knew *about* God. It's very difficult when you hear God talked

339

Oswald, Biddy, and Kathleen at the
Bible Training College in London, in 1915

about your whole life and God talked about sort of easily. . . . He
becomes a part of your life like He's part of your parents' life."

Indeed, Kathleen's spiritual journey had mirrored her parents'.
Eventually, she said, she'd had to find her way past what she'd been
taught about God, and to arrive at God Himself. The revelation

had come to her while she was working at a hospital in London, and it had to do with a young mother who'd recently lost her baby. Kathleen had loved children and had wanted nothing more than to have some of her own. But it was not to be. And there was something in this—the dissolving of our most cherished dreams, the failure of God to honor them—that had led to her spiritual awakening. She related the story like this:

It sort of hits you full tilt the kind of God you have got to equate to what you see happen. You see a woman who's waited all her life to have a baby. She's had miscarriages and she has a baby and it dies and she can't have any more children. You see old people who are just breathing and living day after day after day and you have to look after them and there's never any hope they'll ever be any different. Death could come for them and it wouldn't make any difference, it would be a release for them. For this woman, with her baby, death came. It all seems wrong. The God you thought was a God of love, you've got to realize what kind of God you've got to face up to. . . .

I realized that I didn't know God at all and I had to read the Bible and everything and know God in a completely different angle and a different way. My father had come to know God in his way and my mother in her way. I had to come to know God in my way and realize that as my father said, "God has a will and a permissive will," and you have to understand that He's there whatever He allows to happen. It may not be His will that certain things happen, but if He allows them to happen, He's still there with you in it. You can't ask God to protect you. You just have to ask Him and know that He's going to be there and there's never any place you can go to where He's not there.

It was interesting to me that Kathleen had wound up with the same sort of unblinking realism about God that her parents had embraced. I wondered if she'd absorbed it through their teachings, or if this was where any honest seeker was bound to arrive once the rosy glass had cracked, once the world, in all its imperfection, had been faced full on. How, after such a rude awakening, did one continue in faith? How did one worship once the old ways had become suspect? *Where* did one worship when one's original church had lost its sheen? The questions were particularly compelling in the case of the Chambers family, whose members had each combined a distrust of institutionalized religion with a dazzling ability to build and maintain religious institutions, their skepticism matched only by their glee and determination.

The answer, I thought, lay in *Utmost.* Not in the text of the book, but in the way the book was intended to function, as a daily ritual performed privately but also as part of a society: it was a book to share with friends. Against grand, abstract forces—churches, religions, nations, civilizations—the Chamberses embraced the intimate, the personal, and the communal.

This struck me powerfully as I thought over the final years of Oswald's and Biddy's lives. In the desert in 1917, Oswald was striving to strip life to its essential components—tragedy, sin, and redemption—for the benefit of soldiers. In London, thirty years later, Biddy was striving to keep a nonprofit publishing endeavor afloat, for the benefit of all. Both by this point had acquired a vivid awareness of the haphazard; both had known despair and exhaustion. Each day, they worked hard, and when they weren't working, they made themselves available to others. The doors to their homes were always open, and a steady stream of guests poured through them. They never ate dinner or took tea alone. In the mornings, they kept up with a steady flow of correspondence: family and friends living afar required tending, too. There was no such thing as a private life for the saint, Biddy wrote and Oswald said. They talked to each other constantly.

The energy for their lives was generated in the mornings, before breakfast, before correspondence. Each morning, Oswald and Biddy arose before dawn. Oswald walked from his tent to a high sandy hill in the desert; Biddy walked to the roof of a nearby building. They watched the sunrise while they communed with God. They recorded every sunrise—"daily poems of eternal worship," Oswald called them—in their minds, and very often in their journals. The power of the sunrise would have to last them through the rest of the day. "Ah, the dawn!" Oswald wrote one morning,

> Some mysterious vast sprite tumbled a myriad amount of giant pale pink rose petals over the most delicate azure bowl of the night, and as the petals got near the horizon, a golden glory transfigured them into isles of translucent heavenliness, and among all the rose petals was the weeest pure tip of a clear moon.

After the dawn, they would read from a daily devotional. Things were so difficult that, as their friends would later remember, it was necessary to focus the mind on the few precious gifts God gave each day to keep from going mad. It was necessary to obey His natural cycles, to read the words He sent through His children. Nature and literature: in the end, these were the things which quieted the Chamberses' minds. But only nature and literature confronted ritually, as prayers. They loved a passage by the eighteenth-century French Catholic theologian and mystic Jean Nicolas Grou:

> Give a fixed daily time to God, during which His Presence is our sole occupation, and in which we listen to Him and talk with Him, not with the lips, but in the heart. This is real mental prayer. . . . It is well to select such books as touch your heart, and rouse it to fervour. . . . Your spiritual reading should be in some respects like a meditation, that is to say, you should watch for God's action within you, and pause when you feel your heart touched by what you read.

They liked this idea; they lived this idea, and yet, when it came time to preach and to write, they did not focus on this idea. Instead, they embedded it in a technology, a book broken down into daily readings, which shepherded people into a specific way of life, a specific mode of communing with God.

∾

I'd started my journey with a few questions in mind: Why did my grandmother and I, so different in our ideological, political, and intellectual outlooks, both love *Utmost* so much? Why, if we were both sincere Christians (and Christians of the *Utmost* variety), was there such a divide between us? How could it be closed?

The questions had come to me first in this very place, in the garden my grandmother had tended every day for thirty years and where I now sat alone, waiting for her to return. She was not here at the moment, but neither was she absent; I could not sit here without feeling her presence, around me and inside me. She was in my mind and my matter both; she was in the soil that held me, the pecan tree that had fed me, the thoughts that arose. If there was a definitive answer to the questions I'd asked, a definitive solution to the problem of our cultural estrangement, our differing conceptions of reality, I'd not yet discovered it; indeed, I'd begun to think, with Oswald, that problems of this kind could never be completely resolved this side of heaven. But I had found a satisfying way of thinking on the issue, one related to my grandmother's garden.

There was a passage in Virginia Woolf's memoirs which captured it. Her life since she was a child, Woolf wrote, had passed in a "cotton wool." She could not see reality clearly, could not understand the relationship of one thing to another, one part to the whole. Then one day she received "a sudden violent shock":

> I was looking at the flower bed by the front door; "That is the whole," I said. I was looking at a plant with a spread of leaves; and it seemed suddenly plain that the flower itself was a part of the earth; that a ring enclosed what was the flower; and that was the real flower; part earth; part flower.

In his diary, Oswald copied out a passage along the same theme. It was by the Scottish theologian John Alexander Hutton. "The look of Jesus," Hutton wrote,

> is never a thing by itself, but always something which is in harmony with all that is best in our life and in our memories. Happy are they for whom, down in their hearts, there is some one, or the memory of some one . . . that even to

look across at such an one, or to throw back their minds towards some sweet intimateness of the spirit, is alone enough to end the strife, to banish a legion of devils, to settle the matter in favour of God, and purity, and honour! Happy are they, and safe, upon the whole, who have thus God woven into the very texture of their souls, so that in some hour of stress the Divine strands will hold! Happy are they and safe who have memories, reminiscences, past contacts with Christ hidden in their lives.

This, finally, was the essence of *Utmost*'s importance to me. Whenever I thought of it, I thought of my grandmother, and also of my mother. I thought of seeing them sitting high up in their beds at night, reading and praying, powerful in their devotion. The feeling I'd had as a child, watching them, was the feeling I still got each time I opened the book.

"I am ever grateful," Oswald wrote in his diary, "when I can associate those I love with books which will last as long as my mind will, it forms a fine kingdom on the inside, unassailable by anything external."

There were also others I associated with the book, others who dwelled inside my *Utmost* kingdom. Sherri, Holamon, Stefan, Munro, the White Witch, Mr. Beaver, Peter, Rhonda, Tom, my preacher, the mountaineer. They were entwined with its story, as it had unfolded over the course of my life. This was a curious thing, since some of these people had been nonbelievers, and some had even been combative. Yet they were part of the book, inscribed permanently in its pages. It was only when I thought of *Utmost* with them inside it, rather than struggling to separate it out into a category designated "religion," that I thought clearly. It had to do,

I suspected, with reaching the right perspective or mode of seeing, the one most fully open to and attuned to reality.

∾

And this, I realized, rising from my spot beneath the pecan tree, was as close as I could get to *Utmost.* I could draw no closer to it than Oswald and Biddy and Kathleen and the parade of editors, translators, publishers, and readers who had carried it through the years. I could draw no closer to it than my own family and friends, and my own memories and thoughts. It and they would last, as Oswald said, as long as my mind would. I hoped that this was true, both for myself, poised as I was to launch out into a new, distant reality, and for my grandmother, who, having outlasted her own mind, needed others to carry forth its most important contents. Perhaps one day I would find myself in her position, eager to express things for which I no longer had the words.

If such a thing came to pass, I hoped that I might find a writer or a thinker, someone alive to the possibilities and committed to the viewpoint, someone who would say what I couldn't. "The author who benefits you," Oswald said, "is not the one who tells you something you did not know before, but the one who gives expression to the truth that has been struggling for utterance in you." We spoke each other's words, read each other's minds, prayed each other's lives. "Our lives, my life, is the answer to someone's prayer, prayed perhaps centuries ago." That was Oswald, but it was something I myself would have said, had I known how.

Why could I draw no closer? I looked at the ground, strewn with pecans and the shells of pecans (my mother and I had spent the day before filling bags to take to France, as Christmas gifts for the mountaineer's parents). Most of us, Oswald wrote in his diary, wanted to "make the corn of wheat stand alone." We wanted to hold a kernel of wheat in hand, to look upon it and say, "Look what I have in hand! It is a kernel of wheat. That is what I have." But this wasn't reality. Reality was a grain of wheat falling to the ground and dying and bringing forth fruit. One could never hold that in one's hand.

I stood beside the tree, looking at the house, at the peculiar orange-red tint of its bricks, the window above the sink where the cat had always perched, the window beside it that had been perfect for sneaking out of in high school. I looked up at the branch from which a swing had been suspended in earlier days but which was empty now. I felt strange. Was I saying goodbye? How far was France from this heaven?

As always, it was other people's voices that answered. I heard, first, Kathleen's. She read from Psalm 139, choosing it because it had often brought her comfort in moments like these. My mother read it with her, for it was also one of her favorites, one she'd recited to me often in the past:

Whither shall I go from thy spirit? or whither shall I flee from thy presence?

If I ascend up into heaven, thou art there: if I make my bed in hell, behold, thou art there.

If I take the wings of the morning, and dwell in the uttermost parts of the sea;

Even there shall thy hand lead me, and thy right hand shall hold me.

If I say, Surely the darkness shall cover me; even the night shall be light about me.

Yea, the darkness hideth not from thee; but the night shineth as the day: the darkness and the light are both alike to thee.

For thou hast possessed my reins: thou hast covered me in my mother's womb.

I will praise thee; for I am fearfully and wonderfully made: marvellous are thy works; and that my soul knoweth right well.

I heard Biddy's voice, too, speaking from her diary. She was echoing Oswald, saying that he was right beside her in the desert, in the unseen world that "*is* the real." And I heard Oswald, as always, telling me not to be afraid, but to leap, leap, leap again. "As we go forth into the coming year," he said,

let it not be in the haste of impetuous, unremembering delight, nor with the flight of impulsive thoughtlessness, but with the patient power of knowing that the God of Israel will go before us. . . . Let the past sleep, but let it sleep on the bosom of Christ.

Leave the Irreparable Past in His hands, and step out into the Irresistible Future with Him.

Acknowledgments

Numerous people offered invaluable support, guidance, and company during the preparation of this manuscript. Without David McCasland, I'm not sure anything would have been accomplished at all. In addition to assembling the Oswald Chambers archive at Wheaton, he provided me with an advance copy of Biddy's diary, put me in touch with his fellow council members at the Oswald Chambers Publications Association, helped me with securing permissions, and for years on end was always willing to answer my questions, no matter how challenging or ridiculous. His enthusiasm and kindness were truly sustaining.

Many other members (present and former) of the Oswald Chambers Publications Association—Rob Wykes, Mary Pearson, Geoffrey Bennett, Iain Cant, Carol Holquist, and Nicholas Gray—were incredibly generous with their time and observations. The volunteer work they do in promoting Oswald's words around the globe is a labor of love and a leap of faith, undertaken with the greatest seriousness and devotion. It's exactly the kind of endeavor Oswald would have appreciated. I am also grateful for the support of Ed Rock, at Discovery House Publishers, who made the process of securing rights extremely smooth and who handled all my

Acknowledgments

many queries with patience and grace; and to David Malone, who did the same at the Wheaton College archives—without David, I would not have known where to begin with Oswald's papers.

My agent, Zoë Pagnamenta, helped to shape this book from the start, when neither of us was certain what a project about *Utmost* might look like. Her enthusiasm showed itself in numerous discussions, readings, and rereadings of proposals and rough drafts, and keen editorial insight (in addition to all the regular duties of an agent!). I am very fortunate to have had her by my side.

I owe her thanks, too, for having had the insight to take the proposal for this book to my editor, Ann Close, at Knopf, whose support, generosity, and wisdom made the editorial process a true delight. Ann's willingness to take a chance on an unknown writer and her steadfast confidence in me were invaluable, as was her eagerness to bring Oswald's story to a new audience. Her energy and attentiveness were critical in bringing this book from rough draft to finished version, and to her goes a good deal of the credit.

My friends and family kept me sane and sustained throughout. First and foremost is my mother, Deborah Rutledge-Hilkmann, without whose generosity, hospitality, and support (financial, emotional, and spiritual) I couldn't have written a single word— either of this book or of anything else. To her and to the rest of my uniformly supportive family—my grandmother, Marjorie Macy Rutledge; my stepfather, Dirk Hilkmann; my sister, Alexandra Halford; and my brother, Preston Halford—I owe a large debt of gratitude.

I am grateful to Roger and Kathy Turner, who gave me a place to stay in Wheaton, as well as many fine meals and conversations; to Leo Carey, who kept me in booknotes; to Dana Marino, who read early chapters and (in landlord guise) always charged me below-market rent in Queens, kept the place open for me while I was off galavanting around France, and then let me stay with her on many occasions—in addition to just having been awesome in a general sense for the twenty years I've known her. And to Jenna Krajeski, who read, consoled, advised, visited, G-chatted, and basically went through the entire experience of writing this book with me.

Finally, Thierry Artzner, who met me in the rough, rough-draft years, had to do an untoward amount of listening, reading, and reassuring. He also housed, fed, and amused me, and kept a very *acoté* attitude throughout.

Further Reading

Readers who are interested in learning more about Oswald Chambers have a variety of options at their fingertips. Most of Chambers's individual books can be found in *The Complete Works of Oswald Chambers*, published by Discovery House and available in both physical and digital editions. The group biography edited by Biddy Chambers is out of print, but a more thorough accounting of Oswald's life than I have given here can be found in David McCasland's *Abandoned to God: The Life Story of the Author of "My Utmost for His Highest."* That book has laid the groundwork for all future books on Chambers, thanks to McCasland's tireless research and assembling of the Chambers archive at Wheaton College in Wheaton, Illinois.

For readers who wish to delve more deeply into the history of modern Evangelicalism and fundamentalism, a few classic books serve as fine introductions. David W. Bebbington's *Evangelicalism in Modern Britain: A History from the 1730s to the 1980s* is essential, as are George M. Marsden's *Fundamentalism and American Culture* and Mark A. Noll's *The Scandal of the Evangelical Mind.* InterVarsity Press's History of Evangelicalism series commences with Noll's *The Rise of Evangelicalism: The Age of Edwards, Whitefield, and the Wesleys* and proceeds through four excellent volumes. The series, which will conclude with Geoff Treloar's forthcoming *The Disruption of Evangelicalism: The Age of Mott, Machen, and McPherson,* has helped to meet a glaring need for a comprehensive history of the movement. Randall Balmer has explored the intersection of Evangelicalism and American politics in depth in several volumes, among them *Thy Kingdom Come: How the Religious Right Distorts Faith and Threatens America*. In *The Righteous Mind: Why Good People Are Divided by Politics and Religion*, Jonathan Haidt offers compelling explanations for things that often seem inexplicable.

The history of the Holiness Movement and its influence on Pentecostalism and other charismatic forms of Christianity is a richly complex subject still bursting with potential avenues of exploration. Charles Edwin Jones's *Perfectionist Persuasion: The Holiness Movement and American Methodism, 1867–1936* is a fine entry point, as is Vinson Synan's *The Holiness-Pentecostal Tradition: Charismatic Movements in the Twentieth Century*. If parsing the complexities of the Sanctification doctrine sounds like an entertaining way to pass an evening, Marvin Easterday Dieter's *Five Views on Sanctification* is the book to consult.

For those intrigued by End Times and other historical-futuristic schemes, the recently published collection *Mapping the End Times: American Evangelical Geopolitics and Apocalyptic Visions* provides welcome context on the situation in America, while Isaiah Berlin's fantastic *The Sense of Reality: Studies in Ideas and Their History* tells of the many individuals and schools that have searched for "the key" to history, among them Marx, Vico, Hegel, and Comte—an odd undertaking, Berlin concludes (in words Oswald would have appreciated), since "no attempt to provide such a 'key' in history has worked thus far."

In thinking about devotional texts and what it means to be a devoted reader-consumer of spiritual literature today, two books were incredibly useful to me: Candy Gunther Brown's *The Word in the World: Evangelical Writing, Publishing, and Reading in America, 1789–1880* and David Paul Nord's *Faith in Reading: Religious Publishing and the Birth of Mass Media in America*. Nord likes Stanley Fish's conception of "interpretive communities," and so do I. It can be found in Fish's *Is There a Text in This Class? The Authority of Interpretive Communities*. Finally, Marilynne Robinson's *When I Was a Child I Read Books* is, like everything she's written, a revelatory, intimate, essential work.

Select Bibliography

Balmer, Randall. *Thy Kingdom Come: How the Religious Right Distorts Faith and Threatens America.* New York: Basic Books, 2007.

———. *God in the White House: A History: How Faith Shaped the Presidency from John F. Kennedy to George W. Bush.* New York: HarperOne, 2009.

Bebbington, David W. *Evangelicalism in Modern Britain: A History from the 1730s to the 1980s.* London: Routledge, 1989.

———. *The Dominance of Evangelicalism: The Age of Spurgeon and Moody.* Downers Grove, IL: InterVarsity Press Academic, 2005.

Berlin, Isaiah. *The Sense of Reality: Studies in Ideas and Their History.* New York: Random House, 2012.

Blom, Philipp. *Fracture: Life and Culture in the West, 1918–1938.* London: Atlantic Books, 2015.

Brown, Candy Gunther. *The Word in the World: Evangelical Writing, Publishing, and Reading in America, 1789–1880.* Chapel Hill: University of North Carolina Press, 2004.

Carpenter, Joel A. *Revive Us Again: The Reawakening of American Fundamentalism.* New York: Oxford University Press, 1999.

Carruthers, Gerard, David Goldie, and Alastair Renfrew. *Scotland and the 19th-Century World.* Boston: Rodopi, 2012.

Claussen, Dane S. *The Promise Keepers: Essays on Masculinity and Christianity.* Jefferson, NC: McFarland, 2000.

Couch, Mal, ed. *Dictionary of Premillennial Theology.* Grand Rapids, MI: Kregel Publications, 1997.

Dieter, Melvin Easterday. *Five Views on Sanctification.* Grand Rapids, MI: Zondervan, 1996.

Select Bibliography

Dittmer, Jason, and Tristan Sturm, eds. *Mapping the End Times: American Evangelical Geopolitics and Apocalyptic Visions*. Abingdon: Routledge, 2016.

Dochuk, Darren. *From Bible Belt to Sunbelt: Plain-Folk Religion, Grassroots Politics, and the Rise of Evangelical Conservatism*. New York: W. W. Norton, 2010.

Haidt, Jonathan. *The Righteous Mind: Why Good People Are Divided by Politics and Religion*. New York: Vintage, 2013.

Hankins, Barry. *Uneasy in Babylon: Southern Baptist Conservative and American Culture*. Tuscaloosa: University of Alabama Press, 2003.

Harris, Jason Marc. *Folklore and the Fantastic in Nineteenth-Century British Fiction*. Farnham: Ashgate, 2013.

Haykin, Michael A. G., and Kenneth J. Stewart. *The Advent of Evangelicalism: Exploring Historical Continuities*. Nashville: B & H, 2008.

Hopkins, Mark. "The Down-Grade Controversy." *Christianity Today* 29, 1991.

Jones, Charles Edwin. *Perfectionist Persuasion: The Holiness Movement and American Methodism, 1867–1936*. Lanham, MD: Rowman & Littlefield, 2002.

Kostlevy, William. *Historical Dictionary of the Holiness Movement*. Lanham, MD: Scarecrow Press, 2009.

Krapohl, Robert H., and Charles H. Lippy. *The Evangelicals: A Historical, Thematic, and Biographical Guide*. Westport, CT: Greenwood, 1999.

Lineham, Peter. "Methodism and Popular Science in the Enlightenment." *Enlightenment and Dissent* 17:104–25, 1998.

Löwy, Michael, and Robert Sayre. *Romanticism Against the Tide of Modernity*. Durham, NC: Duke University Press, 2002.

Luhrmann, T. M. *When God Talks Back: Understanding the American Evangelical Relationship with God*. New York: Alfred A. Knopf, 2012.

Mack, Phyllis. *Heart Religion in the British Enlightenment: Gender and Emotion in Early Methodism*. Cambridge: Cambridge University Press, 2008.

Marsden, George M. *Fundamentalism and American Culture*. New York: Oxford University Press, 1980.

———. *Understanding Fundamentalism and Evangelicalism*. Grand Rapids, MI: Wm. B. Eerdmans, 1991.

Martens, Britta. *Browning, Victorian Poetics and the Romantic Legacy: Challenging the Personal Voice*. Farnham: Ashgate, 2011.

McDermott, Gerald. *The Oxford Handbook of Evangelical Theology*. New York: Oxford University Press, 2010.

McKnight, Scot. "Christian Realism." *Jesus Creed*. http://www.patheos.com/blogs/jesuscreed/2014/11/14/christian-realism/, 2014.

Mears, Henrietta C., and Earl Roe. *Dream Big: The Henrietta Mears Story*. Ventura, CA: Gospel Light Publications, 2012.

Menand, Louis. *The Metaphysical Club: A Story of Ideas in America*. New York: Macmillan, 2002.

Morgan, Sue, ed. *Women, Gender and Religious Cultures in Britain, 1800–1940*. London: Routledge, 2010.

Noll, Mark A. "Common Sense Traditions and American Evangelical Thought." *American Quarterly* 37, 1985.

———. *The Scandal of the Evangelical Mind*. Grand Rapids, MI: Wm. B. Eerdmans, 1995.

———. *The Rise of Evangelicalism: The Age of Edwards, Whitefield, and the Wesleys*. Downers Grove, IL: InterVarsity Press Academic, 2010.

Nord, David Paul. *Faith in Reading: Religious Publishing and the Birth of Mass Media in America*. New York: Oxford University Press, 2007.

Parsons, Gerald. *Religion in Victorian Britain: Traditions*. Manchester: Manchester University Press, 1988.

Phillips, Paul T. *A Kingdom on Earth: Anglo-American Social Christianity, 1880–1940*. University Park: Pennsylvania State University Press, 2006.

Pokki, Timo. *America's Preacher and His Message: Billy Graham's View of Conversion and Sanctification*. Lanham, MD: University Press of America, 1999.

Pollock, J. C. *The Keswick Story. The Authorized History of the Keswick Convention*. London: CLC, 1964.

Putnam, Robert D., and David E. Campbell. *American Grace: How Religion Divides and Unites Us*. New York: Simon & Schuster, 2012.

Reardon, Bernard M. G. *Religion in the Age of Romanticism: Studies in Early Nineteenth-Century Thought*. Cambridge: Cambridge University Press, 1985.

Savage, Ruth. *Philosophy and Religion in Enlightenment Britain: New Case Studies*. Oxford: Oxford University Press, 2012.

Sharlet, Jeff. *The Family: Power, Politics, and Fundamentalism's Shadow Elite*. New York: HarperCollins, 2008.

Stanley, Brian. *The Global Diffusion of Evangelicalism: The Age of Billy Graham and John Stott*. Downers Grove, IL: InterVarsity Press Academic, 2013.

Stone, Alison. *The Edinburgh Critical History of Nineteenth-Century Philosophy*. Edinburgh: Edinburgh University Press, 2011.

Synan, Vinson. *The Holiness-Pentecostal Tradition: Charismatic Movements in the Twentieth Century*. Grand Rapids, MI: Wm. B. Eerdmans, 1997.

Thornbury, Gregory Alan. *Recovering Classic Evangelicalism: Applying the Wisdom and Vision of Carl F. H. Henry*. Wheaton, IL: Crossway, 2013.

Select Bibliography

Turner, John G. *Bill Bright and Campus Crusade for Christ: The Renewal of Evangelicalism in Postwar America*. Chapel Hill: University of North Carolina Press, 2016.

The W. A. Criswell Sermon Library. http://www.wacriswell.org/, 2016.

Wauzzinski, Robert A. *Between God and Gold: Protestant Evangelicalism and the Industrial Revolution, 1820–1914*. Teaneck, NJ: Fairleigh Dickinson University Press, 1993.

Wolf, Herbert C. "An Introduction to the Idea of God as Person." *Journal of Bible and Religion* 32, no. 1, 1964.

Wolffe, John. *The Expansion of Evangelicalism: The Age of Wilberforce, More, Chalmers, and Finney*. Downers Grove, IL: InterVarsity Press Academic, 2007.

Yrigoyen, Charles, and Ruth A. Daugherty. *John Wesley: Holiness of Heart and Life*. Nashville: Abingdon Press, 1999.

PERMISSIONS ACKNOWLEDGMENTS

Material from *My Utmost for His Highest* ® by Oswald Chambers, © 1935 by Dodd Mead & Co., renewed © 1963 by the Oswald Chambers Publications Association, Ltd., is used by permission of Discovery House, Box 3566, Grand Rapids, MI 49501. All rights reserved.

Material from Oswald Chambers's other published works, including *God's Workmanship, Biblical Ethics, The Moral Foundations of Life, Conformed to His Image, Called of God, Our Brilliant Heritage, The Place of Help, Approved Unto God, The Ministry of the Unnoticed, Studies in the Sermon on the Mount, Biblical Psychology,* and *Baffled to Fight Better,* can be found in *The Complete Works of Oswald Chambers,* © 2000 by the Oswald Chambers Publications Assn., Ltd., and is used by permission of Discovery House, Box 3566, Grand Rapids, MI 49501. All rights reserved.

Material from the Oswald Chambers archive is used by permission of the Wheaton College Archives and Special Collections, Buswell Memorial Library, Wheaton College, 501 College Avenue, Wheaton, IL 60187-5593.

Material from *Oswald Chambers: His Life and Work* © 1933 is used by permission of the Oswald Chambers Publications Association, Ltd., St. Paul's Centre, Hightown, Crewe, U.K. CW 1 3BY.

Material from the minutes of the Oswald Chambers Publications Association, Ltd., used by permission of the Oswald Chambers Publications Association, Ltd., St. Paul's Centre, Hightown, Crewe, U.K. CW 1 3BY.

Photographs used by permission of Oswald Chambers Papers (SC-122), Buswell Library, Special Collections, Wheaton College (IL).

A NOTE ABOUT THE AUTHOR

Macy Halford was born and grew up in Dallas, Texas. She graduated from Barnard College and later worked at *The New Yorker,* where she edited and wrote the online book review. This is her first book. She now lives in Paris.

A NOTE ON THE TYPE

This book was set in Minion, a typeface produced by the Adobe
Corporation specifically for the Macintosh personal computer and
released in 1990. Designed by Robert Slimbach, Minion combines
the classic characteristics of old-style faces with the full complement
of weights required for modern typesetting.

Typeset by Scribe,
Philadelphia, Pennsylvania

Printed and bound by Berryville Graphics,
Berryville, Virginia

Designed by Soonyoung Kwon